Guthrie's Guide to Better Legal Writing

SECOND EDITION

SECOND EDITION

Guthrie's Guide to Better Legal Writing

Neil Guthrie

IRWIN LAW

Guthrie's Guide to Better Legal Writing, second edition

Published in 2021 by

Irwin Law Inc
Suite 206, 14 Duncan Street
Toronto, Ontario M5H 3G8
www.irwinlaw.com

ISBN: 978-1-55221-569-2 | e-book ISBN: 978-1-55221-570-8

Library and Archives Canada Cataloguing in Publication

Title: Guthrie's guide to better legal writing / Neil Guthrie.
Other titles: Better legal writing
Names: Guthrie, Neil, 1963– author.
Description: Second edition. | Includes bibliographical references and index.
Identifiers: Canadiana (print) 20210124865 | Canadiana (ebook) 20210124903 | ISBN 9781552215692 (softcover) | ISBN 9781552215708 (PDF)
Subjects: LCSH: Legal composition. | LCSH: Law — Canada — Language.
Classification: LCC KE265 .G88 2021 | LCC KF250 .G88 2021 kfmod | DDC 808.06/634—dc23

Canada

ONTARIO CREATES | ONTARIO CRÉATIF

Printed and bound by CPI Group (UK) Ltd, Croydon, CR0 4YY

1 2 3 4 5 25 24 23 22 21

Contents

CHAPTER TWO

Preface

This book began out of frustration.

Frustration at the turgid, pedantic, Latin-filled, jargon-ridden, misspelt, ungrammatical, and inelegant writing that issues from the pens and keyboards of lawyers, law students, and those who come within their orbit (assistants can have an unfortunate tendency to replicate the bad habits of those they work with).

My working title was *Please Don't Write Like a Lawyer*, but my publisher counselled against using that, in case it alienated the book's main audience. It nevertheless provides an accurate insight into my motivation and method.

Why is legal writing so bad? People come to the profession from various academic and other backgrounds, and early on they feel as though they have been initiated into not only a mode of reasoning but also of writing: the art — or mystery perhaps — of law is attended by its *terms of art*. These are a hodge-podge of words, phrases, and habits of expression that have accreted over the centuries, mixing Law French with Latin, the English of the early modern period, memorable phrases from the case law, and defined terms from statutes. Fluency with the lingo is seen, especially in law school and the early years of practice, as a proxy for knowledge of the law itself (whether this is true or not). Being a generally conservative and cautious bunch, lawyers are reluctant to change any wording they have learned or which practice has sanctioned, preferring the certainty of the known to potential ambiguity or uncertainty in something new, even when it is closer to current non-legal usage. This may explain the (sometimes justified) reluctance to adopt plain language in contractual or statutory drafting. Lawyerly caution results in passive constructions, hedged with qualifiers and exceptions. Modern education does not seem to include basic grammar and spelling, so the faults of lawyerish writing are now compounded by technical faults that would not have been present forty years ago. All these things make legal writing the mess it is today.

But lawyers are not drafting only for other initiates into the mysteries: they write for clients and members of the wider public, who are not lawyers and who care not at all for the linguistic arcana of the law. Lawyers forget this, importing the language of contracts or wills into their marketing pieces — or they think that they need to impress non-lawyers with a parade of their mastery of the craft. Non-lawyer readers are probably not impressed, and may be left bewildered.

Ever one to tilt at windmills, I embarked on a series of weekly writing tips at my former firm, with a view to improving the written communications of lawyers and students with each other and with the non-lawyer public. This was my announcement for the series:

> We could all use some help with our writing, and help is on its way.
>
> Every Friday, I'll be sending a short, practical tip on effective writing in a legal context.
>
> This is not contractual drafting or written advocacy (although some of what you'll see will be applicable there), but advice on how to blog, how to stand out from the crowd, how to express yourself clearly and correctly.
>
> A bit of strategy, some grammar and spelling, and a lot of style.

The response was good (the odd curmudgeon aside), so I asked the editors of slaw.ca if a wider readership on the Slaw Tips blog might be interested. A reader enquired whether those tips might be collected for easy reference. I made a proposal to Irwin Law, and here we are.

This book is neither comprehensive nor programmatic. There are far better books on grammar and spelling, and some of them are identified in the bibliography. *Guthrie's Guide* is a selective response to the deficiencies in legal writing that seem to me most in need of fixing; you'll need to look at other books for complete treatment of the subjunctive mood or the correct use of the comma (although both are touched upon in these pages). And before you point it out, I don't always follow my own advice. And I do repeat myself, especially when it matters.

The book is also about legal *writing* (letters, memos, publications for external audiences) as opposed to legal *drafting* (contracts, factums, opinions), although there are some drafting points here and there (and, when I look at the table of contents, rather more of them than I had thought).

The *Guide*'s format, loose arrangement, and liberal use of first-person pronouns reflect its origin as a series of largely unplanned, occasionally repetitious email messages, although the table of contents and index will help readers find what they are looking for (or realize that they need to look elsewhere).

Readers will soon identify my biases: no points for figuring out my preference for the British over the American (although I do try to arrive at a happy Canadian middle ground). My debt to HW Fowler will be apparent — although I also acknowledge other models. On Fowler, I rely more on the second edition (1965, revised 1983) than the third (2004) because I've used it longer and because there is more of Fowler himself in it — and I admit I am myself resistant to change.

Readers are invited to send queries or comments to the author at info@guthriesguide.ca. Replies requiring thought or research may take a while, but I shall respond to all as quickly as I can. Comments and questions are also welcome on Slaw Tips (tips.slaw.ca), Slaw (slaw.ca), or LinkedIn.

★ ★ ★ ★ ★

The second edition collects the material I have written for Slaw Tips since the publication of the first edition. I post there fortnightly, and everything is reposted to the main Slaw blog (slaw.ca) and then shared with whoever reads me on LinkedIn. In *Guthrie's Guide* 2.0 I have also corrected the original text in places, added minor points that didn't warrant blog posts of their own, and inserted new references to articles and cases.

Acknowledgements

From the first edition

Some words of thanks: to Bennett Jones LLP for indulging me on Fridays during my time there, and for permitting me to inflict my views on the public, both on Slaw and here; to Jeff Miller, Alisa Posesorski, and Lesley Steeve at Irwin Law; to Steve Matthews and Emma Durand-Wood at Slaw and Stem Legal; to Shaunna Mireau of Slaw and Field Law; and to the many readers who have agreed and disagreed with me, suggested topics and encouraged me to keep going (notably, my parents, Joan Bilsland, Celia Chandler, Joseph Petrie, James and Louise Reed, Barb Sheperd, and Angela Swan). My sister and best reader Gay Guthrie provided helpful non-lawyer comments. Michael Motala also reviewed the manuscript and made good suggestions. For the index, I am grateful to John Barkwell (freelanceindexing.com), who also spotted some typos and infelicities.

For help of various kinds and permission to quote, I am grateful to Borden Ladner Gervais LLP; Matthew Butterick; Keith Sipe and Carolina Academic Press; Mary Bergin-Cartwright, Tom McKibbin, and Shelagh Phillips in the permissions department at Oxford University Press; Karen L Charney in Alumni Relations and Development at UC Davis; Judith Fischer; Barry Glaspell; Ross Guberman, Christopher Howse; Icon Books; the Hon Mr Justice John Laskin of the Court of Appeal for Ontario; O'Connor's; John O'Neill and Fraser Nelson of *The Spectator*; Lynne Truss and David Higham Associates;

Thomson Reuters; University of Chicago Press; Alison Warner at the Ontario Court of Appeal; Dot Wordsworth; and Bruce and Judy Wydick. Material from the *Oxford English Dictionary Online* and the second and third editions of *Fowler's Modern English Usage* is quoted by permission of Oxford University Press.

It will be apparent from my paraphrase where permissions were not forthcoming (or proved too expensive).

Errors of fact and judgment are mine alone.

★ ★ ★ ★ ★

For the second edition

For permission to quote material in the second edition, I am grateful to Borden Ladner Gervais LLP, Keith Sipe and Linda Lacy at Carolina Academic Press, Laura West at David Higham Associates (*Eats, Shoots & Leaves*), Judith Fischer, Barry Glaspell, Kathryn Walsh at Hachette Book Group, the Hon John Laskin, Rebecca Matzek at Thomson Reuters (*Black's Law Dictionary*), Matthew Butterick's *Typography for Lawyers*), and Judy Wydick.

With regret, I have cut back on quotations from the *Oxford English Dictionary* and *Fowler's Modern Usage*, as the permission fees already charged by Oxford University Press will far exceed my royalties for both editions of this book, and I needed to rein things for the second. If you want the full flavour of the quotations, they're still in the original edition.

Many people have helped with the second edition, including Jakub Adamski, Matt Aleksic, Johanne Blenkin, Ari Blicker, Quentin-Alexandre Brigaud, Graham Brown, Simon Clements, Jim Frank, Chris Graham, Gay Guthrie, Michael Haddad, Matt Helfand, John Hightower, Graeme Imrie, Neill Kalvin, Brendan M Kenny, Caroline Mandell, Ben Mayer-Goodman, Anne Marie Melvie, Jenny Mercer, Will Mercer, Codie Mitchell, Matthew Ponsford, Jennifer Prouse, James and Louise Reed, Zale Skolnik, Angela Swan, Douglas Tsoi, Lionel Tupman, the team at Irwin Law, and numerous readers of Slaw Tips, Slaw, and LinkedIn.

Neil Guthrie

chapter one

Get Writing!

A. INTRODUCTION

The first email tip to my gentle readers was simple: get writing! Or, more to the point, get blogging and posting to social media.

Blogged content has high visibility and much higher readership than content that is distributed by email. Unless you have a very targeted and well-maintained email distribution list, it's unlikely that a publication sent by email will be opened (much less read) by more than 5 percent of its recipients.

Contrast that with material that is posted on a blog, which can easily get views in the four digits. Blog posts also have the advantage of being picked up by aggregators (Lexology, Mondaq) and can be reposted to LinkedIn and JD Supra, which widens your readership even further. By way of example, Lexology's analytics once told me that a blog post of mine had been read by someone in the airport lounge in Perth, Australia. (The poor sod must have been at a loose end.)

Lest you doubt the power of social media, after I posted a short announcement on LinkedIn that I was publishing this book, the post was viewed nearly 8,400 times (I had only about 1,300 people in my network at the time), and it received lots of "likes" and comments. Let's hope all the viewers buy a copy.

So, what to post about? Recent developments in the law, of course, but give them a practical spin. Don't just announce some new decision or legislation—explain why it's relevant to your clients or potential clients. Give your perspective on industry trends or market developments. A fresh take on things is more likely to attract readers.

There are a lot of lawyers out there, and writing something that will resonate with existing and potential clients is a great way to build your profile, demonstrate your abilities, and advertise your services.

B. SO WHAT SHOULD I WRITE ABOUT?

The law, for starters — but there is a bit more to it than that.

Here are some suggestions, adapted from the Law Society of Upper Canada's (now known as the Law Society of Ontario) *A Guide to Business Development for Women Lawyers* (they are equally applicable to men):[1]

- Choose your topic carefully
  - Write about something you actually practise, know about, or want to develop as an area of specialization.
  - Don't allow people to think you're an expert on the basis of one article.
- Recycle old work
  - A memo for a file could be the basis of a client piece, but:
    - be careful to remove any information that could identify your client;
    - strip out technical terms, footnotes, and citations; and
    - make sure you bring things up to date.
  - The same piece can (within reason) be published in more than one place, often with only minor adjustments.
- Get your piece in front of the right audience
  - A legal journal, magazine, or newspaper may be read by other lawyers but not by business people.
  - Think about industry/trade publications or general news outlets — you have a better chance of being read by non-lawyer clients.

1 The Justicia Project Business Development Working Group, *A Guide to Business Development for Women Lawyers* (Toronto: The Law Society of Upper Canada, 2013), online: www.lsuc.on.ca/uploadedFiles/Equity_and_Diversity/Justicia/Business_Development_2013.pdf.

- A descriptive piece on recent developments in a particular area of law is always good, should be easy to write, and can get broad readership.
- Be timely
  - Publish as quickly as you can on breaking developments, but don't sacrifice care in thinking, writing, fact-checking, vetting by someone more senior, editing, and proofreading.
- Include a picture and brief bio
  - Your piece should be accompanied by a professional headshot wherever possible.
  - Include a short bio (short!); bonus marks if you can be distinctive without being gimmicky.
  - Link to appropriate social media (LinkedIn profile, maybe your Twitter handle, but not Instagram or Facebook).
  - If you're writing for an external publication, add a disclaimer that the views expressed are your own and not necessarily your employer's, and do not constitute legal advice.
- Other ideas
  - What challenges are your clients facing? How do other industries cope with similar challenges? Tell a story based on real examples.
  - What are the current trends in an industry or area of law you know about?
  - What kinds of questions have you been getting from clients or readers?
  - Avoid writing about "developments" that aren't really new ("Court reaffirms long-standing common-law rule that . . ."), even if this seems like a way to keep in front of your public (they'll lose interest).
  - What have you read lately, and what can you add? (But don't be catty about other people or present law as a world of insiders commenting on each other.)
  - What interests you about your practice area? (But remember that not everyone may share your enthusiasm for the law of drainage — you may have to make that interesting for other people, or at least explain why it might actually be important to them.)

- What mistakes have you made and what did you learn? (Careful with this one, though; don't alarm a client or your insurer.)

1) Advice for Associates and Students

Do you feel nervous about publishing something? You should, a bit — but don't let it put you off.

Here are some things to bear in mind:

- Get a partner to vet your idea and your draft, for technical accuracy.
- Defer to the senior person on points of law (unless you can show you're right), but not always on stylistic matters (as an articling student, I stood my ground when a partner insisted that *theirself* was a word).
- Check whether your firm acts for any party you're talking about — you don't want to say anything a client might not like.
- Be cautious in taking positions on public issues — your firm may represent parties with interests at stake, even if those parties aren't mentioned specifically in your blog post or update.
- Humour is good, but be careful; it can backfire.
- Consider anti-spam legislation (basically, no commercial electronic messages to parties with whom you don't have an existing business relationship).
- If available, have any marketing or communications people review the formatting of your piece and then run a draft by you before publication.

On a more positive note:

- Write about something that clients will find interesting.
- Pitch it at a level that will engage, not alienate, your reader.
- Write plain, understandable prose — not Latinate legal mumbo jumbo (which will alienate your reader).
- Explain why this new case or statutory provision (or whatever) is relevant: what does the client need to do, be aware of, avoid?

Now that I think of it, many of these are useful pointers for partners, too.

So, get writing.

2) Some Guidance for the Reluctant Legal Blogger

In the distant past, lawyers used to send printed client updates by snail mail. Those days are long gone. Then came email, rapidly reaching the saturation point.

You don't want to clog up your clients' email in-boxes more than you need to, so push things their way through a brief and punchy blog post.

Blog posts can be published on your firm's website and distributed to a phenomenally large audience through aggregators of online content (as mentioned before; the big ones are Lexology, Mondaq, and JD Supra).

Novice blogger? Fear not — here are some tips:

* Don't write about the law; write about how the law affects the people you serve.
  * Why should the reader care about this information?
* A good way to think about blog-writing is to consider it a proxy for speaking.
  * If you were asked about a particular topic in an elevator, what would you tell the person in thirty seconds?
* To be engaging, your blog post should do some or all of the following:
  * educate, inspire, or entertain
  * not be boring — no one wants a tedious and overly technical piece with dozens of footnotes
  * have a specific client (or type of client) in mind
  * share and initiate a conversation
  * introduce why the reader should read the post (online content is judged largely by its headline, especially when readers usually see a list of headlines in their feeds)
  * provide quick, practical information on how the content affects the reader

    - make the reader want to ask you for further information
    - be short (600–1,000 words)
- Blog-writing is a way of sharing your personality (this may be a challenge for some; try, anyway):
    - make it distinctive, without being gimmicky or jokey
    - a conversational tone may be effective
- Additional resources to help you:
    - Learn from others who do this well — JD Supra collects pieces by its top blog authors.[2]
    - JD Supra also has a helpful guide to preparing and scheduling topics.[3]
    - As does Lexology.[4]

Helpful (but not Always Reliable) Software Tools

Oh, Microsoft, Apple, and your ilk! You think you're being helpful when you release new tools and updates, but you sometimes wreak more havoc than you bring clarity and certainty.

Herewith some views on some various writing "solutions" (to use the lingo of Silicon Valley).

Auto-correct

I am a terrible typist, so in some ways a feature that automatically corrects obvious typos is a blessing.

But it is also a curse. The auto-correct feature that you get with the standard Microsoft products could not have been devised by lawyers, nor is it set up to work in a Canadian setting. It can also defy common sense and good English.

Microsoft Word thinks that *tortious* (relating to a civil wrong) must be *tortuous* (twisty), dislikes *honour*, *offence*, and the like,

2 See JD Supra, "Meet Our Top Authors" *JD Supra*, online: www.jdsupra.com/readerschoice/2016.

3 Adrian Lurssen, "How One Simple Question Leads to 3 Months of Solid Writing Ideas for Attorney Bloggers" (29 April 2016), *JD Supra*, online: www.jdsupra.com/legalnews/how-one-simple-question-leads-to-3-83086.

4 See Chris Riley, "Help — They Won't Write! Engaging Lawyers in Content Marketing Programmes" *Lexology* (24 July 2018), online: www.lexology.com/library/detail.aspx?g=d24f9aa4-6830-4360-865c-9d339d100ffa.

assumes I mean *paragraph* © not *paragraph (c)*, and insists I want 5th instead of *5th* (the superscript is incorrect in legal citations).[5]

You can reset the language from US English to Canadian (or Caribbean, or Australian, or UK) English, but that's a bit fiddly to do — and what dictionaries are they relying on? If the word "Oxford" isn't in the title, it's not a proper dictionary, to my mind.

The auto-correct feature that comes with Apple's version of Microsoft is even more aggressive. And texting is worse: no wonder there used to be a website dedicated to frustrating (and funny) iPhone auto-correct failures.

Auto-fill and predictive text

How many times have you sent an email to the wrong person because some other name was automatically pulled out of your contacts or your list of previous recipients?

Often this isn't really an issue (although your mother may wonder why you're asking her to join the gang for drinks on Friday night), but if you're a lawyer it can be very scary indeed.

Many a privileged email has wound up with the wrong party as a result of the auto-fill feature, and that is clearly A Bad Thing.

Predictive text is your worst enema, as the saying goes.

Blacklining (or sometimes redlining)

In the olden days, a pair of articled clerks would sit together with two versions of a document. One would read aloud the new version and the other would mark the changes on the old, striking through deletions, writing in additions and then underlining them. A red pen was typically used, hence redlining. With the advent of the monochrome photocopier, this became blacklining.

How quaint! But not so far into the mists of antiquity. We now have software that does all this with a few keystrokes, and very effective it is, too. It also eliminates the human error attributable to sleepy, hungover students. It can be a useful way to see if you've made errors in the new material.

5 See "How to Prevent That Annoying Autorrect of (c) to ©" *Slaw Tips* (18 August 2020), online: http://tips.slaw.ca/2020/technology/prevent-that-annoying-autocorrect-of-c-to.

Just make sure you save the marked-up version as a new document, so you preserve the record of the document comparison.

Workshare Compare seems to be the market leader, but there are other products.

Spell-Check

Same comments as for auto-correct. No, I don't mean *cheese* when I type *cheque*.

In a legal document, you'll end up with lots of wavy lines under technical terms or regional spellings that Word just doesn't recognize. Spell-check may not catch errors in words that are all in capitals. And I haven't yet managed to figure out how to add a (correct) spelling to spell-check's dictionary.

Use this feature with caution —it's never a substitute for printing off a hard copy and doing some proper proofreading.

Microsoft Word Proofing

This is a bit buried. Go to the Review tab in the top toolbar in Microsoft Word, then Review > Language > Language Preferences > Proofing.

You'll get a menu that allows you to select your auto-correct options (you can turn off the automatic correction of *(c)* to ©, for example).

You can also run a check of grammatical and stylistic problems or errors, including misused words, run-on sentences, sentence fragments, clichés, colloquialisms, gender-specific language, passive constructions, unclear phrasing, and overly long sentences.

Another option is to get readability statistics — and I bet you most lawyers will get high scores for the number of passive constructions (which isn't good).

A lot of subjectivity there, but at least you can accept or reject the suggested changes. It's doubtful that the software is attuned to legal terminology, but it may help you avoid some obvious problems.

WordRake

This one isn't free, but it may also be helpful.

WordRake says it "tightens, tones, and clarifies your writing" (like calisthenics for prose?), aiming for both "clarity and brevity." By clicking "the 'rake' button . . . the in-line editor ripple[s] through your document, suggesting edits to remove clutter and improve unclear phrasing, just like a live editor."

Sounds great! In a recent demo with a real lawyer's document, WordRake picked up a lot of boring, passive constructions and suggested more concise alternatives to verbose phrasing. But it failed to pick up the (ghastly) *facilitative* and didn't always handle idioms well. It won't catch grammar and spelling issues.

Like all the other tools, it is helpful as far as it goes, but unreliable. Other tools that are commercially available include Grammarly (shouldn't that be Grammatically?), Praktio, and Hemingway. Use with caution.

BriefCatch

Unlike WordRake, this software is aimed squarely at lawyers, specifically their "briefs" for court. (It's an American product, so uses US terminology.) It will spot flabbiness in your prose, passive constructions, excessively long sentences, jargon, repetition, citation errors (US only?), inconsistencies in formatting, and typos; it also generates a grading of your document's flow, style, and readability.[6]

BriefCatch will give a score out of a hundred for:

* reading happiness (use of active voice, word and paragraph length, and the like)
* sentence length (including excessive length, variation in length)
* flow index (use of effective transitions and other sign-posts)
* punchiness (verbiage-catcher)
* plain English

Ross Guberman, the promoter of the software, has entertaingly used BriefCatch to assess the quality of judicial decisions, particularly those from SCOTUS.

There is a companion product called ContractCatch, which will spot potentially ambiguous wording, inconsistent terminology, grammar and spelling errors, and plain-English issues.

Both tools suggest edits, which can be accepted or rejected.

6 Online: BriefCatch.com.

Contract Companion

A neat product that whizzes through a document (not necessarily a contract) and locates problems like capitalized defined terms that lack actual definitions, unpaired quotation marks, spacing variations, and inconsistent numbering of sections and paragraphs.

Fiddly stuff that the human eye may well miss, in other words.

Users say the software does come up with some false positives, but it finds a lot that human review will overlook.

Microsoft now offers a similar product called Contract Tools.

Track Changes

This comes with Microsoft Word, and some people love it. I don't.

Track Changes does offer the ability to make marginal comments as well as revisions to the text, but also requires the reviewer of the document to accept or reject the previous editor's comments and edits.

That process is annoying — or I think so, anyway. And any subsequent changes, even if those don't involve input from another person, result in a marked-up document.

You also have to be very sure you have cleaned all the metadata from your document when you send it to someone external; otherwise, the recipient will see all those marginalia saying things like "Not sure this is a good argument but let's try it anyway!"

3) Think of Your Reader

A lot of writing by lawyers is clearly only intended for other lawyers, and there is a lot of it on Lexology. This is fine if your target market is a lawyer at another big firm — except that probably isn't your target market. Your readers may well be in-house counsel, so things of purely lawyerly interest may work for them.

But wouldn't it be better if your in-house counsel readers could distribute your blog post (or whatever it is) to all the business people they support, with no requirement for translation into plain English?

To expand your reach, it's better to pitch things to a more general, non-lawyer audience. Some tips:

* Use plain language wherever possible
* Avoid legalese — or use it once, explain, and move on
* No Latin!
* Be practical in focus — why is this legal development important to someone outside the rarefied world of law? What action does your reader need to take (or avoid)?
* Don't go into too much detail — you want to give the highlights without giving away all your wisdom *and* without miring your reader in the minutiae (which can be a bit boring)
* As a wise person has said, good writing makes your reader feel intelligent; bad writing, stupid.

a) Plain Language

A few more words about plain language. My discovery of Richard Wydick's *Plain Language for Lawyers* was serendipitous.

I had started sending out weekly writing tips by email at my firm and was in constant need of new material (which remains the case).

Someone on my street had left a box of books at the curbside, for passersby to take what appealed to them. On the top of the pile was the fifth edition (2005) of Wydick's excellent book.

Its messages are simple and important:

* omit surplus words
* use base verbs, not nominalizations
* prefer the active voice
* use short sentences
* arrange your words with care
* choose your words with care
* avoid elegant quirks
* punctuate carefully

Richard Wydick died in 2016, and I was very grateful to receive permission from his family and publisher to quote from the fifth edition in the previous edition of this book (which collected those weekly emails).

A sixth edition of *Plain Language for Lawyers* has now appeared (2019) thanks to Amy E Sloan of the Baltimore School of Law.

It preserves the basic structure and "classic features" of the 5th, but adds a new chapter on document design, updates to some of the material, and new exercises.

Recommended reading for all legal writers. And if you can't find a free copy among a neighbour's discards, it's only US$25 from Carolina Academic Press.

b) TL;DR

Translation: "Too long; didn't read."

This is the verdict, Aaron Orendorff argues, on most work-related writing. Orendorff, a writer and editor, suggested a while back in the *New York Times* that your work colleagues really don't want to read anything you write in a professional setting.[7]

It's not that they don't like you or that you write badly; it's just that they (like you) are inundated with reading material.

He offers eight strategies to get people to read what you send them (because some of it actually might be important):

- write less often
  - scarcity is more valuable
  - keep personal conversations separate from professional channels
  - wait before you send or reply, sometimes up to 24 hours — or don't send at all
- keep it short
  - brevity is the soul of wit (Shakespeare's joke being that it is the tedious old bore Polonius who says that in *Hamlet*)
- put action words in the subject line of your email
  - not "Budget attached" but "APPROVAL REQUIRED FOR ITEMS 9–12: Budget attached"
- listen rather than talk
  - ask clear, concise questions that invite answers
- ask, don't answer

7 Aaron Orendorff, "Your Colleagues Don't Read Anything You Write. Here Are 8 Ways to Change That" *New York Times* (9 March 2020), online: www.nytimes.com/2020/03/04/smarter-living/your-colleagues-dont-read-anything-you-write-here-are-8-ways-to-change-that.amp.html.

   - "use one or two sentences to describe the situation; then ask a single question and let the team chime in"
- "lead with the need"
   - skip opening niceties and cut to the chase
   - move the final sentence of your first draft to the top and then cut most of the rest
- provide an executive summary
   - call it "TL;DR," even
   - especially useful for memos, agendas, and group emails
   - say who needs to do what by what date
   - if this covers everything, omit the rest of the draft
- think of your readers
   - is what you're writing interesting or relevant *for them*?
   - include your reader by referring to *we* not *I* or even *you*
   - asking for someone's opinion invites criticism; try to build on a shared identity

These eight points won't make people hang on every email you compose, but you may at least get their attention.

4) Keep Your Cultural References Current and Universal

This is intended mostly for baby boomers.

If you're writing a client piece, it's often tempting to jazz things up with a reference to sports, popular music, TV, or movies. This can be effective, both in conveying an image and in making the writer look human (which isn't always easy in legal writing). There are some pitfalls, however.

Those born before 1965 may have to come to the shocking realization that there is a now a generation for whom The Beatles are just some old band their grandparents bore on about. Trying to look hip can also backfire, as John Tory, the current mayor of Toronto, found out when he lauded Kanye West as a "proud product of our music industry." Whatever his other foibles, the late Rob Ford probably wouldn't have made the same mistake.

I know the day will come when my Advanced Legal Research and Writing class fails to recognize The Smiths. This is inevitable but regrettable, not only because the band helped to define my late adolescence, but also because their squabble over money is a such a nice illustration of basic principles of partnership law.[8]

Sports references can be vivid, but also problematic. American writers make the mistake of assuming that the entire world loves baseball as much as they do. (The term “World Series” appears to originate not from the sport’s purported global reach but from early sponsorship by the *New York World* newspaper.)

By the same token, Canadians may want to avoid too many hockey references if they have potential readers in Australia or Hong Kong — or Canadian readers who grew up in cultures in which the dominant sports aren’t hockey and (North American) football, but cricket or (what the rest of the world calls) football. Many Americans will not have played games that involve the offside rule, so using *offside* to describe improper behaviour may give rise to blank looks. Female readers may (but may not) be put off by sports analogies of any kind, which may reek a little too much of the (male-dominated) locker room.

And we’ve all met that tiresome guy (and it is usually a guy) who can repeat whole episodes of *Monty Python*, *Seinfeld*, or *The Simpsons*. Remember that not all who read your client piece will have seen the particular episode you find hilarious (or if they have, have found it hilarious).

It’s best to stick to references that everyone will get — which is no easy thing.

5) Plagiarism

Long, long ago, when the interweb was new and I was an articling student, I had to write a conference paper for a partner — one of those pieces that ended up with his name as author and mine in a footnote.

I was doing research in the firm’s library and among my sources were conference papers by other lawyers. At one point, I said to myself, “Oh, wait — I’ve read this one before, haven’t I?” When I

8 See *Joyce v Morrissey and Others*, [1998] All ER (CA) 556, and a rather different account of the facts in Morrissey, *Autobiography* (London, UK: Penguin Classics, 2013).

checked the pile of binders on the table, I realized I had read the paper before — but it was ostensibly by a different author at a different firm from the one whose work I had just looked at.

I realized at once what had happened. Another stressed-out articling student with a looming deadline had just copied an earlier paper, *holus bolus*, and slapped the instructing lawyer's name on it. Both papers dated from the same year, so which was the original and which the plagiary? There was no way to tell, so I cited both in my footnote and left readers to draw their own conclusions.

For a generation of articling students who have never known a world without the internet, and whose notions of copyright are perhaps a bit flexible, the opportunities for copying others' work are legion. And deadlines from lawyers are no less pressing. How embarrassing it would be to have someone from another firm call you up and point out that your blog post or conference paper is in fact something she wrote last year, repackaged as your original work.

When I'm marking law school assignments, if a phrase sounds too polished or too technical to be the work of a 2L, I run the excerpt (in quotation marks) in the search box for legal blogs at legalresearchandwriting.ca or slaw.ca, and in Google. There are also some tools — some of them free — to be found by searching for "plagiarism checker" on Google. So, see what your students have been up to.

And better yet, write your own original content.

C. GET TO THE POINT

A short primer on what is called "point-first" writing.

You might be tempted to keep your reader in suspense about your conclusion or even the very subject of your blog post or client update, but that would be a mistake — you aren't aiming to write a mystery novel or a cliff-hanging thriller. Like most people, your client is busy and has a short attention span — so get to the point. Point-first writing is also effective in memos, factums, and letters.

Start with your conclusion and then explain how you got there. Begin by expressing the general rule, and proceed to the exceptions. Open with the general, refine with the specifics.

This will tell the reader what your piece is about, up front. The reader can then decide to read on in order to get the details or the nuances. The reader can also decide to come back to your piece later (or not at all).

A clear sense of direction right from the opening line guides the reader: the last thing you want to do is force the reader to ask, "What's this all about and where is it going?"

It's also helpful to wrap up at the end with a restatement of your general point, to make sure the reader hasn't lost the plot in the mean time.[9]

It's hard to improve on what John Laskin, formerly of the Ontario Court of Appeal, has to say in "Forget the Wind-Up and Make the Pitch":

> Of all of my suggestions, I consider point-first writing the most important. Point-first writing, more than anything else, will improve the clarity and persuasive[ness] of your writing.
>
> State your point or proposition before you develop or discuss it. Do not write your factum like a mystery novel in which the conclusion is revealed only in the final paragraph, if at all. In other words, give the context before discussing the details. Indeed, point-first writing puts into practice the principle of context before details. Point-first writing should be used throughout your factum, both in the facts part and in the law part, and within those parts, in every section and in every paragraph. Whenever you are about to dump detail on the reader, give the reader the point of the detail first.
>
> We see far too many factums that contain long meandering paragraphs, in which the point of each paragraph is never stated, or almost as bad, is stated three paragraphs later. This is not reader-friendly advocacy. You can fix this problem in these ways. At the beginning of the paragraph, tell the reader what topic or idea you are going to discuss in the rest of the paragraph. Try to restrict each paragraph to one main idea or topic. Then, in the first sentence or two of each paragraph, articulate the point of the paragraph, usually your conclusion or submission on the issue. The remainder of the paragraph will discuss the

9 On *mean time* and *meantime* see Chapter 2, Section D, "Miscellaneous Things That Annoy Me."

> submission, elaborate on it, support it, or qualify it. This is point-first writing.
>
> Unfortunately, too many factums contain either point-last writing or no-point-at-all-writing.[10]

Laskin thinks point-last writing may sometimes be effective — perhaps when the story involves an unfolding drama or the overarching point is controversial and needs development in order to persuade a judge — but believes it should be employed sparingly. In any event, he advises providing the context first, then the details.[11]

This is equally applicable to other kinds of legal writing.

To recapitulate: point first; conclusions up front; explain; repeat conclusions.

1) Catchy Headlines and Openers

Just as blogs get more readers than emails, articles with catchy headlines and enticing openers are more likely to be looked at than, well, boring ones.

Here is a post from LinkedIn that illustrates the point:

> A recent case from the ONSC clarifies the law on whether municipalities can regulate boathouses and whether the *Building Code Act* applies to same, finding that (i) municipalities have jurisdiction to zone Ontario lakes and apply zoning by-laws to lakes, regulating construction of boathouses and other structures; and (ii) the *Building Code Act* applies to such structures, where not otherwise prohibited by the by-laws and the *Public Lands Act*.

Descriptive and relatively clear (despite the legalese) — but a bit dull? Especially when the underlying facts are rather good: Toronto lawyer objects to a neighbouring cottage's rogue boathouse; municipality and province refuse to step in and regulate; lawyer sues governments; judge clarifies "murky waters" (his phrase) of planning rules for boathouse construction.

10 Hon John I Laskin, "Forget the Wind-Up and Make the Pitch: Some Suggestions for Writing More Persuasive Factums" (1999), Court of Appeal for Ontario, online: www.ontariocourts.ca/coa/en/ps/speeches/forget.htm.

11 Email from Hon John I Laskin to the author (6 August 2020).

Lexology is littered with similar examples. I had hoped to quote some of the more sleep-inducing ones, but (not surprisingly) permission to do so was not forthcoming from the law firms from which these tedious pieces had emanated (although I did have a pleasant exchange with a nice person in the marketing department of one law firm).

In a way, it isn't even necessary to quote real examples, because they are formulaic. Some made-up, but true-to-life examples:

> **OSC staff publish draft amendments to National Instrument 45-105**
> Boring and Boring LLP
> On June 18, 2015, staff of the Ontario Securities Commission published draft amendments to National Instrument 45-105 — *Trades to . . .*

> ***Spence v BMO Trust Company*, 2016 ONCA 196**
> Dull, Duller and Dullest LLP
> In this recent decision, the Ontario Court of Appeal reversed a decision of the Superior Court of Justice, which had . . .

Lexology shows just a headline and the opening words of your piece, so make them enticing — give the reader a sense of what the post contains and why it is worth reading, not an impenetrable title and a repellent intro. No one cares about the specific date of a decision or regulatory instrument!

And let's rewrite that first example: *Judge clears up "murky waters" — you can't just build a boathouse anywhere.*

2) Capitals, Defined Terms, and Acronyms

Go easy with these.

a) Capitals

Where there are too many words with capital letters, the visual effect is jarring and over-emphatic.[12]

12 Bryan Garner, "LawProse Lesson #217: When Do You Capitalize 'Federal' and 'State'?" *LawProse* (2 July 2015), online: www.lawprose.org/lawprose-lesson-217-when-do-you-capitalize-federal-and-state.

Above all, Resist the Temptation to Capitalize Important Words, which can look a bit *Winnie the Pooh* ("I have been Foolish and Deluded . . . and I am a Bear of No Brain at All.").

By all means, write that *the Government of Canada issued bonds*, but when the reference is more general, you can lose the uppercase: *The government wants to extend tax breaks to . . .* (or, *the federal government*). Similarly, *The Province entered into an agreement with . . .* but *former president Bill Clinton*. And, except as a defined term in a legal document, *the board, the company, the chair*.

Litigators, take note: outside the context of a factum or other formal document, you do not need to stick a capital on every instance of *judge*, *justice*, and *court*. Do refer to *Justice Cromwell*, but in your legal update it is cleaner and more modern to write *The judge ordered . . .* and *The court decided . . .* A capital letter in these cases is not the sign of respect it is sometimes said to be (*The Judge is an idiot?* — or perhaps that's *Idiot*); it's a just hold-over from the days when *all* nouns were capitalized in English. Nouns still take the uppercase in German, but the practice began to fall out of general usage in all but lawyers' English after about 1750. Resist the temptation to write *Will* (in the testamentary sense) and *Act* (in the legislative).

The names of the seasons and *world* don't need a capital; *Earth* and *Sun* as the names of celestial bodies do, I suppose (*The Earth revolves around the Sun*), but not otherwise (*Where on earth? Everything under the sun*).

I do like the official use of a capital T in *Her Majesty The Queen*, however — but you'll need to convince me why *internet* needs an uppercase I.

Oh, and no capital after a colon (unless the word would have one anyway, like *Canada*). The *Globe & Mail* does this, and it irritates me. The colon doesn't indicate the end of a sentence: it marks the pause before you deliver what was promised before it.[13]

b) Defined Terms

A related issue.

13 RW Burchfield, *Fowler's Modern English Usage*, 3d ed, revised (Oxford, UK: Oxford University Press, 2004) at 159.

Remember that if you're writing a client-friendly blog post or article, a thicket of defined terms is off-putting, and often unnecessary. You aren't drafting a contract that needs to have airtight, interlocking terminology.

If Alvin Chang is suing Jonathan Cohen, and there are no other Changs or Cohens in the picture, please don't do this: *The plaintiff, Alvin Chang ("Chang"), alleged that the defendant, Jonathan Cohen ("Cohen"),* . . . If the dispute with Cohen is about a contract, and one contract only, there is no need to define it as *(the "Agreement")*. Just call it ***the contract*** or ***the agreement***. Heck, mix things up and call it both; it will add a little variety.

c) Acronyms

Acronyms can be useful, but they become annoying — or even impenetrable — if overdone. Common ones are fine, because they will cause no confusion: *CBC*, *NAFTA*, *IBM*, *NATO* are more well-known in that format than they would be spelled out in full. Others, like *USA PATRIOT Act*, stand for things no one much cares to know, having been concocted by legislators looking for a catchy statute title.[14]

But if you're talking about specialized terms, entities, or concepts, the appropriate acronym may simply leave your readers wondering. There was a lot on Lexology about *TRID* at one point. It turns out this stands for the *TILA-RESPA Integrated Disclosure* rule — whatever that is, and whatever *TILA-RESPA* is. Maybe your readers know this, but odds are they don't, and aren't likely to want to find out. Wouldn't

14 It stands for the *Uniting and Strengthening America by Providing Appropriate Tools Required to Intercept and Obstruct Terrorism Act of 2001*. The *SPEECH Act* is another example (*Securing the Protection of our Enduring and Established Constitutional Heritage Act*). Bureaucrats in the armed forces seem to be fond of contriving acronyms, like *MAGIC CARPET* (*Maritime Augmented Guidance with Integrated Controls for Carrier Approach & Recovery Precision Enabling Technologies*) for a piece of software to enable landing on aircraft carriers (see Dave Majumdar, "Landing on a U.S. Aircraft Carrier Is About to Get Easier" *War is Boring* (23 March 2017), online: http://warisboring.com/landing-on-a-u-s-aircraft-carrier-is-about-to-get-easier/#.8d011v5rf). More fun was a British Army project named *MARILYN* (*Manning and Recruitment in the Lean Years of the Nineties*): see Parliamentary Business, "Column 363" (23 October 1989), *Publications & Records*, online: www.publications.parliament.uk/pa/cm198889/cmhansrd/1989-10-23/Writtens-10.html.

it be better to describe it as something like the *"know before you owe" rule for consumer lending transactions*?

3) CAPS

Not hats: capital letters (or, in typographical parlance, uppercase).

a) Don't Shout at People

When the interweb and email were new, it took (some) people a while to figure out that typing your message all in caps is the typographical equivalent of shouting. Compare: *please don't forget to do this* (gentle reminder) *versus* PLEASE DON'T FORGET TO DO THIS (angry, hectoring, perhaps a bit desperate, possibly crazy). Everything in upper case in the subject line of an email is particularly alarming.

Used sparingly, capitals can be an effective way to express emphasis (especially if you're not typing in HTML or rich text) — but the key word here is "sparingly"; if everything is emphasized, then nothing is (the lawyer who cried "urgent"?). Or you look like you're shouting.

b) Proper Names

That is, names of persons and places (*Beyoncé*, *Tennessee*), which always take an initial capital — unless done otherwise for typographical (or other) effect (authors e.e. cummings, bpNichol, and bell hooks come to mind).

Sometimes proper names can lose their initial capital when they become disassociated with an actual place or person: you would not be wrong to write *brussels sprout*, *china cup*, *danish pastry*, *french letter*, *french window*, *roman type*, *venetian blinds*; and to put a capital on *boycott* or *shrapnel* (both derived from surnames) would look strange.

c) Titles

Old-fashioned usage is to go all out with capitals on these; it's more modern to ease up.

When referring to a specific person by title, it may be better to use uppercase: "Ladies and gentlemen, please welcome the Prime Minister of Canada!" Publications like *The Economist* are going the other way, although I suspect its preference for *the queen* in reference to The Queen is more republican than orthographical. Seeing something like that or *the duke of Devonshire* is ambiguous, to my mind: is the latter the chap whose formal title is *Duke of Devonshire* or just any old duke, perhaps one of many, who hails from Devonshire (where, incidentally, the Duke does not)? The French have long done it this way, however: *le duc de Devonshire*.

When you're using a job or other title as a generic description, the capitals can go: "When Sir John A Macdonald was prime minister, there were less rigid rules about conflicts of interest."

Similarly, it's not necessary to capitalize every routine instance of *president*, *chair*, etc. Or words like *state* or *province*, unless you're referring to the government of the jurisdiction in a legal or technical sense: *He was born in the state of Alabama*, but *The Province of Newfoundland and Labrador has issued bonds*.

It is *not* (or perhaps that should be *NOT*) necessary to use an uppercase J every time you write the title *judge* or *justice*. Yes, *that speech at Brandeis by Justice Abella was inspiring*; but, *there are nine justices of the Supreme Court of Canada* and *the judge gave brief oral reasons*. Same thing with *court*: capital C when it's a specific court (especially the one to which your factum is addressed), but not generically.

In the humanities and social sciences, capitals are disappearing from titles of books and articles (except for the first word and any proper names); it's also generally regarded as better design to omit capitals in headings and headlines (although not house style with the publisher of this book). This may yet come to the law.

d) Abbreviations

Periods were once *de rigueur* but now may be omitted for a cleaner look: *ABA*, *FWB*, *LCBO*, *NAFTA*, *MP*, *QC*, *St*, *UK*, *USA*, *WTF*, etc. My publisher also omits periods after abbreviations such as Hon, Mr, and Dr.

And then there is the odd habit of treating non-abbreviations as though they were: *APP* (for "application"), *FOB* (when something like a key fob is meant; it's fine as an abbreviation for "free on board" in shipping), *MAC* (no, your laptop is a *Mac*), *VISA* (OK as a trade name for the credit card, but I've seen it in an immigration context, which is wrong), *CAP rate* (should be *cap*, short for *capitalization*).

e) Capitals for Important Words

Please resist the temptation to slap a capital letter on a word as a form of emphasis: see Section C(3), "CAPS," above.

4) Euphemisms

These are round-about ways of saying something you don't want to express directly, whether it's for reasons of delicacy, discomfort, or discretion.

A classic example is the rather old-fashioned *unmentionables*, which people used to say before they felt they could talk about *underwear*. But even *underwear* is a euphemism, isn't it? It refers obliquely to what it's worn beneath and not to what it covers (the French *cache-sexe* comes to mind).

Is there a problem in using euphemisms? Well, yes. They can sound mealy-mouthed, obfuscating, wishy-washy, coy, cowardly, immature, disingenuous, dishonest.

Not desirable if you want your prose to be plain, honest, and direct — but sometimes there may not be many alternatives.

a) Bodily Functions

Where we perform these is one of the most euphemistically hedged areas of vocabulary.

In the United States, people ask to use the *restroom* — but they aren't going to lie down and have a nap, are they?

Here in Canada, *washroom* or *bathroom* is conventional — and a bit more to the point, because handwashing is (ideally) part of what you're going to be doing; though you are less likely to have a bath as well. The main objective remains obscured by both terms.

The British *lavatory* is a fancy, Latinate way of saying *washroom*. *WC* (short for *water closet*) is similar, and serviceable. The colloquial British *loo*, of uncertain and much-disputed origin, is useful and inoffensive. *Public conveniences* is coy and possibly deceptive.

Toilet is the one that gets people agitated: in both the United Kingdom and North America, it's regarded as *déclassé*, even vulgar. It's quite fun to watch people squirm by asking for the *toilet*. It is in fact as euphemistic as any other term; you aren't typically going to be performing a *toilette* worthy of Marie Antoinette in the *john* at the truck stop or even in the *powder room*, are you?

Comfort station is bad too; the public kind are seldom comfortable.

Less objectionable, perhaps, are *men's room* and *ladies' room* (and note the placement of the apostrophes in each case) — although the latter is freighted with class issues in a way that *the gents* somehow is not. As places like this become gender-neutral, however, these terms may prove problematic.

Or perhaps we should think like the French who, when not looking for *les toilettes* or *les cabinets*, can use the plain and direct (if less polite) *pissoir* or *pissotière*. But please, never *the little boys'* (or *girls'*) *room* or other coy substitutes.

b) Breaking the Bad News

In performance reviews, the phrase *constructive criticism* is often used, but it generally means all the negative comments nobody thinks you'll be able to address, right? And those who are *transitioning* (in an employment sense) are generally those who were pushed out the door. *Learning opportunities*? Those are the things you got reamed out for and will never put right.

Another one is *interesting*, which you do not want as the reaction to your idea, proposal, or plan. If this is someone's response, it usually doesn't mean the person is interested in the slightest: the subtext is more like "overly technical," "hare-brained," "are you kidding me?," "wildly impractical," or "completely crazy."

Noted as a response to a request is also one to avoid, especially if you're an underling; it unmistakably conveys "consigned to the circular file," complete with dismissive eye-roll.

These are all versions of the *English no* (English as in England) — that is, a positive statement that means its exact opposite if you read correctly between the lines. Examples: *You really must stay with us the next time you're in town*; *Let's have lunch soon!*; *It's not you, it's me* (or, if you want to sound dramatic [or pedantic], *it is I*).

c) The Great Beyond

The end of life is a bit scary, which is presumably why many people prefer a range of oblique expressions to the simple, direct, and explicit words *dead*, *death*, and *die*. The Toronto Police, in tweets and news releases, now say that accident victims are *pronounced at the scene* rather than the more direct (and less ambiguous) *pronounced dead*.

And really, *pass away*? This is vague and fuzzy, with an air of séances and crystal balls. *Pass on*? It's as though the *deceased* has handed something off, like a parcel. Worse is just saying *pass*: *So-and-so passed* makes it sound like the *dear departed* has taken a course and written the test. *We lost so-and-so last year* — but did you look everywhere you could have? Please just use the solid Anglo-Saxon *D* words, which have a suitable ring of finality to them. This isn't just a problem in English. The French will say someone has *disparu* ("disappeared"), *nous a quitté* or *laissé* ("has left us"), or is *éteint(e)* ("extinguished').

And then there is *casket*. *Coffin* is just too blunt for the unctuous *undertaker* (another circumlocution; *corpse-technician*, perhaps?), so *casket* is the invariable term in the funeral business. That's wrong, however: a *casket* is a little box or coffer suitable for jewels, letters, or other small things of value — not bodies. That *–et* ending should be your clue: like *–ette* in French, it signifies something diminutive, not cadaver-sized.[15]

On a related point, what to do when a colleague or client experiences the death of someone close? Many feel they should stay silent, ostensibly so as not to intrude, or remind and exacerbate the other person's grief. I say "ostensibly" here because more often than not the impulse to refrain from communicating arises from an awkwardness about the whole subject of death and its phraseology. It's almost always better to express sympathy; nine times out of ten, the bereaved will appreciate the human connection. Avoid mention of *death* if you absolutely must, but do write. You can keep it brief: *I am so sorry to hear about the death of your husband. Thinking of you and your family*, with an appropriate closing would be just fine. A hand-written note is always best, especially if you know the recipient

15 For entertaining takes on the mortuary industry and its hideous euphemisms, see Jessica Mitford's *The American Way of Death* (New York, NY: Simon & Schuster, 1963) and Evelyn Waugh's *The Loved One* (London, UK: Chapman & Hall, 1948).

more as a friend than only professionally, but even an email is better than nothing (as with thank-yous these days).

d) What This Means for Legal Writing (There Is a Point to All This)

Aim for plain language that is free from lawyerly circumlocutions and obfuscations. Think of Lord Denning's vigorous and vivid prose: short sentences, active constructions, and simple and direct language.[16]

D. WORD CHOICE

1) Banish Business Jargon

Many aspects of the working day are kind of boring. In response, people in business seem to want to jazz up the English language, often with words suggesting action when there isn't much (*jump on a call, heavy lifting*). The result can often be a collection of expressions that were bizarre to start with and hackneyed soon after.[17]

If everyone is using them, you don't want to. Instead, dazzle your reader (or listener) with language that is clear, precise, and original.

In the world of business jargon, some patterns emerge (my commentary in square brackets).

---

16 See Carmine Gallo, "Why Every Leader Should Take a Page from The Fed's Plain English Campaign" *Forbes* (18 June 2018), online: www.forbes.com/sites/carminegallo/2018/06/18/why-every-leader-should-take-a-page-from-the-feds-plain-english-campaign/#66d7d947222f.

17 See also Freelance Writing, "Top Reasons to Avoid Business Jargon," online: www.freelancewriting.com/business-writing/top-reasons-to-avoid-business-jargon; Laura Brown, "Write in Plain English: Lose the Jargon and Connect with Your Reader" *Forbes* (30 May 2019), online: www.forbes.com/sites/laurambrown/2019/05/30/write-in-plain-english-lose-the-jargon-and-connect-with-your-reader/#2ed01efd6748. For a reminder that jargon is not confined to law and business (and that it can be worse in other fields), see *Philosophy and Literature*, The Bad Writing Contest, press releases (1996–98), online: www.denisdutton.com/bad_writing.htm (I am grateful to Ben Mayer-Goodman for the reference).

a) Metaphors That Were Once Vivid

"Once" being the operative word — they are now just clichés.[18] Examples:

- *action items* [*tasks* would work just fine, no?]
- *adding value*
- *anytime soon* [not specific to business, but hackneyed]
- *at the end of the day*
- *availability* [*when are you free?* (or even *available*) is so much better than *what's your availability?*]
- *back of a napkin*
- *baked in*[19]
- *bandwidth*
- *boil the ocean*
- *bring me up to speed*
- *bring to the table*
- *buy-in*
- *C-suite*
- *circle back*
- *close the loop*
- *connect the dots*
- *core* [as bad as *key*]
- *decision point*
- *deck* [you mean *the slides* not *the deck*]
- *deep dive*
- *dial it back*
- *double down*
- *drill down*
- *drink the Kool-Aid*
- *ducks in a row*

---

18 This website could be satirical, but it's hard to tell: Yumi, "Consulting Jargon: Low-Hanging Fruit and Granular" *The English Farm*, online: https://theenglishfarm.com/blog/consulting-jargon-low-hanging-fruit-and-granular. The *Dilbert* cartoon reproduced in it certainly is.

19 Does this have its origin in that vacuous remark by the sometime MP Belinda Stronach about baking "a bigger economic pie" (whatever that was intended to mean)? I don't know, but please stop talking about things being *baked in*; you're a lawyer, not a baker.

- *ecosystem* [in biology, sure; you mean *jurisdiction*, *regime*, *scheme*, *system*]
- *face-time*
- *fall through the cracks*
- *feedback*
- *flip* [as in *flip me an email*; always suggests haste and lack of thought to me; *send* or forward *instead*]
- *gain traction*
- *game-changer*
- *grow the business*
- *guru* [*expert* or *specialist*, please]
- *hard stop*
- *heads-up*
- *heavy lifting*
- *herding cats*
- *high-level*
- *hill to die on*
- *hit the ground running*
- *impactful* [*forceful* or *effective*]
- *in my wheelhouse* [why on earth do people say this? Just what is a *wheelhouse*?]
- *in the loop*
- *jump/hop on a call*
- *learning curve* [and they're only ever *steep*, aren't they?]
- *low-hanging fruit*
- *mindset* [how about *mind* or *way of thinking*?]
- *move the dial/needle*
- *moving parts*
- *my gut tells me* [please, no one wants to know what your digestive tract is doing, much less telling you]
- *next steps* [for the love of pity, can we not refer to these at the end of *every* meeting? We can't take *previous steps*.]
- *ninja* [see *guru*]
- *on the same page*
- *open the kimono* [racist, sexist, more than faintly creepy]
- *optics*

* *page-flip* [see *flip*, above; greater care is suggested by *read*, *review*, or *go through*]
* *pain-point*
* *paradigm shift*
* *patch me in*
* *peel the onion*
* *piece* [as in *the employment piece* or *the environmental piece*; why not just *the employment issues* (or *aspects* or *components*)?]
* *pivotal* [tiresome in its ubiquity and betraying an inherent teleological fallacy in assuming the inevitability of whatever resulted from a supposedly *pivotal* moment; *important* is all that is meant]
* *point-person*
* *push the envelope* [unless you are a test pilot]
* *reach out* [you didn't reach out; you just emailed][20]
* *reinvent the wheel*
* *relatable* [meaning "easy to relate to," which is better anyway; properly, it refers to the ability to be narrated, brought into relation with something else, or to possess a mutual relation]
* *rock star* [for heaven's sake, you're a lawyer, and certainly not a rock star]
* *run it up the flagpole*
* *scalable* [like a mountain, a fish that needs cleaning, or a tea-kettle with lime depsoits? Better: *adaptable*, *extensible*, *flexible*, *variable*]
* *secret sauce*
* *serial entrepreneur* [doesn't this suggest a string of failures masquerading as success? A slum landlord turned real estate developer, TV personality, and politician comes to mind.]
* *singing from the same songbook*
* *skill up*
* *space* [as in *the banking space*; just say *banking*]
* *special sauce*

20 As many have pointed out, only the Four Tops are allowed to reach out. And please, could we replace *can I grab* with *may I please have*?

- *spidey sense*
- *stakeholder* [always makes me think of Dracula; shopworn in other contexts, although admittedly a pithy synonym is hard to think of]
- *strategic* [don't be strategic, just do things]
- *suit up*
- *synergies* [pseudo-scientific for *opportunities for co-operation, affinities, associations, links*]
- *take it offline*
- *take it to the next level*
- *take-aways*
- *the devil is in the details*
- *think outside the box*
- *timeframe* [can usually be avoided by some formulation with *time* or *when: When do you need it?* Not *What's your timeframe?*]
- *touch base* [actually, all sports analogies][21]
- *touch-point*
- *trial balloon*
- *tweak* [*revise* or *edit*][22]
- *unpack*
- *value-add* [*value* or *benefit*; is there such a thing as a *value-subtract*? Not yet, anyway . . .]
- *value proposition* [how about plain old *value* — or asking, *What is it worth? What does this offer?*]
- *view from 30,000 feet*
- *walk you through it* [are you going to hold my hand? and what if I want to run?]
- *window of opportunity*

21 There is the NSFW meaning you probably don't wish to invoke: see Urban Dictionary, online: www.urbandictionary.com/define.php?term=touchbase.

22 Originally, to *tweak someone's nose* was to pull and twist that person's proboscis. It came to be used figuratively, and at some point (in the 1960s?) it was applied to the making of fine adjustments to a car or other machine, and from there to legal documents. Not sure how or why; and again, it's OK in principle but worn out from use. Find a new metaphor or go back to a plain, non-metaphoric description. (More recently, to *tweak (out)* is to become twitchy from using amphetamines or meth. Not to be confused with *twerk*.)

b) Verbs That Aren't (Or Shouldn't Be) Verbs

Examples:

- *action*
- *architect*
- *cascade* [unobjectionable in respect of water, horrid in relation to email distribution within an organization]
- *conference*
- *courier* [which leads to the awkward-sounding *couriering*]
- *error* [no, the judge *erred*]
- *impact* [except in a dental or medical sense, like an *impacted* bowel; probably rendered a verb in more general use because people can't figure out the difference between *affect* and *effect*]
- *incent*, *incentivize* [*incent* is not even a word]
- *language* [ugh]
- *leverage*
- *liaise* [like *incent*, not even a word]
- *plain-language* [double ugh]
- *pronunce* [from LinkedIn, which is offering to "Let people know how to *pronunce* your name. Add name pronunciation"; one also occasionally hears the pronunciation *pro-NOUN-ciation*]
- *reference* [and *above-referenced* is an abomination worthy of the sixth circle of hell]
- *repurpose*
- *scale*
- *scope*
- *skill* [fine when used to describe things like *skilled trades*, not when it refers to getting additional training; worse are *reskill* and *upskill* (does one ever *downskill*?)]
- *task*
- *transition*
- *trial*
- *vision* [as dreadful as the strategic-planning sessions and team-building exercises it emanates from; you mean *plan*, *see*, or *envision*]
- *whiteboard*

One fabricated verb I do like is *voluntell* (past and past participle *voluntold*), which expresses so well how things get done in law firms. Another is the very useful *text*.

c) Weird Nouns

Examples:

* *ask* [a verb that isn't a noun]
* *deliverable* [adjective not noun, and not to be pluralized]
* *learnings* [never; nor should you talk about *a learning*]
* *spend* [ditto; you mean *cost*, *expenditure*, *expense*, or *spending*]
* *trainings* [ditto]
* *value-add*

d) Noun-Accumulation

Examples:

* *business process outsourcing*
* *change-management*
* *mission statement*
* *process-improvement*
* *project management*
* *quality assurance*
* *thought leader* [why not just *thinker*?]
* *workflow*

e) Bad HR Jargon

Other fields of endeavour are guilty of polluting the language with their specialist lingo.

Human resources (itself a piece of HR jargon; it used to be *personnel* or, in a more sexist age, *manpower*) comes to mind. Here are some examples of HR jargon to avoid; there are many more.

Diverse

Americans often refer to a *diverse attorney* when they want to describe a lawyer (as we would typically say in Canada) from a background that is other than White, male, straight, and middle class. But in a room full of Brown lesbian barristers, there is no diversity (at least on the basis of race, sexual orientation, or area of practice). We are diverse only in relation to others and collectively.

What the adjective means in *diverse lawyers* is, less concisely but more accurately, *historically disadvantaged or underrepresented in the legal profession*. That's a bit of a mouthful, so perhaps *diverse* in this context serves a purpose.

But I still don't like its imprecision.

Feedback

Originally, *feed-back*; and used to describe the return of electrical output from one segment of a circuit or amplifier to an earlier stage of input — like the *feedback* from the speakers when you're rocking out on an electric guitar.

Starting around the 1940s, the word began to be applied metaphorically to a response to any kind of process, often in relation to the kind of behavioural conditioning associated with the American psychologist BF Skinner.

More recently, and in HR-speak, *feedback* has come to mean commentary on someone's job performance.

Given the origins of the term in circuitry and behavioural science, where *feedback* is involuntary or automatic, rather than thoughtful or considered, its extension to performance reviews is somewhat unfortunate. Couldn't we just ask for *comments*, *views*, or *a review*? But this is a losing battle; *feedback* in its HR sense is here to stay.

Proactive

This is a recent coinage, much loved by those who give (but perhaps not receive) performance reviews.

It was invented as an opposite for *reactive*, a quality that is perceived as a weakness and in need of a forward-looking alternative (even though reacting is often all one can do when events are unforeseen or unforeseeable, as they often are).

Even those with foresight don't *proact*, they simply *act*; if one is both thinking ahead, one *anticipates*. Seen in a positive light, *proactive* means thoughtful or careful; more neutrally, merely fortunate in predicting an outcome (or in making it look as though one saw it coming).

Either way, *proactive* is overused HR jargon that is best avoided.

Team

This is another piece of weary HR-ese, with unpleasant overtones of organized fun, forced collegiality, and top-down decision-making. (*Andrea and her team* just makes me think it's all about Andrea, somehow.)

Or maybe I'm just not a team player.

f) Miscellaneous Jargon

Interface

Bad enough as a noun, worse as a verb.

The noun just means something like *connection*, *contact*, or *common ground*; the verb (especially as used outside the IT context) is a silly way of dressing up old-fashioned words like *meet* or *talk*.

Surface

This is from the world of technology, a jargon-generator if ever there were one.

As in, *This AI solution will surface all the relevant case law.*

Please, techies, stop calling every product or service a *solution* for one thing; but also, stop using the verb *surface* in this way.

Things *surface*, but one does not generally *surface* things. Here, it means nothing more than plain old *find*.

Just say that.

Transparency

Blame NGOs and civil servants for this one, I think.

It was once a vivid metaphor to describe a refreshing new approach to government (or business, or what have you) that has nothing to hide.

It's tired now (1,579,993 hits on the Government of Canada website!) — and in this new world of big data, we are all probably skeptical of the claim anyway.

Why not say *openness*, *candour*, or even *honesty*?

But perhaps that is the point: things aren't hidden, exactly, but do they fall somewhere short of complete disclosure?

Wellness

If my hunch about *transparency* being almost-but-not-quite honesty is correct, *wellness* is definitely along the same lines.

It isn't the same as *health*, with which it is often twinned but thereby juxtaposed: see, for example, www.studentlife.utoronto.ca/hwc/contact-us.

Promoters of *wellness* may say the concept is meant to seem wider and more *holistic* than *health* (*holistic* being a New-Age sort of word from the 1930s that I don't much like either).

I suspect the underlying rationale is that *wellness* is often the domain of the unlicensed; and the standard by which it is assessed is more subjective, more nebulous — and therefore intended to be less susceptible to litigation?

g) Meaningless Platitudes

Examples:

* *core competencies* [are we interested in peripheral ones? just say *job requirements* or *skills* — and not *skill set*]
* *functionality* [instead of *it has these functionalities*, why not just say *it does x, y, and z*?]
* *going forward* [let me know when we can go back in time]
* *it is what it is* [well, yes]
* *solution* [in the IT sense, this is just a product or service — and often a "solution" in search of a problem anyway]

h) Awful Adjectives

Examples:

* *core*
* *granular*
* *high-level* [which just means *superficial because I couldn't be bothered to read the document and think about it*]
* *iconic* [please stop using this word, especially when describing things that aren't images; *emblematic* might be a fresher alternative, but really all people mean when they say something is *iconic* is that it's *distinctive*; and something cannot be *one of the most iconic* of its kind — it's iconic or it isn't]

- *impactful* [um, how about *effective*?]
- *key* [*let's leverage our key learnings*! no, let's not]
- *major*
- *proactive*
- *robust* [fine for coffee or red wine, but not regulatory compliance]
- *seamless*

Dress code

Judging by the way they write, you might think that many lawyers wear the business clothes of plutocrats in the cartoons of the 1930s: morning coats, top hats, spats. Their prose is stuffy, pompous, outdated.

What you want to aim for is a more modern feel in your writing (and your wardrobe). Not a three-piece pinstripe suit and fancy tie with little animals on it, or a female equivalent that might have hung in the closet of Margaret Thatcher, because that's a bit too formal. More like David Cameron's slim-cut suit and open-necked shirt (but with better judgment) or, better yet, Emmanuel Macron's slim-cut suit and skinny tie. Professional without being uptight; conversational; accessible. Don't get too casual, though: unless you're in tech or the not-for-profit sector, you don't want your writing to come off as the equivalent of a tank top and flip-flops.

How do you match the sartorial and the written? Excise the Latin, technical terms, and legalese that you picked up in 1L to sound cool (*absent, in sum, therein*, and the like), convoluted constructions, lawyerly qualifiers like *generally*, citations that no one cares about, and anally retentive defined terms.

Your readers will thank you — or, rather, you will *have* readers.

i) Bad Business Jargon

We've seen this already (see Section D(1), "Banish Business Jargon"), but it just won't go away.[23] It should.

Here are some further examples you should expunge from your vocabulary.

23 See also Lucy Kellaway, "Lucy Kellaway's Jargon Awards: Corporate Guff Scales New Heights" *Financial Times* (8 January 2017).

Around

All of a sudden, it seems, we're having issues *around* XYZ, conversations *around* ABC, discussions *around* PQR.

No, no, a thousand times no. You mean *about* or *on* or *related to*. See Chapter 2, Section D "Miscellaneous Things That Annoy Me."

Conversations

And while we're on the subject of *conversations*, why is it that everything is now a *conversation*?

When I call my bank to complain, when I read an online newspaper, when politicians or citizens debate issues, it's a *conversation* — presumably in an attempt to make things sound folksy and approachable (or *relatable*, to use another dreadful piece of jargon).

As Elvis once said, a little less conversation. It's now trite.

Going forward

Or, worse, *on a go-forward basis*.

Human life and the progress of time move ahead, never back, so it's unnecessary (and, if you think about it, vapid) to point out the obvious and inevitable realities of time's fiendish progress.

Granular, granularity

Once upon a time, this seemed like a vivid metaphor, I guess — although I'm not convinced that sand or salt is such an apt analogy for a high level of technical detail (grains of sand or salt all look pretty much the same).

In any case, it's a tired expression that has long passed its "best before" date.

Grow

I'm sick of hearing about *growing your business*, as though it were some cash crop. Try *increase*, *expand*, *augment*.

Hygiene

People are now talking about things like *docketing hygiene* and *document-retention hygiene*, when all they mean are *good practices*. Just say that; nothing was dirty before, merely less efficient.

Key take-aways

Because of its ubiquity, this dreadful phrase merits a few words.

Ubiquity, for starters. The phrase appears in nearly 5,000 posts on Lexology, which to me suggests one word: hackneyed (and therefore to be avoided).

It's also unnecessary, as there are perfectly good, plain alternatives: *lessons* or *important points* come to mind (but, please, not *learnings*).

And if you have readers in the United Kingdom, you may occasion some scratched heads: a *takeaway* is a takeout meal or the establishment from whence it came — so your reader in London may be wondering, "Does she mean 'really important curries'?"

The language of war

Why the bellicose metaphors in the boardroom? *Attacks, campaigns, offensives, marching orders, strategy, tactics, war rooms* — isn't this all a bit 1980s corporate-warrior-ish? And more than a little testosterone-fuelled.

Meetings

People used just to *meet*. Now, they *take a meeting, have a meeting, hold a meeting, do a meeting*, even *meet together* (can they meet separately?). Let's return to plain old *meet*.

Metrics, optics

More clichés meant to make the language of business sound sexy or scientific or something.

Avoid them: *data* or *figures* and *perceptions* or *appearances* work quite well.

Narrative

If *conversations* are now everywhere, so are *narratives*. Unless you're writing or talking about a work of literature, keep *the narrative* out of it; this is a now-tired piece of media/PR-speak.

Powerful

IT people routinely describe every product (or as they would say, every *solution*) as *powerful* — to the point where the description is losing its vaunted power. *Useful, helpful, effective*, or just plain *good* would get the point across more successfully.

Role

A bit of recruiter-speak that suggests play-acting: it would better to do your *job*, once you've taken up a *post* or *position*.

Socialize

This has three usual meanings: to civilize; to engage in social activity; and to bring under state or public ownership.

Plus a fourth we now hear, meaning to seek consent or agreement. Couldn't we just say that? It's so much clearer.

Speak to

At meetings, people now *speak to an agenda item* or *speak to an issue*. And it is a question of now; this usage doesn't seem to have been in evidence before about 1990.

It has always seemed weird to me, because it has overtones of childhood discipline (*Your father will be speaking to you about the state of your room when he gets home.*).

Speak about something, *address* or *raise* an issue.

Takeaways

Please, no more *takeaways*; no more *key takeaways* in particular. *Important lessons, salient points, major conclusions*: all better and more elegant.

Touchpoint

This one is proliferating, and that is not a good thing.

A *touchpoint* is, apparently, contact or interaction between parties, typically buyer and seller. Couldn't we just say that, instead of this touchy-feely and faintly icky compound? I feel like I'm being poked or prodded.

2) Lawyerly Compounds

By this, I don't mean where partners spend their weekends. Instead, I have horrors like these in mind, all of which suggest drafting with a quill pen by candlelight:

- *aforementioned* [or (shudder) its bastard progeny, *above-captioned* and *above-referenced*; *this* or *that* will often suffice]
- *herein*
- *hereinafter*
- *heretofore*
- *herewith*
- *hitherto*
- *inasmuch as*
- *notwithstanding*
- *therefrom*
- *therein*
- *thereinafter*
- *thereof*
- *thereto*
- *therewith*
- *whereas*
- *wherein*
- *whereof*
- *whereupon* [can always be replaced by *at which*, *on which*, or simply, *then*]

As Richard Wydick puts it, these words "give writing a legal smell, but they carry little or no legal substance. When they are used in writing addressed to non-lawyers, they baffle and annoy. When used in other legal writing, they give a false sense of precision and sometimes obscure a dangerous gap in analysis."[24] It's very easy to lose sight of what a *hereof* or a *therein* refers to in your sentence.

Avoid words like these in your client piece — and think about ways to do that in legal drafting too.

24 Richard Wydick & Amy E Sloan, *Plain English for Lawyers*, 6th ed (Durham, NC: Carolina Academic Press, 2019) at 64.

Please tell me you don't write letters like this

This is adapted from an actual letter received from a lawyer. The style and terminology of the original have been preserved, but the precise wording has been altered to maintain the confidentiality of the matter and to shroud the identity of the scribe with a justly deserved veil of anonymity:

> We acknowledge your recent correspondence of the 11th instant with thanks, same being forwarded herewith by the writer to our client for reference and review... We appreciate your consideration herein and ...

* *Instant*? No one has used that for "of the current month" since about 1870.
* *Same*?! Ugh, ugly commercialese — and, logically, it refers here to *thanks* not *correspondence* (which the writer presumably had in mind).
* *Herewith*? Archaic. And it's not entirely clear to what this refers.
* And *the writer*??!! You're a lawyer, not Queen Victoria — there's no need to refer to yourself in the third person.
* *Consideration herein*? In this document? This matter?

I fear this lawyer also writes to clients in the same vein.

Here's a proposed translation, which has the advantages of being shorter, clearer, and not drafted by some scrivener in a novel by Dickens:

> Thank you for your letter of [month] 11, which we have sent to our client.... We'd be grateful for your attention to this and ...

Less egregious, but equally Dickensian (in a bad way):

* *please find attached/enclosed* (even in the days of physical letters, the *please find* business was weird and archaic; you can simply say *I have attached the X* or refer to *the X, which is attached*)
* *please do not hesitate to ...* (the readers are grown-ups and can figure out whether they want or need to do that; this is meaningless and faintly patronizing)

- *this is to acknowledge* (just say *thank you for* whatever it is; by doing that, you've acknowledged it)
- *govern yourself accordingly* (the worst kind of wannabe Perry Masonism; it should be clear from your letter, if you're writing to a lawyer, that the recipient should be on notice about something, and if you aren't writing to a lawyer, it sounds even more cheaply menacing)

Please avoid these (and other) worn-out phrases, which have altogether too much of the inkwell and the quill pen about them.

3) Lose the Latin

Bryan Garner, editor of *Black's Law Dictionary* and a legal writing expert, blogged on the exciting topic of when italics should be used for Latin words and phrases and when they can be in roman (plain) type.[25] It must have been a slow day in the blogosphere.

He suggests that you can skip the italics when the word has become fully naturalized into English. So, "habeas corpus" and "prima facie," but *sensu stricto* and *in pari materia*.

In a waspish mood, I left a comment on Garner's blog, asking whether it wouldn't be better to write "strictly speaking" and "on the same subject" for the last two of those, since our clients don't generally converse in Latin. Mr Garner doesn't seem to have liked the comment, because it was "awaiting moderation" on his site for months and then vanished into the ether — but I stand by it.[26]

If you're acting for the Vatican or writing for an audience of learned monks, Latin is fine. Otherwise, use it only when it cannot

25 Bryan Garner, "LawProse Lesson #215: How Do You Decide Which Latin Phrases to Italicize?" *LawProse* (17 June 2015), online: www.lawprose.org/lawprose-lesson-215-how-do-you-decide-which-latin-phrases-to-italicize. See also, Thu-Huong Ha, "Bilingual Authors Are Challenging the Practice of Italicizing Non-English Words" *Quartz* (24 June 2018), online: https://quartzy.qz.com/1310228/bilingual-authors-are-challenging-the-practice-of-italicizing-non-english-words.

26 Mr Garner, or at least his people, also do not seem to reply to requests for permission to quote from the blog, which is too bad, considering its authority and comprehensiveness.

be avoided or is so widely understood that it doesn't look like a dead, foreign language.

This point seemed lost on many of the students in my Advanced Legal Research and Writing class, who thought *prima facie* was a helpful thing to say in their third written assignment, an update on a recent case for owners of small businesses. They learn bad linguistic habits early.

Supra and *infra* should yield to plain *above* and *below* — or omit that entirely and just say *See paragraph 16*; it will be obvious whether it is up or down in the text.

A Latin expression that is hard to lose is *stet* ("let it stand"), used by legal editors when they cross something out and then realize it should stay the way it was originally. It's difficult to think of an English equivalent of equal succinctness. *Stet* won't typically be seen outside the confines of a law office, and never once your piece has had its final edit, so you can let it stand.

Lawyerly use of Latin has its pitfalls, if you get things wrong. American lawyers use *scienter* as a noun ("degree of knowledge that makes a person legally responsible for the consequences of his or her act or omission; the fact of an act's having been done knowingly, esp. as a ground for civil damages or criminal punishment").[27]

To a classicist, *scienter* is an adverb ("knowingly" or "skilfully, expertly").

Better to stick to the language you and your readers know than to try looking all edjumacated.

4) Repetition

Judicious use of repetition can be a very effective rhetorical device, especially in written and oral advocacy. *Judicious* use, mind you.

Winston Churchill made memorable use of repetition: *We shall fight on the beaches, we shall fight on the landing grounds, we shall fight in the fields and in the streets, we shall fight in the hills.*

Lawyerly writing, on the other hand, tends to repeat things because the writer doesn't want to allow an iota of uncertainty by

27 Bryan A Garner, ed, *Black's Law Dictionary*, 10th ed (St Paul, MN: Thomson Reuters, 2014). Quoted with the permission of Thomson Reuters.

substituting a pronoun like *it* or *that*, or a synonym — or because the writer hasn't taken the time to edit.

Ask yourself, for example, whether you really need to repeat a defined term *ad nauseam*. You may in contractual drafting, for the sake of certainty, but in a case comment or client update the context may make things clear without dull duplication. If you're careful, *it* or *that* can work just fine.

If you read your piece aloud, you will be more likely to spot the kind of repetition that makes your prose leaden rather than lively.

5) Gender and Pronouns

a) Go Gender-Neutral

Strive for neutrality, or at least balance.

As Richard Wydick suggests, "many readers, both women and men, will be distracted and offended if you use masculine terms to refer to people who are not necessarily male."[28] People have begun to recognize this even in the fusty realm of contractual drafting, where the old-style phrase about *the masculine shall include the feminine* is being replaced with something more like this:

> Where the context requires, the singular shall include the plural, the plural shall include the singular, and any gender shall include all other genders.

Wydick also notes that it's equally distracting to use "clumsy efforts to avoid masculine terms," for example, using only feminine terms to redress imbalance or alternating between male and female.[29] This may have a sort of law-school ring to it, which may not be what you're aiming for.

Ways to go gender-neutral:

28 See Wydick & Sloan, above note 24 at 59. See also British Columbia Law Institute, *Gender-Free Legal Writing: Managing the Personal Pronouns* (July 1998), online: www.bcli.org/project/gender-free-legal-writing-managing-personal-pronouns; Kati Pajak Strzelczyk, "How to Write Gender-Neutral Contracts" (27 January 2020) *Mintz* online: www.mintz.com/insights-center/viewpoints/2911/2020-01-how-write-gender-neutral-contracts.

29 See Wydick & Sloan, above note 24 at 59–61.

* use both masculine and feminine: *each client will need to consider his or her own circumstances* (or indeed, *her or his*)
* omit the pronoun altogether: *the client will need to make the decision* (or *a client*) instead of *the client will need to make his own decision*
* use *you* instead of *he* or *she*: *as a consumer, you'll need to make your own choice* rather than *each consumer must decide for himself*
* use *it* instead of *he* or *she* (this may often work, if many or even most of your clients are not natural persons): *the bank's customer will need to decide for itself* not *the bank's customer will have to decide for himself or herself*
* use the plural: *bank customers will need to decide for themselves*
* repeat the noun: *a client will have to decide whether this is appropriate for that client's particular circumstances* rather than . . . *for her circumstances*
* alternate between masculine and feminine: this can look awkward and artificial, however, and you can mess up where a pronoun should be gendered, thereby giving someone an accidental gender swap
* use the passive voice: not recommended, as it weakens the impact of your writing (see Chapter 3, Section A(3), "Take a Pass on the Passive")
* terminology: *chair* not *chairman*, *representative* not *spokesman* (although *fisherfolk* sounds silly, and *fishers* not much better — nor would I recommend referring to *the four horsepersons of the Apocalypse*)

Ways not to:

* *he/she* or *his/her*: ugly (don't even get me started on *(s)he*)
* *their* or *themselves*: fine if your antecedent is plural (*clients will need to assess their needs themselves*) but not if it's singular (*a client will need to assess its needs* or *his or her needs*); but see Section D(4)(b), "The Problem with Pronouns," below, and see Chapter 3, Section A(4)(b), "Let's Get Personal."[30]

30 It just seems weird to write *A woman could be in business, they could be an engineer, they could be a lawyer, they could be a doctor*, as found in a Lexology

b) The Problem with Pronouns

Have you been to a meeting yet where people announce, or add to their name tags, what their preferences are in terms of the personal pronouns you should use in relation to them? This isn't common on Bay Street, but it's all over the university and not-for-profit sector.

The choices these days are not strictly binary. Some people now prefer to be referred to as *they* or *them*, or go for truly gender-neutral neologisms like *ze*, *ey*, *hir*, or *xe*. It may take some time for those to make it to the financial district and the big law firms, but the singular *they* is (like it or not) here to stay.[31]

We should recognize that pronoun use has always been fluid in English: remember *thee* and *thou*, which passed out of common usage by the end of the seventeenth century? And there are literary instances of the singular *they* before our own century. If someone asks to be called or referred to as something specific, obviously you should do so — it would be rude not to.

I don't entirely like the singular *they* — when it's used in a lazy way. *A tax lawyer should never be without* ***their*** *copy of the Income Tax Act* is lazy; at the risk of offending the gender-fluid, *his or her* is preferable, at least grammatically. Ninety-nine times out of a hundred, the intent behind such *their* constructions was not gender-neutrality or concern for the intersex; it was just sloppiness of thought.

If you must use the singular *they*, it should be based on a desire to be inclusive of the transgendered, the gender-fluid, and the gender-questioning (which is probably not what most people are up to when they talk about *a tax lawyer and* ***their*** *copy of the Income*

---

post (12 March 2019), online: www.lexology.com/library/detail.aspx?g=e3233557-0fcb-4b99-8597-140f943acaoc.

31 See also Gretchen McCulloch, "The Year Marks a New Language Shift in How English Speakers Use Pronouns" *Quartz* (21 December 2015), online: https://qz.com/578937/this-year-marks-a-new-language-shift-in-how-english-speakers-use-pronouns; "English Has a Traditional Solution to Gender-Neutral Pronouns" (1 April 2017), *The Economist* online: www.economist.com/news/books-and-arts/21719768-praise-singular-they-english-has-traditional-solution-gender-neutral-pronouns?frsc=dg%7Ca; "Who Do They Think They Are?" *The Economist* (16 January 2020), online: www.economist.com/books-and-arts/2020/01/16/who-do-they-think-they-are?frsc=dg%7Ce.

Tax Act, or LinkedIn when it invites you to congratulate someone on ***their** work anniversary*).

As ever, English is more complicated than other languages—many of which don't use gendered pronouns (or even pronouns at all, in some instances): Armenian, Bengali, Chinese, Finnish, Hungarian, Japanese, Korean, Persian, Turkish. Others have a neuter pronoun that can be repurposed for our newly gender-sensitive era (German, Icelandic) or have invented a third, gender-free option (Swedish). In Romance languages (French, Italian, and Spanish) there are gendered pronouns, but it isn't the gender of the person involved who determines what you use in possessive constructions. The gender of the object governs, not the subject: in French, it's *son livre* (a masculine noun, which must therefore take a masculine pronoun), whether the book belongs to a man, a woman, or a differently gendered person.[32]

c) Gendered Job Descriptions

Does it still strike you as odd to see Cate Blanchett or Meryl Streep described as an *actor*?

Actress is in fact a relatively new word in English, because no women performed on stage in England before the seventeenth century (although the *Oxford English Dictionary* (*OED*) does say that *actor* was applied to both sexes in the early days of the mixed stage).

Even now, not everybody is using *actor* for both women and men. There are more than 75,000 women who describe themselves on LinkedIn as an *actress*. Oscars are not yet awarded to the best *female actor*—much less to the best *actor*, regardless of sex (or gender).

Other *–ess* words faded away longer ago. It would be rare nowadays to ask to speak to the *manageress* of a shop. Even early in the twentieth century, the terms *poetess* and *sculptress* fell from use because they sounded faintly derogatory (*OED* quotes a passage in which *poetess* is described as becoming old-fashioned in 1903). *Waitress* is disappearing—but so too is *waiter*, both largely displaced by *server*. One would still use *priestess*, but only in relation to a non-Christian, possibly historical religion ("the *priestess* of Diana

32 The gendering of nouns often seems arbitrary in French, especially if you think of the names (both standard and colloquial) for body parts involved in sexual activity; these are not always intuitively designated masculine or feminine.

at Ephesus"), rather than for a female ordained in the Anglican churches that have them.

If you are still using legal Latin, you may still also be referring to a *testatrix*, *executrix*, or (possibly) *administratrix* (although Ontario's *Succession Law Reform Act* uses the *–tor* forms for both men and women). *Aviatrix* is as dead as Amelia Earhart, but *dominatrix* is firmly entrenched (perhaps because no one would dare mess with one).

United States *congressmen* have been joined by *congresswomen* since the early twentieth century, but *congresspersons* or *congresspeople* never gained much terminological traction. (Do you remember *Saturday Night Live*'s send-up of The Village Persons?)

If the trend in English seems to be going towards the gender-neutral (or, actually, to the terms formerly applied only to men, like *priest*), continental languages have gone the other way.

In the days when there weren't many, a female lawyer in France or Quebec used to be *un avocat*, just like her male counterpart; one now sees *une avocate*. In traditional European French, a female judge was *madame le juge*; *madame la juge* was the polite way to refer to the wife of a male judge. Quebeckers — either less polite or more egalitarian, depending on how you look at it — dropped *madame la juge* for the judge's wife, and started using it for a *Madam Justice*.

A woman lawyer in Italy is an *avvocatessa*, and a female academic is a *dottoressa* or *professoressa*.

In Germany, the feminine equivalent of a *Rechtsanwalt* (lawyer) is a *Rechtsanwältin*, although the Federal Lawyers Code uses the masculine form as a "gender-neutral" term. In academic circles, one is either *Frau* or *Herr Doktor* (or, if super-qualified, *Herr* or *Frau Doktor Doktor* or *Professor Doktor*).

d) *Trans* and *Cis*

As a result of popular culture (as much as anything else), most people are now aware of the meaning of *trans* (or *transgender*).

It refers to someone who was assigned a gender at birth but who later takes steps to affirm another gender that more closely aligns with their true identity.

The *trans* part is derived from Latin and means "across" or "on the other side." We see it in words that involve crossing boundaries, barriers, and other things: *transatlantic*, *transgression*, *transition*, *translation*.

A bit less familiar is the expression *cis*, now used to refer to people who were assigned a gender at birth that they remain OK with. For example: *Cis White men make up the majority of partners at law firms*.

Cis is the Latin opposite of *trans*, and means "this side of."

So *Cisalpine Gaul* was the part of the province on the Roman side of the Alps; to get to *Transalpine Gaul*, the Romans had to cross the mountains. (The Gauls would have seen things differently, of course.)

In the early twentieth century, *Cisjordan* and *Transjordan* were used to describe the territories on either side of the River Jordan. The former is now more usually called the West Bank, although the French still refer to it as *Cisjordanie*. The early twentieth-century Emirate of *Transjordan* became the modern Kingdom of *Jordan*.

Those who really know their history will recognize *Cisleithania* as a name for the non-Hungarian parts of the Austro-Hungarian Empire, the Leitha being a small tributary of the Danube that marks the historical border between the Archduchy of Austria and the Kingdom of Hungary.

Note that in all the geographic senses, the definition of what is on this side and what is across the way is determined by the perspective of the more powerful group, and I suspect those who identify as trans might say the same thing.

e) *Womxn*

No, that isn't a typo.

The spelling is deliberate, an attempt to decouple *woman* and *women* from that male-sounding second syllable.[33]

And indeed, the Anglo-Saxon origins of the traditional spelling of the word are pretty sexist: *woman* (originally *wifmane*) is a

33 See, for example, Saavriti, "Why We Should Use the Word Womxn and Not Women" *SheThe People* (2020), online: www.shethepeople.tv/home-top-video/use-word-womxn-women.

combination of *wife* and *man*, as though heterosexual marriage were defining.

Womxn isn't the first attempt to neutralize those gendered overtones. In the 1970s, some feminists started to refer to themselves as *womyn* or *wimmin* (the latter is also an old, regional English spelling of *women*).

More recently, we have seen *Latinx* as an inclusive substitute for *Latino*, *Latina*, and *Latino/a*.

Female would need to be revisited on this logic. The word derives from the Old French *femele* (or *femelle*), which in turn comes from the Latin *femella* and *femina*, but the *–male* ending arose in Middle English by association with the obviously masculine *male*.

Unlike *Latinx* (la-TEE-nex), *womxn* is unpronounceable. It also may be unclear whether it refers to a single person or more than one, although the context should usually clarify that.

It's doubtful we'll see *womxn* in contractual or statutory drafting soon, but it may happen; the days of the masculine gender being defined to include the feminine are not so far behind us.

6) Other Terminological Issues

a) Race, Ethnic Origin, Disability

Terminology associated with these terms is fraught with peril these days, not least because the terminology changes — and sometimes rapidly. Forgive me if I put a foot wrong!

Indian is not a term one should use, except in relation to people from India (and I'm guessing people from the *West Indies* may prefer *Caribbean*). Having said that, *Indian* is (for now) a term of art in the *Indian Act* ("a person who pursuant to this Act is registered as an Indian or is entitled to be registered as an Indian," section 2(1)). *Indigenous* now seems to be the acceptable term, although it's not strictly accurate if the ancestors of our *First Nations* peoples came originally from Asia across the Bering land bridge; something that is *indigenous* to a particular location has always been there (the French *autochtone*, used in relation to this continent's First Peoples, is to the same effect). *Aboriginal* seems to have passed out of favour in Canada (but Australians still refer to *Aborigines*), as has *Native* to some extent. *Eskimo*, a derogatory term, is now universally *Inuit*, in Canada at least.

For people whose ancestors came from (sub-Saharan) Africa, *Black* is still used (*Black Lives Matter*), as are *African-American* and *African-Canadian* — although the latter two would probably not be used to describe people from the top part of the continent, like Berbers or Egyptians. Terminology with ugly historical associations is to be avoided, although there are some holdovers (the *National Association for the Advancement of Colored People* has not changed its name, and I think one can still talk about *Negro spirituals*).

People of colour is a useful (if imprecise) description for non-Caucasians (who aren't actually colourless). *Caucasian* is a bizarre term to begin with, based on a since-exploded eighteenth-century theory that the "White races" (and some others) originated in the Caucasus region between the Black Sea and the Caspian Sea.

I still haven't managed to get my aged parents to substitute *Asian* for *Oriental*; they don't seem to get that there is no centre of the world in relation to which people are eastern or western. (The *Middle East*, by the bye, used to refer to the region roughly from Mesopotamia to Burma, when London saw itself as centric; as the axis of global power shifted westwards to Washington, the Middle East did too. Things may be shifting back eastwards, but past London.)

Scotch used to be the usual description for someone or something from Scotland, at least to a Sassenach (English person); it's better now to say *Scottish* or *Scots* (the latter, particularly, in reference to the country's distinct legal system). Vestigial uses of *Scotch*: *Scotch bonnet*, *Scotch broth*, *Scotch egg*, *Scotch mist*, *Scotch whisky* (which I would just call *whisky*, all other types needing an identifier like *Irish* or *rye*; the Irish variety is more usually spelt *whiskey*).

People with disabilities understandably prefer that term to *disabled people*, so as to place the emphasis on the person not the disability.

Capitalize terms denoting race? Sometimes it's useful (*White privilege* is more pointed than *white privilege*), but it's not always necessary (*Why aren't there more brown partners at your firm?*). An uppercase B for *Black* is now preferred.

When in doubt, the best policy is to ask someone's terminological preference in these matters and be willing to be educated. We all make mistakes, but not everyone seeks to learn from them.

b) Corporate Names

As many readers will know, the Law Society of Upper Canada rebranded itself in 2017 as the Law Society of Ontario (LSO).

A new logo also appeared on the LSO website in place of a stylized version of the Society's coat of arms, together with pictures of a Black man and an Asian woman with a nose-ring.

Presumably all of this was an attempt to shake off a perceived stuffy image, part of a larger effort to appear (and perhaps even be) more relevant to the general, non-lawyer population. We'll see about that, but I'm doubtful.

The new logo, which consists of three concentric circles, could just as easily be that of a pharmaceutical company or a credit union. Bland! And no amount of stock photography is going to solve the legal profession's diversity and inclusion problems.

There can be value in keeping a seemingly outdated name. The National Association for the Advancement of Colored People remains resolutely that, reminding us of historical struggles and also continuing challenges. Sadly, some things haven't changed, but sticking to the old name is an effective way to convey that. The New-York Historical Society retains its antique hyphen, suggesting a strong historical sense while indicating in a tiny way that the past is, as one historian put it, a foreign country. It is no bad thing to keep that in mind, without imposing a sanitized version of the present.

For those who prefer incremental change, the Law Society of Canada West might have been an option.

In any case, a rose by any other name …

E. EMAIL AND OTHER CORRESPONDENCE

1) Email Pointers for the Millennial Generation (and Others)

Millennials are said to favour more new-fangled methods of communication like WhatsApp, Snapchat, and Facebook Messenger to old-fashioned email. As a result, they may be a little more casual in their communications than some of their stuffier older colleagues may like. But even the older types need some pointers on this subject.

Mary Beard, everyone's favourite classicist, perceptively notes that old-fashioned correspondence offered subtle gradations in formality, which we haven't got quite right with electronic mail. Beard finds email inappropriately informal, strangely unpersuasive, often annoying, and not conducive to genuine expressions of thanks.

Writing a letter also involved a helpful cooling-off period because you had to make the effort to find a stamp and then post your letter; this gave time for second thoughts about sending it at all.

To save her from those late-night missives sent after one glass too many, Beard wishes her laptop had a function that blocked sending anything after 11 p.m., followed up by an "Are you sure?" message in the morning, or a built-in breathalyzer.[34]

a) Caution

Don't reply in haste, much less in anger. Think twice before sending something you think is funny.

Proofread; don't rely on spell-check.

Beware of "bcc," "reply all," distribution lists, and auto-fill for recipient names — especially when you are dealing with privileged and confidential information. Make sure metadata are scrubbed from attachments (they may not be when you use a mobile device).

Think about who needs to be copied (and who does not).

You represent your firm and yourself in every email sent to third parties.

b) Content

The "subject" field should contain a brief but meaningful summary of the content of the message. This helps the recipient find the relevant email later, when it's buried amidst the other thousand things in the in-box. It's also helpful to summarize the message in the first line or two of the message itself.

34 Mary Beard, "I Hope This Email Finds You Well" *BBC Sounds* (20 October 2017), online: www.bbc.co.uk/sounds/play/b098ns34.

Proofread (again). There is research that suggests a direct correlation between grammatical mistakes in the subject line of an email and lack of reader response.[35] Errors in the body of the email won't help matters either; the recipient's confidence in the quality of your content will be undermined by technical faults.

One subject per email (this makes them easier to file and retrieve later). Short sentences, short paragraphs, short emails. Headings are useful.

Attachments can be annoying (especially if there are other emails containing their own attachments or other attached email messages).

Use the "high priority" flag very sparingly, if at all.

c) Courtesy

Be responsive, even if it's only to acknowledge receipt and say you'll respond later at greater length.

Know when email is not appropriate. If the senior partner calls you on the phone, respond in kind.

Don't use your mobile device in meetings. It's rude. If you have to check email or deal with something, excuse yourself discreetly and step outside.

Think about timing: don't send and then vanish. Also remember that many people sleep with a mobile device on the bedside table. Your 4 a.m. ping may wake a sleeping client or partner.

Don't ask recipients to check a box acknowledging that they've read your email: it's passive-aggressive and annoying.

Always set an "out of office" message when you're not around; this helps to manage expectations. Your level of seniority can dictate how much you push back in the message about responsiveness (or lack of it). Or perhaps your location: *I am travelling by yak in a remote region of Outer Mongolia with no access to email.* If you respond when you say you won't, you've undermined any buffer that geography, time zones, and ostensible lack of connectivity may have given you.

35 See Sarah Kessler, "The Most Unforgiveable Email Mistake if You Want a Response" *Quartz* (3 January 2018), online: https://qz.com/877111/whats-the-worst-email-mistake-to-make.

On the subject of "out of office" messages, both recorded and electronic, could we avoid the formulation *I'll get back to you as soon as possible* as soon as possible? *Get back* is a bit colloquial for professional use, and it has more than a slight tone of the dismissive: if someone says *I'll get back to you on that*, odds are it won't be soon, or at all. Just say you'll *reply* or *respond*. At the other end of the tone spectrum is *as soon as I am able*, which is, like *Should you wish to leave a message* in recorded voicemail greetings, merely fancy for the sake of it; plain old *as soon as I can* or even *soon* would be fine.

Remember to turn off your "out of office" message as soon as you're back (if only to forestall that irritating person who will point out that it's still on) — but you may wish to wait until you've cleared through your in-box and whatever else has piled up in your absence.

d) Emoticons and Emoji

Tone can be difficult to convey in an email. What you intended as light-hearted banter can be interpreted by the recipient as a snarky comment. So, you might be tempted to resort to one of those cute little pictures that proliferate in your text messages to indicate that it's all intended in fun.

By way of taxonomy, an *emoticon* is a graphic representation of a facial expression, using punctuation marks, letters, or numbers (a semi-colon and a closing parenthesis for a wink, a colon and a capital D for a grin); *emoji* are pictographs that do the same work (the smiley face image being the most well-known, but there are many more now, and they are increasing in number and complexity).[36]

Don't succumb to the temptation to use these if (a) the recipient of your email is older than you are, (b) the exchange is professional rather than personal, or (c) both (a) and (b). Use smiley faces all you want with your assistant, your friends at another firm, or the other associates in your group (but only when you're scheduling after-work drinks, not when you're talking about a file).

Otherwise, NO emoticons or emoji.

36 *Emoji* is plural in Japanese, I gather, but one also sees *emojis* as a plural in English.

e) Formality

In a business setting, email can be a bit more casual than a letter or opinion, but you may want to clothe it in more formal dress when providing advice or replying in a thoughtful way. One-word or one-sentence replies are one thing, but if the message or the recipient is important, your email should be more like a traditional letter.

Always use proper punctuation, capitalization, and grammar. Professional email is no place for LOL, LMFAO, srsly, WTF, and the like.[37]

"Hi Dave" may be an appropriate opener when you're writing to your peer at another firm, but probably not when it's some crusty senior partner. "Dear So-and-so" may seem a bit weird in an email, but fear not that it may suggest that an affectionate relationship is being claimed. (See Section E(3), "Beginnings and Endings," below.)

f) Format

Don't experiment with fonts and formatting. Stick to a standard template (especially if you are working in a firm or corporate setting), and always include your signature block (with a link to your LinkedIn profile and your firm's social media, if appropriate).

37 That said, at least two of the abbreviations beloved of texting millennials have an older provenance than you might imagine.

IDK, short for "I don't know," turns out to be US military slang from the First World War. The *New Courier* of Athens, Alabama, reported on 17 August 1918 that *IDK* was "the latest American soldier slang . . . which stands for 'I don't know' in reply to fool questions asked by recruits and men who have just been landed." Or perhaps by partners in law firms. See online: https://twitter.com/sophcocooper/status/1024667840320815106?s=11).

OMG ("Oh, my God/gosh!") is of roughly the same vintage, having been used by Admiral Lord Fisher in a letter to Winston Churchill (then Minister of Munitions) on 9 September 1917. While the admiral explained that it stood for "Oh! My God!," he was using it as a short form for a fanciful new order of knighthood, jokingly modelled on the existing Order of St Michael and St George (the grades of which are abbreviated as CMG, KCMG, and GCMG). So, not quite how the kids are using it now. See online: www.smithsonianmag.com/smart-news/the-first-use-of-omg-was-in-a-1917-letter-to-winston-churchill-145636383.

g) Swearing

You may have noticed that lawyers, especially the baby boomers, use colourful language quite a lot. This might be nerds over-compensating, but that's just a theory.

In any event, use profanity *only* if you know your readers are OK with it, and only in something not related to work, especially when dealing with external parties.

h) Taming the In-Box

Create folders, arranged by client or subject. Save email to your document-management system, if you can. Ruthlessly delete the unnecessary. I never have more than ten messages in my in-box, if I can help it.

i) Titles

Admittedly, you may not be using all of these in regular correspondence.

Judges

Stephen Waddams observes in *Introduction to the Study of Law* (my edition is 1992) that it is not proper to refer to a judge as *Your Honour* (or *My Lord/Lady*, where that is still used) outside the courtroom. He advocates just plain *Mr Wagner* or *Ms Karakatsanis*, or failing that, the old-fashioned *Judge* (without the person's surname) when you encounter one in a social setting. Most Canadian lawyers will probably say *Justice So-and-so* at a cocktail party, if they are not on first-name terms, and this also has the sanction of historical usage.

As pointed out elsewhere, it's *Madam* (emphasis on the first syllable) *Justice*, not *Madame Justice*. In England, it's *Mrs* (or less commonly *Ms*, occasionally *Miss*) *Justice* for women High Court judges. (Canada did a better job of capturing the dignity of the bench with *Madam.*) In the Court of Appeal for England and Wales, it is *Lord* or *Lady Justice Who's-it*; in the UK Supreme Court, *Lord* or *Baroness* (or *Lady*, depending on preference) *What's-it*.

Retired judges in Canada and England are often still referred to by their former judicial titles, as a courtesy, but it is not wrong to call the former *Justice Binnie* just plain *Mr Binnie* now that he is back in private practice. Beverley McLachlin, though retired from the Supreme Court of Canada, is still *Justice McLachlin* (although not *Chief Justice*) because she now sits on Hong Kong's Court of Final Appeal. And an envelope addressed to her would not have *Ms Beverley McLachlin* on it; she is *The Rt Hon Beverley McLachlin*, as a former CJC — and in writing Mr Binnie gets *The Hon Ian Binnie*.

Government officials

Ministers of the Crown are now referred to as *Minister Freeland* or *Minister Elliott* — and, *mutatis mutandis*, so are mayors, police chiefs, dog catchers, what have you. This is an unfortunate American habit. In the good old days in our loved Dominion, the Minister of Whatever was simply called *Minister* to her or his face and referred to as *Mr*, *Ms*, etc., as the case might be. Somewhere along the way (and I think it was in the 1980s), we began imitating the US convention of calling officials in the executive branch *Secretary Baker* and *Assistant Under-Secretary Butcher*. (This happened in eighteenth-century England, too, where the Speaker of the House of Commons would be called *Speaker Onslow* or what have you.)

Another weird thing (among many) that Americans do is to keep calling former office-holders by the title they used to hold. In Canada and the United Kingdom, a former prime minister goes back to private life and relinquishes all the trappings of office, including the title (although, in the United Kingdom, they might get a peerage or knighthood, like *Baroness Thatcher* or *Sir John Major*). It's *Ms Kim Campbell* and *Mr David Cameron* (although both are, more formally, *The Rt Hon*). Whereas south of the 49th parallel, *President Carter*, *President Bush* (times two), *President Clinton*, and *President Obama* are still kicking around. As well as that orange person.

And while we're on the subject, Amurricans still say *Mr President*, *Ms Secretary*, etc. We dropped the M-preamble long ago: it's *How do you do, prime minister?* when you meet our head of government, not *Mr* or *Ms Prime Minister*.

Royalty

The person represented on the coinage isn't *Queen Elizabeth*: that was her mother, *Queen Elizabeth, The Queen Mother*. It is simply *The Queen* or *Her Majesty* on your Canadian quarter.

Prince Charles is what we call the heir apparent to the Canadian throne colloquially, but he is properly *The Prince of Wales* (in Scotland, though, he is *The Duke of Rothesay and Lord of the Isles*). His first wife was never (correctly) *Princess Diana*; she started her married life as *The Princess of Wales* and after her divorce became *Diana, Princess of Wales*. Wife number two is not *Camilla, Duchess of Cornwall*, which would imply she is a widow or a divorcée. Just *The Duchess of Cornwall*; same deal with her step-daughters-in-law.

If their husbands had not been created royal dukes, Kate and (pre-withdrawal) Meghan would be respectively *Princess William of Wales* and *Princess Harry of Wales*. If that sounds odd, think of the old-fashioned way of addressing a married lady: *Mrs John Smith* (and of *Princess Michael of Kent*, whose first name is Marie-Christine). In any event, never *Princess* (or *Duchess*) *Kate* or *Meghan*, even though they are both princesses (and duchesses) by virtue of marriage.

Note, by the way, those official uppercase Ts in the titles of senior royals. And you should stick *HRH* before the title of a prince or princess, *HM* for the Boss.

2) Email Disclaimers

Nerd alert: I love assessing the email disclaimers that individual lawyers and law firms use, especially as they relate to matters privileged and confidential.

The laziest of these notices merely assert that the content of the email is privileged and confidential. But wait, you're my lawyer friend and you've just asked me by email if I'm free for a beer on Friday. That's privileged and confidential? Of course it isn't. In most cases, this isn't an issue, but on a big litigation file you might find yourself struggling before a judge to say why something contentious *is* privileged and confidential when it becomes apparent that you routinely slap the disclaimer on everything you send, drink invitations included.

A bit more thoughtful is the disclaimer that the contents of the email *may* be privileged and confidential. But only a bit; you've admitted that not everything a lawyer sends will be privileged or confidential, but it still looks like you haven't thought about whether the actual communication is or not. This isn't better than saying everything's privileged and confidential, if push comes to shove.

It is preferable to have no boilerplate disclaimer at all, and to label something as privileged and confidential when it truly is, in the subject line of the email and at the top of the underlying message, as well as in the fine print underneath. Putting this into practice would be a nuisance, however — and would require some thought.

And you must think about whether what you send is privileged at all: I think it drove a former general counsel boss of mine crazy when I identified information as confidential only, but I was correct as a matter of law; only actual legal advice is privileged, not facts or even suggestions for your readers to consider legal issues and reach their own conclusions.

The other thing that kills me in standard email disclaimers is the assertion that disclosure of the contents of an email that wasn't intended for you is *strictly prohibited.*[38] By what, exactly? If you can tell me, I'll buy you a Negroni. No, two. Doubles.

3) Beginnings and Endings

Openings and closing of business correspondence, that is.

My late father, an old-fashioned lawyer if ever there was one, once said there are only two ways to start and close a business letter: either *Dear Sir/Yours faithfully* or *Dear Mr So-and-so/Yours truly*, depending on one's level of acquaintance with the recipient. (And not *very truly*: one is true or one is not; no more, no less.) There is a certain simplicity to that, and it can be made female-friendly without difficulty.

My own views follow.

a) Beginnings

Younger folk appear to have this strange view that *Dear* at the start of a letter somehow suggests affection.

38 I have even seen a warning that disclosure is not only *strictly prohibited* but also *may be illegal.*

Dear Sir is a little warmer than just *Sir*, but it's by no means touchy-feely (*Dear Sir, Your account now being considerably in arrears . . .*).

That said, *Dear* may look a bit old-fashioned in a more casual email, where *Hello Neil* or *Hi Neil* seems to have largely displaced *Dear Neil*.

Just using someone's first name without *Hi* or *Hello* before it could sound a bit stern, however.

> *Neil, I want to talk to about this* sounds like I'm in trouble.
>
> *Hi Neil, I want to talk to you about this* is much chirpier and therefore less ominous.

I would confine the *hi* and *hello* business to purely casual exchanges, and inject more formality into an email message that contains considered legal advice.

Dear Mary in a business letter? If you want — but a more elegant way to do it is to type *Dear Ms Wang*, cross that out in pen and write in her first name. In England, it's usual in business letters to leave out the salutation and the *Yours truly* bit entirely, leaving blank space which the writer fills in by hand, with whatever degree of formality seems appropriate.

If you are at the *Dear Sir* level, the female equivalent is *Madam*. Not *Madame* — although the plural of *Madam* (in this context) is *Mesdames*, not *Madams* (which is the plural form for women who run brothels). And on that note, it's *Madam Justice*, not *Madame*; she's running a court, not a bordello (although it may seem that way at times).

One sometimes used to see *Gentlemen* as a substitute for (*Dear*) *Sirs* in letters addressed to a firm in general (typically, opinion letters). The gender-neutral equivalent should be *Dear Sirs and Mesdames*; the formulation *Ladies and Gentlemen* that people sometimes use has (to me, anyway) an air of the circus tent to it (*Ladies and gentlemen, boys and girls! The greatest show on earth!*).

For the love of pity, avoid the leaden *I hope this finds you well* as an opening line; surely you can think of something more interesting, and it's always better to get to the point instead of this waffle. Almost as bad is *I (just) wanted to . . .* (Do you not still want to?) In thank-you emails (or letters, if people still send those), the most boring opener is *Thank you for . . .*

b) *I hope this email finds you well*

More on this. Beloved of vendors of products and services you probably don't want and with whom you are unacquainted, it is puzzling.

What *do* they mean?

The first possibility is that the sender hopes (or pretends, for the sake of fake-friendliness) that when the email finds me, I am *well*; that is, healthy, in a state of contentment, etc.

That interpretation is unlikely not only because it presupposes the sincerity of the wish, but also because I am 99.999% sure that the sender would use *good* (not the grammatically correct *well*) in response to the question "How are you?"

The only other possibility is that the sender is hoping that the email finds me *well* in the sense of its having travelled directly or without difficulty to me through the ether. However, now that we've entered the third decade of email's widespread use as a communications tool, it is wholly unnecessary to be asking that very 1990s question, "Did you get my email?"

Oh, it found me all right (and I wish it hadn't). If it hadn't, you'd have received a bounce-back.

Since the possible meanings of *I hope this email finds you well* are either unlikely or inane, can we please consign this leaden opener to the dustbin of sales clichés? But perhaps this is being harsh.

As it turns out, however (and as Mary Beard notes in the BBC video cited above), it's not much different from the *SVBEV* (or *SVBEEV*) used as an opener by writers of letters in ancient Rome, which stood for *Si vales bene est* [ego] *valeo* ("If you're OK, that's good; I am too").[39] And Alexander Pope, one of the best letter-writers ever, used the *I hope this finds you well* formulation (although obviously not by email).

Mary asks, are the old clichés the best clichés? I actually think not — they're all terrible and to be avoided.

39 See above note 34.

c) Endings

I think my father was correct that these should be on the formal side. Save (*Yours) sincerely* for social correspondence.

And, if I could, I would banish *regards* of all sorts (*kind, warm, warm personal, best, fond*, whatevs). You're never going to send regards that are unkind, lukewarm, cold, impersonal, worst, not quite best.

Apparently in India, however, one often sees *Unfeigned regards* as a sign-off. That one would even think to say this suggests the ridiculousness of the whole *regards* thing: are regards that are said to be *kind, warm*, or *best* inevitably insincere? Perhaps it's better not to send any of these in the first place. I confess, though, that I do sometimes add *Best wishes* or just *Best* (occasionally *All best*) if the email needs to sound a bit friendlier — but I cringe inwardly while doing it.[40]

Similarly, avoid worn-out and meaningless phrases like *Please do not hesitate to contact me* . . . The reader may well be inclined to think "Of course I won't hesitate — what sort of shrinking violet does she think I am?" or alternatively, "I'll hesitate if I bloody well want to; you charge by the hour and I'll only get in touch if necessary." Either way, it's useless.

Closings like *have a good* [or *great*, etc.] *day* or anything that smacks of the motivational/inspirational should be avoided.

Always include a standard signature block with your contact information in emails that are going to external parties. It's useful to include relevant professional information with that, like links to your LinkedIn profile and Twitter feed.

I don't put a comma after *Yours truly* and the like. I also omit one (or a colon) after *Dear So-and-so* at the top of a letter. More modern, cleaner typographically, with no loss of sense.

40 For a compelling case to omit all this sort of stuff, see Rebecca Greenfield, "Why Signing Your Emails with 'Best' Is Actually the Worst" (3 June 2015), *Mashable*, online: http://mashable.com/2015/06/03/best-email-signoff.

d) Thanks!

I used to work with someone who might fairly be described as curmudgeonly. This person detests people who reply to an email with a one-word *Thanks*.

Needless replies are a bit annoying, but it's also hard to know when to terminate an email exchange. The advice I give to law students in my seminar on email in a professional setting is to err on the side of politeness, especially in relation to more senior peeps — even at the risk of irritating a curmudgeon.

e) Attention!

The other day I received that now rather unusual thing, a letter. On the envelope, beneath my business address, was typed *Attention:* with my name after it.

Why is this — or why was it ever — necessary? I suppose it helped postal delivery persons and mailroom workers a bit, but surely not that much. My name at the top with the address after it would reach me with no problem, just like a non-business letter sent to me at my home address.

While we're on the subject, I like addresses to go from the particular to the general:

Box, office, or floor number
Building
Street address
City, province/state
Code
Country

F. WHAT SHOULD IT LOOK LIKE?

1) Think About Layout and Design

If you are fortunate enough to have them, this will largely be a job for the marketing or communications departments who prepare pieces for publication, but there are some design aspects you should be thinking about too.

a) White Space

Dense blocks of text are hard on the eyes. Too many words will repel readers. Think about breaking up long paragraphs and sentences so your piece is easier to read, especially if it will be viewed on a small screen. Vary the length of your sentences.

b) Headings and Sub-headings

A useful way to impose order when you're writing, and to guide the reader when the piece is published.

c) Block Quotations

Avoid long quotations. As Matthew Butterick says in his illuminating book, *Typography for Lawyers*, don't assume anyone will read a big chunk of quoted text:

> Lawyers often dump text into a block quotation intending to signal "This source is really important, so I've quoted a lot of it!"
>
> Instead, the actual signal a reader often gets is "Here's something long and dull from another case whose meaning and relevance you'll have to figure out for yourself because I can't be bothered to summarize it!"[41]

Readers tend to skip over block quotations in any event. You're better to quote only the essential bits, integrate the rest into your own text or, if a long quotation is indispensable, explain what it says before you quote (on the assumption the reader won't be bothered to read the quotation).

41 Matthew Butterick, *Typography for Lawyers: Essential Tools for Polished and Persuasive Documents*, 2d ed (Houston, TX: O'Connors, 2015) at 147 (quoted with the permission of Thomson Reuters). For more on fonts, see online: http://tips.slaw.ca/2019/practice/its-not-what-you-say-its-how-you-say-it-using-typefaces-to-write-more-persuasively. See also Adeline Cheok & Andrew Lumsden, "The New World of Legal Design" (2019) *Michigan Bar Journal* 42, online: www.michbar.org/file/barjournal/article/documents/pdf4article3756.pdf; Wydick & Sloan, above note 24 at 105–17.

d) Bulleted and Numbered Lists

These are helpful:

- they're easy to read
- they provide emphasis
- they break up your text

Keep each item in the list short, though. Punctuation optional after each item (more modern and elegant without it).

Make sure the grammar of each bullet point syncs with the others (they should start with the same part of speech, verb tense, etc.) and any internal punctuation works (if you introduce your list with a colon, the bullet points can't have periods or colons within them).

e) Boldface and Italics

Use sparingly. As Butterick points out, "if everything is emphasized, then nothing is emphasized."[42] Bold and italics are also harder to read than roman (regular) text.

f) Fonts

Legal writers should think about fonts in their own documents so their written work is easier to read and more compelling.[43]

Some fonts are more readable on a screen than on a printed page, and vice versa. Others are better suited to contracts than presentations. Some fonts look professional; others (Comic Sans) do not.

Butterick hates Arial; and, while "it's not that Times New Roman is a bad font," he doesn't exactly love it (the United States Supreme Court forbids it).

The book also discusses punctuation marks, spacing, formatting, and layout, with elegant sample documents and practical advice.

Fonts can be of forensic value as well. In *Re McGoey*, a bankrupt argued that two properties had been placed in trust for his children in 1995 and were not part of the assets available to his creditors in 2018. The trustee in bankruptcy produced an expert in design and typography, who testified that the fonts of the purported trust deeds (Cambria and Calibri, respectively) were developed by Microsoft in

42 Butterick, above note 41 at 81 (quoted with the permission of Thomson Reuters).

43 See *ibid* for guidance.

2002 and not released to the public until 2007. No one in 1995 could have used them.[44]

On the strength of that evidence, the judge concluded that the trusts were a sham, and fraudulent preferences intended to defeat creditors.

2) Footnotes[45]

Go easy on these.

Unless you're writing for the *Harvard Law Review*, your readers probably don't want to wade through the hundreds of footnotes found in a typical academic law journal (and maybe not even then). Nor do they want to have to trace dozens of cross-references to find some simple information, like a previous citation.

In a legal memorandum, it's more helpful to have a citation in the main text — especially if it's that beautiful thing, a neutral citation (example: 2017 SCC 1).

Even a longer, traditional citation is more usefully placed in the body of the text, rather than buried in a footnote (or endnote). The reader can quickly see the year, jurisdiction, and level of court, all of which are helpful in judging the weight of the authority cited. A thicket of footnotes that say things like "*supra* note 138" will annoy rather than illuminate your reader.[46]

Could we just dispense with *supra* and *infra* while we're at it? It's much easier for the reader to see the title of the case or statute being cited (even if that gets repetitious) than a Latinate cross-reference. These hold-overs could all safely go the way of the seldom-seen *op. cit.*, *loc. cit.* and *q.v.*

44 2019 ONSC 80.

45 Ha! Made you look.

46 For judges who take a dim view of overdoing the footnoting (and yes, I'm doing this in a footnote), see *Conference of State Bank of Supervisors v Officer of the Comptroller of the Currency*, No 17-CV-763, Doc 8 (DDC, 2 August 2017); *Equal Employment Opportunity Commission v Darden Restaurants Inc*, No 15-cv-20561, Doc 237 (SD Fla, 25 July 2017); and C Ryan Barber, "Judge Busts Banking Agency for 'Excessive' Footnotes, Strikes Court Brief" *National Law Journal* (31 July 2017), online: www.law.com/nationallawjournal/almID/1202794321435.

Footnoting like there's no tomorrow may also drive your assistant (if you have one) or you (if you don't) to the point of insanity: as formatting gets complicated, errors can creep in — especially if you want to do a lot of cross-referencing. For everyone's sake, keep it simple.

A preference for in-text citations is to some, however, a heretical and dangerously radical position. Bryan Garner, the US expert on legal writing and the editor of *Black's Law Dictionary*, finds in-text references distracting.[47] On the other hand, *The Bluebook*, and no less a mind than retired Chief Judge Richard Posner of the 7th Circuit, prefer them to footnotes.[48] I'm generally with Posner.

This is not to say that footnotes are always out of place. They're useful if you need to refer to a bunch of things, like a laundry list of cases or statutory provisions; or for discussion that is digressive or otherwise not central to your main argument (but ask yourself whether that is necessary to include, even down below).

If you're writing a piece intended for non-lawyers, on the other hand, an in-text citation is more likely to throw them for a loop: footnoting is fine, if kept to a minimum (or omit the nerdy lawyer stuff altogether).

Acknowledgments — if not placed directly below the title of a published piece — make a good first (or even sole) footnote. Less than good is the all-too-common practice among some lawyer "authors" of using that footnote to thank the poor law student or junior associate who actually wrote the article; at the very least, give the kid credit as co-author.

G. NAVIGATING SOCIAL MEDIA

Everyone is doing it now: you should too, although with caution.

47 Bryan A Garner, "Textual Citations Make Legal Writing Onerous for Lawyers and Non-lawyers Alike" (1 February 2014), *ABA Journal*, online: www.abajournal.com/magazine/article/textual_citations_make_legal_writing_onerous_for_lawyers_and_nonlawyers.

48 *Ibid*.

1) Choose Your Distribution Channel Appropriately

The best social media for business and professional purposes are LinkedIn and, probably to a lesser extent, Twitter. Use Instagram and Facebook for pics of vacations, amazing restaurant meals, your kids, and the dog.

2) Manage Your Presence

If you have a social media presence that is purely personal (vacations, amazing restaurant meals), that doesn't mean it can be unprofessional. Don't post things via a non-work account that you wouldn't want your employer or your clients to see. Everybody has Google, and someone is bound to find those pics of you at the kegger with your pants down.

Don't reveal confidential client information or say negative things about a client (or your employer). You should also exercise caution in speaking out on public issues that a client may have an interest in — even if this does have the effect of clipping the wings of your commentary. An "all views my own" disclaimer may not be sufficient when someone is upset.

Join appropriate groups on LinkedIn.

Don't feel you must accept every LinkedIn connection request. There are a lot of spammers and other opportunists out there. And think about the people you do connect with: it was a bit off-putting when a professional contact of mine connected on LinkedIn (and perhaps elsewhere) with an adult film star. Similarly, adding every legal recruiter in town to your LinkedIn contacts may send a signal to your current employer.

3) Keep It Short

Twitter famously limited tweeted messages to 140 characters, although this has since been eased to allow longer tweets. That's a shame: the beauty of a tweet is its very pithiness, and a word-limit imposes a healthy discipline.

Keep your posts on other platforms on the short side too. No one is on social media to read the *Encyclopaedia Britannica*, and most will be looking at your update on a mobile device with a small screen. If you do have a longer piece you want to push to people, you can do that by sending a URL (and you can shorten that by using a service like bitly, ow.ly, or tinyurl). Don't send just the link, though; it's helpful to tell your readers why they'd want to open it (and reassure them it's not some phishing scam). On LinkedIn, you can share a piece longer than a brief post by using the "Write an article" option.

4) Don't Overdo It

Regularly posting updates is an effective way to remind your friends, colleagues, and clients that you haven't fallen off the face of the earth, but no one needs minute-by-minute live-tweeting of you doing document review. Don't post for the sake of posting; have something meaningful to say.

5) Use Existing Content

Retweet items from trusted sources to your legion of followers. Like or repost updates on LinkedIn. It helps to introduce or provide the context for something you're passing on from another source (*Great article by my colleague on . . .*).

The only way to build a true personal brand, however, is to post original (and, ideally, thoughtful) content of your own.

6) Link Appropriately

If you are saying nice things about someone, include a link to that person's LinkedIn profile. Include that person's Twitter handle or a hashtag with a company name or keyword.

H. AND FINALLY: THE IMPORTANCE OF EDITING AND PROOFREADING

You've drafted a client piece — now what?

Heed the words of Samuel Johnson: "What is written without effort is generally read without pleasure." Or, as Blaise Pascal wrote of a long letter, "I did not have the time to make it shorter."

In other words, go back and edit; your text could always use some polishing. To continue in the literary vein, this is "the last and greatest art."

Here are some specific tips.

- ★ Sleep on it — you will spot things the next morning that were not apparent the night before, especially if the midnight oil was burning (typos, spelling and grammar, stylistic things).
- ★ Get a second opinion — this will help with correctness, readability, and errors you just aren't seeing because you're too familiar with your text (even after sleeping on it).
- ★ Translate — is it in plain English that a businessperson would understand or Latinate, jargon-ridden legalese? If it's in the latter, you need to change that.
- ★ Watch for repetition — is there a way to avoid using the same word or phrase excessively, but without making it look as though you are straining to find alternatives?
- ★ Think about the flow — do the paragraphs or sections follow each other logically, with nice transitions? Or do you need some headings to impose order?
- ★ Do your sentences vary in length? (They should — and cut very long ones into smaller units.)
- ★ Visual appeal — can you break up the text? (Use shorter paragraphs, headings, bullet points, or graphics.)
- ★ Wield the axe — as the kids now say, "TL;DR" (too long; didn't read).
- ★ Paranoia check — have you said anything about a client, or about an issue that a client might have views on? Has the piece been vetted for correctness? Have you verified names, titles, facts, quotations, and citations (if any)?
- ★ Print it off — proofreading is more effective from a hard copy than on the screen.
- ★ Read it aloud — this will reveal incoherencies, overly long sentences, convoluted phrasing, and clunky style in a way that reading silently to yourself will not.
- ★ Read it backwards — an old proofreading technique; effective because it counteracts your brain's tendency to make your eyes gloss over errors.

- Don't rely on spell-check — it misses things and makes silent corrections (*tortuous* appears in a million legal documents where *tortious* was intended; *form* for *from* and *you* for *your* are other frequent ones).[49]
- Make sure you proofread *everything* — including the title, headings, and author information (things can go wrong where you don't think to look, and it's embarrassing to have an obvious mistake in something like your name).
- Sleep on it again.
- Run it by a second pair of eyes for final review.[50]

1) Case Study 1: The Importance of Profreading

The error in the heading is deliberate, for two reasons.

First, it's a reminder about the point made in the previous section to proofread *everything*, including titles, recipient names in a memo, captions for diagrams or pictures, footnotes. It's particularly embarrassing if you spell your client's name incorrectly or your managing partner's.

Second, *prof* for *proof* is a play on words, prompted by the experience of students at the Faculty of Law at the University of Toronto.

A certain law professor (who will not be named here) copied and pasted exam questions from a previous year.[51] He seems to have failed, however, to ensure that references to parties and other details in the recycled portions matched up with the newer part of the fact-pattern. Exam questions were "so poorly written they were incomprehensible." It sounds like there were problems of composition and editing, as well as proofreading concerns.

49 The last time I checked in CanLII, a search for *tortuous* yielded 1,262 hits in cases, 97 in commentary; at a quick glance, it looked like *tortious* was meant in the vast majority of instances.

50 For proof of the importance of this tip, look no further than Section H(2), "Case Study 2: *Meh*," below.

51 See *Ultra Vires* 20:1 (September 2018), online: https://issuu.com/ultravires/docs/uv_vol_20_iss_1_-_sept_2018.

Issues like this often occur when you adapt a precedent, or cobble together something new from multiple templates: defined terms that aren't defined or are never used, inconsistent terminology, cross-references that don't sync, problems with formatting and numbering.

There is software that will help with this (Contract Companion comes to mind) — but it won't spot that error in the managing partner's surname.

2) Case Study 2: *Meh*

This is an embarrassing example of assuming the junior person who's working for you will have done the proofreading in the first place, and that you don't need to check things yourself.

In *Golo, LLC v Higher Health Network, LLC*, Curiel USDJ sets out the standard of proof required for the claims being advanced. At the end of one paragraph, this comment appears in parenthesis: *meh I need a better rule statement than this.*[52]

The comment is perhaps that of the judge in mid-edit, but more probably that of the hapless judicial clerk who actually wrote the opinion — in which case, evidence of two proofreading failures. (And one of authorship.)

Fans of *The Simpsons* will be happy, though.

52 *Golo, LLC v Higher Health Network, LLC*, Case No: 3:18-cv-2434-GPC-MSB at p 11 (SD Cal Feb 5, 2019).

chapter two

Words Used and Abused

A. INTRODUCTION

Writer is an old Scottish term for "solicitor," and the word is well-chosen. The careful lawyer thinks about what words mean and how they will be interpreted — or may be misinterpreted. And yet, modern lawyers frequently misuse the wordhoard that is available to them, whether this is through force of (unthinking) habit, imprecise thinking, confusion, or simple error.

The meanings of words change over time.

A nice example is *condescending*, which not so long ago meant something along the lines of "being gracious to the underlings" (the King James Bible, Dr Johnson, and Lord Byron use it in this sense). Since the later nineteenth century, it has meant "patronising" (in a bad way; that also once had a neutral or even positive connotation).

Another is *meticulous*, a quality we now seek in new legal hires, but a word which used to mean "timid" or "fearful," then "overly worried about trifles" before taking on its current meaning of "detail-oriented."

Note as well that many superlatives we use colloquially to describe things we love used to have rather different meanings: *awesome, fantastic, incredible, sick, terrific, tremendous, unbelievable.*

Only a pedant would cling to the old meanings; and we must recognize that language is not of marmoreal permanence.

What is different is a misuse or error that sticks, as opposed to a gradual shift in meaning or tone. *I could care less* is an example.

It's just a lazy shortening of *I couldn't care less*, and the difference in meaning is worth preserving.

When usage is changing, we should hang on to an older meaning where the new one lacks precision, logic, or truth.

As events in recent years have repeatedly shown, words and truth matter; they should not be distorted to mean their Orwellian opposite.

B. MISUSE

1) Gruesome Twosomes

What do I mean by this? These are pairs of words that lawyers routinely use together, but would be better not to. These pairs may once have had distinct meanings (in the late Middle Ages?), but now really don't.

And even in the Middle Ages, they may not have: many of these "coupled synonyms" (as the late Richard Wydick called them) join an English word with its (Old) French equivalent, in a belt-and-suspenders manoeuvre — for example, like *free and clear*, which combines the synonymous Old English *freo* and Old French *cler*.[1] Further examples will be discussed below.

a) Redundancy

Linguistic redundancy, not the employment variety. In the linguistic category, there are both legal and non-legal redundancies.

The legal

Legalese is replete with pairs of words that mean the same thing and therefore don't need to be used together (except to create a leaden, lawyerly effect):

* *any and all* [*any* covers one or more, so *and all* adds nothing]
* *cease and desist* [plain old *stop* will do just fine]

1 Richard Wydick & Amy E Sloan, *Plain English for Lawyers*, 6th ed (Durham, NC: Carolina Academic Press, 2019) at 18.

- *closest and most real connection*[2]
- *full and complete* [same comment]
- *if and when*
- *no force or effect*
- *null and void* [how about *of no effect*?]
- *one and the same*
- *plain and obvious* [synonymous]
- *save and except* [one or the other, not both]
- *separate and apart* [except as a term of art in family law]
- *unless and until* [this drives me crazy]

The following expressions require a little more explanation.

CO-CONSPIRATOR

To *conspire* necessarily involves combination or agreement with at least one other person to do something wrong. *Co–* and *con–* come from the same Latin root indicating joint action, so you need only one of them.

Yes, the *OED* cites examples of *co-conspirator* from the 1860s, but they are in a list of *co–* words that are described as either rare or one-offs.

Co-conspirator, as used today, is an ugly and unnecessary creation of the Watergate years. Regrettably, it occurs in Canada in both the federal *Competition Act* and the *Military Rules of Evidence.*

DIRECTLY ON POINT

A case is on point or it isn't, and you wouldn't ever say that one was *indirectly on point.*

SIDEBAR: In England, it is usual to say that a legal authority is *in point*, not *on point*. North Americans do say *a case in point*, but typically (I think) in non-legal usage. *On point* has entered the millennial lexicon as a way of saying something *nails it*, especially in relation to fashion or grooming.

2 I am grateful to my friend and colleague Angela Swan for reminding me of this one.

NULL AND VOID

The two elements mean the same thing, so there is no need to use both.

As a drafting point, it's a dangerous phrase. If doing (or not doing) something renders a contract *null and void* (or *terminated*), you may not be able to sue the breaching party because there is no longer any underlying obligation. You are better to say that the non-breaching party is relieved from performance of the contract (but can still sue on it).

RATE OF SPEED

This phrase appears, according to CanLII, in 4,173 Canadian cases and 126 statutory provisions. Speed is, by definition, the rate at which something moves. So, just *speed.*

These are redundant and inelegant, they don't reflect how normal people (like clients) actually speak, and they make your writing look fussy.

Sometimes what may look like a redundancy is not one: in an Ontario case, a judge held that the two elements of *indemnify and save harmless* had similar but not identical meanings, *save harmless* being broader.[3] The main thing is to think about meanings and determine whether one term will suffice without a synonymous second one — or not.

The non-legal

Writing that is non-lawyerly (or not exclusively lawyerly) also suffers from redundancies. Here are some common ones:

- *absolutely necessary* [you need something or you don't]
- *added bonus* [a bonus is always added]
- *advance notice*
- *advance warning*
- *armed gunman*
- *blue in colour* [no, it's just blue]
- *both* [often unnecessary: for example, as in *The plaintiff seeks both compensatory and punitive damages*]

3 See *Stewart Title Guarantee Co v Zeppieri* (2009), 94 OR (3d) 196 (SCJ).

- *close proximity*
- *comprehensive coverage from 2016 forward*
- *during the course of* [please, just *during*]
- *each and every*
- *exact same*
- *exactly the same*
- *face mask* [where else?]
- *full gamut* [there are no partial gamuts (or *spectrums*, for that matter)]
- *general consensus* [consensus is, by definition, general]
- *mental telepathy* [telepathy is communication from one mind to another; it's always mental]
- *moment in time* [a moment is, perforce, in time]
- *more* or *most fundamental* [you've reached the bottom or you haven't]
- *new recruit*
- *outward appearance* [can there be an inward one?]
- *personal belongings* [unless you're nicking someone else's stuff from the overhead compartment, I guess]
- *personal opinion* [it's no one else's]
- *PIN number* [what do you think the N stands for?]
- *pre-heat, pre-arrange, pre-existing, pre-owned, pre-plan, pre-prepared* [all of these involve a prior action or condition before something else happens; *pre-* is unnecessary]
- *reason why*
- *role model* [just *model*, which doesn't mean only the runway kind — "The rapper is not perhaps the best *model* for young people."]
- *safe haven* [yeah, you want to avoid the unsafe ones]
- *software programme* [that's what software is]
- *sum total* [that's like saying *debit deficit*]
- *terminal building* [a terminal *is* a building]
- *time period* [one or the other; they mean the same thing]
- *United Together* [optimistic but perhaps ill-advised slogan of the 2016 Democratic National Convention; as opposed to?]
- *very* [or any other modifier] *unique* [something is unique or it ain't]

* *very true* [the truth is not relative]
* *weather conditions* [weather is a condition, and *the conditions* would generally include the weather]

The following redundancies could benefit from some discussion.

ACTION PLAN

I suppose there could be a plan to do nothing (an *inaction plan*?), but generally *plan* implies taking action — so the first element in *action plan* is redundant.

BETWIXT AND BETWEEN

They mean the same thing.

Yes, the phrase is used idiomatically to describe situations where one is unable to choose, but it has no place in legal drafting — just *between* in your contracts.

END RESULT

No, just *the result.*

EXACTLY THE SAME, ONE AND THE SAME

Just *the same.*

FORWARD PROGRESS

All progress is forward-looking; that's why it's progress.

FREAK ACCIDENT

As opposed to the deliberate or expected kind?

MORE PARTICULARLY

No, just *particularly*. It's unqualifiable. Better yet, avoid this weak adverb.

OFTENTIMES

I heard this in a meeting recently, but the *OED* says it's "archaic or literary." And redundant: *often* alone will do.

PRE-ROLLED JOINT

This contains two pleonastic elements.

A *joint* is a cigarette containing marijuana (or, as federal legislation still quaintly spells it, *marihuana*). A cigarette is, by definition, rolled into shape (whether by hand or by machine). There are no *unrolled* joints — that would just be loose weed.

Redundancy number 2 is the prefix *pre–*. As in formulations like *pre-heated* and *pre-owned*, that prefix adds nothing useful, because there is an implied priority to the verb. One doesn't *post-heat* or *post-own* or *post-roll*.

To recapitulate, all joints are rolled in advance of smoking. And a joint is rolled anyway.

Just *a joint*, then.

And all *chaps* are *assless*.

THE REASON WHY

Lord Tennyson may be to blame for this one (or CV Wedgwood): "Theirs not to reason why, theirs but to do or to die" (*The Charge of the Light Brigade*).

It's a pretty awful poem, but it's worse to say *The reason why the defendant did this is . . .* ; it's just *The reason the defendant did this is . . .*

And please, never *the reason is because* or, worse, *the reason why is because* (the latter being something heard on the CBC).

The reason is that . . . can work, however.

RELATIONSHIP

A thoughtful reader points out that the *–ship* bit adds nothing.

Compare *trusteeship* or *fellowship*, where the suffix actually changes the meaning of the other part (turning person into thing).

In the realm of dating and marriage, *relationship* is now too entrenched to be dislodged; but you could usefully use *relation* (or *relations*) in your legal writing and drafting to describe the interrelatedness of parties or concepts.

REMANDED BACK

I heard this on the CBC as well, and I'm hoping it hasn't made its way into criminal lawyers' writing: *The suspect was remanded back into custody*.

The *re–* prefix means "back," so it is just *remanded* (and usually *in custody*, sometimes *to*, but not *into*).

Similarly, not *refer back* — just *refer*.

Ditto *revert*, etc.

STILL REMAINS

If something is still around, it simply *remains* (and it doesn't *remain the same*, either — remaining involves sameness; tell that to Led Zeppelin).

TEN-YEAR ANNIVERSARY

No, just *tenth anniversary*.

The *anni–* bit derives from the Latin *annus*, which means "year" and also gives us *annual*.

TIER LEVELS

The actual phrase used by an American professional development manager was *skill sets for tier levels of associates*. Insert Edvard Munch "Scream" emoji.

There's a lot of redundancy going on there: just *skills* would work (and sometimes those come singly, not in groups); and either *tiers* or *levels*, but not both.

TWELVE NOON, TWELVE MIDNIGHT

In both, the *twelve* (or 12) is unnecessary.

2) *That* and *Which*

People have long had trouble with the correct use of *that* and *which*.

Writing in 1926, the grammarian HW Fowler found it difficult to discern consistent rules from the practice of good writers. He came up with a fairly simple approach that people who think about these things have largely followed, which is distilled in the following sections. (If you don't have *Fowler's Modern English Usage*, you must buy it now.)[4]

a) *That*

Use it where the information in the clause that follows is defining.

In other words, what comes after *that* is essential to the meaning of the sentence and limits it: *She gave me a list of books that had influenced her.*

4 See HW Fowler, *Fowler's Modern English Usage*, 2d ed, revised by Sir Ernest Gowers (Oxford, UK: Oxford University Press, 1983) at 626 [*Fowler's*, 2d ed]; and RW Burchfield, *Fowler's Modern English Usage*, 3d ed, revised (Oxford, UK: Oxford University Press, 2004) at 774 [*Fowler's*, 3d ed].

Not just any old books, but a limited selection as defined by *that*. In this scenario, *that* is **restrictive.**

b) *Which*

Use it where there is no particular limitation in the clause that follows; what comes after *which* is not essential to the meaning of the sentence: *I always buy her books, which have influenced me greatly.*

Her books again, but the fact they have influenced me is merely descriptive.

Here, *which* is **non-restrictive.**

Ross Guberman, the US legal writing guru, suggests an easy and workable test: "Use '*which*' if you would pause when reading the sentence out loud. If you wouldn't pause, use *that*."[5]

Whether to include a comma before *which* can also be difficult. Go by instinct as much as anything else.

> *He returned to the work van and removed what we believe was a pail of screws, **which** he carried with his right hand into the rear yard.* [defining *which*, so preceded by a comma]

> *He again bent fully forwards at the waist to pick up an item off the driveway, **which** he immediately threw into the garbage bin.* [defining *which*; without the comma, the sentence would suggest that it was the driveway he threw in the bin, not the item]

But:

> *He bent fully forwards at the waist and collected two empty buckets **which** had been placed next to the garbage bin.* [non-defining *which*, no comma; but you could add a comma and make it defining]

3) Waffle

This was my tenth-grade English teacher's expression for useless verbiage. Other ways to say it: throat-clearing, filler, circumlocution, BS.

5 Ross Guberman, *The Attorney Toolkit* (LegalWritingPro.com, 2014) at 42.

Examples	*(and what to say instead)*
a number of	*some, many*
as a means of	*to*
as prescribed by	*in, under*
at the present time	*now*
at this point in time	*now*[6]
as to whether	*if, whether*
by means of	*by, with*
concerning	*about, on* [and don't misuse *concerning* for *of concern, disturbing, troubling*]
due to the fact that	*since, because*
duly authorized	*authorized* [can something be *unduly authorized*?]
during the time that	*during, while*
for a/the period of	*for*
for the avoidance of doubt	[by saying this, you are acknowledging that your drafting is poor; redraft so there is no doubt]
have an adverse effect on	*hurt, set back, impair*
in a timely manner	*promptly, on time*
in accordance with	*by, following, under*
in addition	*also, too*
in an orderly fashion	[I can't think why you'd want to say this in the first place]
in order for	*for*
in order that	*so*
in order to	*to*
in other words	[remove and rephrase whatever you said before so you don't then have to clarify it]
in relation to	*about, to, with*

6 Worse is *at this juncture in* time, used by the former dean of a law school who should know better: see (2017) 48 *Victoria University of Wellington Law Review* 225–36. See also Mark Nichol, "50 Plain-Language Substitutions for Wordy Phrases" (27 August 2013), online: www.dailywritingtips.com/50-plain-language-substitutions-for-wordy-phrases/; Michael G Walsh, "Tips for Converting Legalese to Plain English (Part I)" *The Practical Lawyer* (August 2016), 7–9.

Examples	*(and what to say instead)*
in sum	[a lawyerism that people picked up in 1L; lose it and just summarize/conclude]
in the event that	*if*
in the process of	[leave it out and don't replace; it adds nothing]
in view of	*because, since*
in/with regard to	*about, on*
including but not limited to	*including* [the *but not limited to* bit doesn't add anything, does it?]
it is interesting to note that	[if you have to say this, it probably isn't interesting; just leave it out]
kindly	[just ask, and add *please* if you need to make it more polite]
make available	*offer, provide*
on a [adjective or adverb] basis	[cut out the *basis* business, which is excess verbiage: *every year*, *annually*, or *yearly* rather than *on an annual* (or *yearly*) basis]
pertaining to	*about*, *of*, *on*
please find enclosed/attached	*I enclose/attach* OR *the* [whatever it is] *is enclosed/attached* [Even in the days of snail mail, was it really ever a challenge to locate the extra thing in the envelope with the letter? Be gone, nineteenth-century nonsense!]
provides guidance to	*guides*
pursuant to	*under*, *according to*
put another way	[see *in other words*; you might also want to rethink *for greater certainty*, even in contractual drafting]
reason why	[no, just *the reason*]
regarding	*about, on*
relative to	*about, on*
set forth in	*in*
subsequent to	*after*
the fact that	[omit and rephrase, so that *The fact that the borrower defaulted* ... becomes something like *The borrower's default* ...]
the question as to whether	*if*, *whether*, *the question whether*

Examples	*(and what to say instead)*
to the extent that	*if, as far as, as much as* [avoid *insofar as*]
until such time as	*until*
with reference to	*about*
with respect to	*about*
with the exception of	*except*

De-clutter your prose by eliminating verbose (and hackneyed) words and phrases.

4) Awful Lawyerisms, aka Legalese

While we're on the subject of waffle . . .

Legalese isn't always confined to lawyers; it permeates the email and speech of law clerks, legal assistants, and students.[7]

Absent

Odds are, the only way you used this word before you went to law school was to describe physical absence: *I was absent from school that day because I had the flu.*

Then, all of a sudden, in 1L you started saying things like *absent evidence to the contrary* because it made you sound all, like, lawyer-y. Please revert to your pre-law ways. *Without* or even *in the absence of* will strike your non-lawyer readers as normal.

And that's a good thing.

7 It happens in French too. A lawyer in Lyons (*Lyon*, to use the French spelling) complained on Twitter about contractual drafting like this:

> *Par ailleurs, si l'Acquéreur envisagé en émet le souhait, celui-ci devra avoir la possibilité de . . .*

Translated literally, that means "Moreover, if the prospective Acquiror indicates its desire to do so, it must have the ability to . . ."

As the lawyer points out, one could simply say, *L'Acquéreur pourra . . .* ("The Acquiror may . . ."). This stuff drives him (and me) *dingue* (crazy). Thanks to Quentin-Alexandre Brigaud for the example.

Advised

The phrase *Please be advised that ...* is one of the most leaden openings of all time. Cut to the chase and just convey the actual information, without the pointless preamble.

And *advise* in this context is, well, ill-advised. On stylistic grounds, for one. It's pompous to say *Please advise me if ...* when you could just say *Please tell me if ...* or *Let me know if ...*

It's also not a great idea to extend your use of the words *advice* and *advise* beyond that which is legal advice in the strict sense.

As soon as I am able

Seen in automatic out-of-office email replies or heard on voicemail.

There is nothing wrong with *as soon as I can*, and it certainly sounds less pretentious.

At first blush and *on its face*

In the first year of law school, students pick up many bad writing habits. Perhaps the chief of these is to use previously unfamiliar phrases that have a (specious) lawyerly appearance.

An example is *at first blush*, which is not commonly used outside the law; and because it's used so much within it, it ought to be avoided as an overused cliché. You could just write *at first*, without the blushing ("This case seems, at first, to be uncomplicated ...")

On its face has a venerable legal pedigree (at least as far back as 1632, according to the *OED*), and referred originally to the words as they appeared on the face of a document — but, like the blushing business, it's a worn-out expression that could happily be dropped.

If the previous two constructions are merely old and tired, the use of *facially* for *on its face* is recent, lazy, and deplorable. I cross it out in student work-product, and wish I could do the same with the 408,000 occurrences in Canadian blog posts (according to Slaw's Canadian Law Blogs Search Engine).

Attend

Oft-seen in emails from harried assistants: *We urgently need a student to attend at the client's office to ...*

Go to would be much more effective in putting a fire under the articling students.

Do dockets still read *attendance to* [*whatever activity*]? Probably time to modernize the accounting software.

For the avoidance of doubt

This phrase is pompous, no doubt about that. It also indicates that you needed to explain things better in the first place.

Don't admit failure: avoid it.

A bright-line test

This phrase is frequently used by judges and lawyers; there are roughly 400 cases in CanLII that employ it. Notable among them is *R v Neil*, where Binnie J applies a *bright-line test* to identify lawyers' conflicts of interest.[8]

We all know what this means (a test that is clear, easily applied, and certain in outcome), but how did we come to use it?

The legal notion of a bright line seems to have its origin in *Girard Trust Co v Commissioner of Internal Revenue*, where Goodrich CJ observes that "[a] bright line between that which brings conviction to one person and its influence on the body politic cannot be drawn." The judge later says, "Nor has the law sought to draw such a bright line between the exercise of private and public influence."[9]

Justice Frankfurter referred a few years later to "a bright line dividing negligence from non-negligence," which is probably where the concept takes off.[10]

If readers are aware of any earlier citations, please share them!

Are lines actually bright, though? Perhaps if they are drawn in bright-red ink.

Or maybe the idea comes from physics, where a *bright-line spectrum* is a discontinuous one composed of lines resulting the radiation of an incandescent vapour or gas; or from photography, where a *bright-line view-finder* is one in which the area of the picture appears

8 2002 SCC 70.

9 122 F2d 108 (3d Cir 1941).

10 *Wilkerson v McCarthy*, 336 US 53 (1949).

framed by a white line. It's unlikely, though, that US judges had these meanings specifically in mind in the 1940s.

In any event, the phrase has, over the decades, become a judicial (and lawyerly) cliché — like the *safe harbors* that US securities lawyers like to talk about, or the requirement for *noisy withdrawal* by a US lawyer from client fraud.

Clichés, while useful shorthand, are tired — and thus to be avoided by writers of lively, engaging prose. Why not just say something like a *clear test* or a *simple test* instead? Your client will get that, but may be left in the dark by the *bright-line* stuff.

The case at bar

See *The instant case*, below.

Commence

This word is unavoidable as a technical term in litigation: one *commences* an action under the *Courts of Justice Act*, RSO 1990, c C43, for example. But don't use the word in normal parlance or non-technical writing, where it sounds fussy and pompous.

She didn't *commence employment* on whatever date; she *started work*.

While we're on the subject, the academic term *commencement* for a graduation ceremony (so, the conclusion rather than beginning of one's course of study) has always seemed strange to me — perhaps because it's a Cambridge term, and more recently an American one. But it's old, going back at least as far as 1387. I guess it's like Cambridge colleges holding May balls in June.

Deemed

This is one of those words with a weird function confined largely to the world of law. The ordinary current meaning of *deem*, according to the *OED* is, essentially, to consider, think, or judge (in a non-judicial way). But lawyers have a special meaning, where *deeming* means treating A as if it were B and not A. Creating a legal fiction, in other words (and that doesn't mean John Grisham).

This comes up in my teaching, where the law school will occasionally stick a *deemed Wednesday* in the calendar in order to make up for an actual Wednesday sacrificed for some reason like a holiday or special event. It also comes up a lot in statutory drafting, where all kinds of things are *deemed* to be other things for legal purposes: the word *deemed* occurs 4,141 times in the *Income Tax Act* (Canada), for example.

Oddly, the *OED*'s other definitions of *deem*, while they involve judgment of some kind, don't quite capture the "treating A as if it were B" meaning that is familiar to lawyers.

One legislative drafter says that the ordinary "consider" usage should be avoided: "Phrases like 'if he deems fit' or 'as he deems necessary' are objectionable as deviations from common speech."[11] It appears that the *OED* would think the legislative use of *deem* is actually the departure from ordinary usage — but intelligent people can disagree.

This division of opinion may cease to matter. Ruth Sullivan suggests that modern legal drafters have already ditched *deem* in the "consider" sense and are starting to say *is considered* or just *is* when they wish to create legal fictions.[12]

Dictated but not read by . . .

We don't send letters the way we used to, but new software has revitalized the practice of dictation. As a result, the old *dictated/not read* formulation is still seen on correspondence — both digital and printed.

It was never good: it conveys a message of "I'm too busy (or, more to the point, disorganized) to take proper care."

One research lawyer in Toronto once jokingly used the phrase to describe a loose-leaf text of inconsistent quality, ostensibly by a senior partner at another firm but largely the work of successive generations of articling students. (Buy me some drinks and I'll identify both lawyers.)

In any circumstance, don't write (or practise) this way. Consider, check, proofread, revise. (And write your own material.)

11 GC Thornton, *Legislative Drafting*, 2d ed (1979) at 83–84, cited in *Black's Law Dictionary*.

12 Ruth Sullivan, *Sullivan on the Construction of Statutes*, 6th ed (Markham, ON: LexisNexis Canada, 2014) at §4.105.

The fact that . . . and *The reality is* . . .

John Laskin, late of the Ontario Court of Appeal, suggests in his "Forget the Wind-Up and Make the Pitch" that although "this advice may cause mutiny among lawyers and judges," you should avoid writing sentences containing "The fact that . . ."[13]

It's much more effective just to state the fact, rather than to state the fact that the fact is a fact. So, not "The fact that my client has accepted your offer . . ." but "My client's acceptance of your offer . . ." The latter is direct, clear, less wordy.

Similarly, eschew *notwithstanding the fact that* in favour of the plain English *although*, and the dreadful *due to the fact that* for good old *because*. As Laskin notes, *The fact remains that* can simply be omitted; it adds nothing but verbosity.

I'm not sure why *The reality is* . . . bothers me as much as it does, but it does. Like *The fact remains* . . . , it's useless. Just state what the current state of affairs is, without the pointless preface. And, please, don't ever say or write *The reality is, is that* . . .

Highly anticipated? Hah!

As I've suggested elsewhere, odds are if you insert the word *clearly* in your sentence you are trying to impose clarity on something that isn't clear at all. If something really is clear, you don't need to say so.

In the same vein is the phrase *highly anticipated* ("This highly anticipated decision from . . ."; "The release of the OSC's highly anticipated rule on . . ."). The phrase gets used a lot: according to Slaw's Canadian Law Blogs Search Engine, it occurs approximately 5,080,000 times in Canadian blog posts.

That sure sounds like overuse — or, in other words, a reason not to use a hackneyed expression.

Not only hackneyed, but also far from the truth. What it usually means is "highly anticipated by a single law nerd or small group of them who need to make this blog post sound more important than it probably is." You can and should do better in your blogging: show your reader why something is important or interesting; don't merely assert.

13 Hon John I Laskin, "Forget the Wind-Up and Make the Pitch: Some Suggestions for Writing More Persuasive Factums" (1999), Court of Appeal for Ontario, online: www.ontariocourts.ca/coa/en/ps/speeches/forget.htm.

In a position

You aren't *in a position* to do X, Y, or Z? Just say *I can't do* X, Y, or Z, which is more direct and avoids suggestions of awkward body poses.

Inasmuch as, in so far as

These pomposities can always be replaced by something simpler and clearer.

Inasmuch as is just a fancy (and archaic) way of saying *seeing that*, *since*, or *because*.

In so far as (sometimes *insofar as*) means much the same thing, or *to the extent that*.

They add nothing to your prose except flab (as does *to the extent that*).

Rephrase.

Indicate

This is an example of three syllables where one or two would suffice: *show*, *say*, *suggest* are all shorter — and actually clearer.

The instant case

This would have been normal, current English in the late eighteenth century, but it has no place in your present-day factum or pleadings.

Say *this case* (and NOT *the case at bar*, which always makes me think of cocktails).

Iteration

Someone recently emailed me *the latest iteration of the presentation* — so much fancier than a good old *draft* or *version*. But seriously, how much *iterating* do you really do?

And *an iterative process* is just work that requires more than one step. (Which is to say, most of what we do.)

Re:

Someone recently made this comment on LinkedIn: *I'm so excited re: the below.* (The colon may or may not have been there.)

Why not *I'm so excited about this* instead of the commenter's mish-mash of somewhat immature enthusiasm and the lawyer jargon of *re* and *the below*?

If you think carefully when you write, something simple like *it* or *this* sounds much more natural than *the above, the below, the latter, the former* — which all sound stiff and pompous.

Dr Johnson counselled against these constructions, saying "As long as you have the use of your tongue and pen, never, sir, be reduced to that shift" — *shift* being an eighteenth-century expression for a shabby expediency or forced measure.

And *re* — do we really need to use this vestigial piece of Latin? While it is usefully concise, if you're composing something like a tweet, *re* has a definite air of "I'm using a word I would never have uttered before I went to law school and I'm only saying it now in order to sound like the real lawyer you may not think I am."

So, to be dispensed with.

Re is a funny word too, as it doesn't quite mean "about" or "regarding" (or didn't originally).

It is one of the grammatical forms (the ablative case, to be precise) of the Latin noun *res*, which means "thing" — and, by extension, "subject," "matter," "affair."

In law reports, *In re* sometimes appears in a style of cause, especially where the litigation is an investigation into the property of a bankrupt or the will of a testator. A famous example from Ontario is *In re Estate of Charles Miller, Deceased*, [1937] OR 382 (CA). The name of that case might also be given as just *Re Miller*.

Use of *re* as a stand-in for "about" goes back a long way (1707 is the earliest example in the *Oxford English Dictionary* (*OED*)), but try to do without it.

Try, particularly if your legal writing is already peppered with random bits of Latin like *per* and the dreadful commercial English of the nineteenth century (*I acknowledge receipt of your letter, same being forwarded to our client for review*). You are only alienating non-lawyer readers and sounding like some scrivener in a bad Victorian novel.

In the heading of your memo, *Re:* can easily be replaced by *Subject:*, which your reader may find more meaningful anyway.

Situate

Seen on email: *A client of ours is looking for real estate counsel situate in Montana.*

While the real estate is (in a technical, legal sense) *situate* in that state, the lawyer you are looking for is just *located* there, or even just *in Montana.*

A structured guide to ...

If you get the Lexology newsfeed by email every morning, you may have noticed the proliferation of *structured guides* to this, that, and the other thing. Maybe it's just a Lexology thing, but it needs to stop.

Dispute resolution in Cyprus! Acquisition financing in Portugal! Art law in California! Advertising and marketing in the United Kingdom!

They all have a structured guide. But so do more than 4,000 other topics if you search for the phrase *structured guide* on lexology.com. That number suggests overkill to me. Yes, you want the reader of your blog post to know what to expect — but would you ever (intentionally) offer up an *unstructured guide*?

Just *guide* or *overview* or *summary*. It should be organized, but just calling it *structured* won't make it so.

Thusly

Oh Lord, no!

While there are some mid-Victorian colloquial examples of *thusly*, the correct adverb is *thus* — and, frankly, that has no place in modern legal writing either. Nor does *thus far*.

Timely

This adjective isn't my favourite. Perhaps it's that weak, adverb-like *–ly* ending. It's unobjectionable in *a timely reminder*, but *in a timely manner* is like fingernails down a chalkboard, somehow. I think that's because of its fussy, needlessly formal tone and use of four words when one or two would suffice. *On time* (or even *early*) would do just fine.

Also unattractive is the American legal usage that turns the adjective into an adverb (as seen in the title of this US blog post): *Does Your Company Timely Respond to All Reports of Potential Misconduct?*

Are there are other ways to phrase it?

* *Promptly*. That works.
* *Timeously*. Very Scottish, so a bit outlandish in North America (or England).
* *Timelily*. Perhaps the weakest of weak adverbs, with that unusual (but correct) –*lily* ending. Don't.

I'd go with *on time*.

And in the *timely reminder* sense, you could also say *well-timed, opportune, seasonable*.

Unto

If you are still using –*eth* as a verb ending, *unto* might be OK. There is no reason to be using it in modern English, however.

Upon

The lawyer said (pompously): *Upon my return to the office ...*

Please, just *When I return* or *On my return*. Or even *When I get back*.

We herein provide you with an update on the status of ...

These opening words from an actual email are a waste of everyone's time. Just say what the status is: *We closed the transaction*, *The court dismissed the appeal*, whatever it is. The preamble is just meaningless filler with a phony air of *gravitas*.

5) *However*

Commonly misused.

First, as a conjunction, which it isn't:

> The Outside Directors and Officers Liability policy held by the firm on your behalf is set to expire on July 30, 2015, however your assistance is required in advance.

Don't do this. It's a bad run-on sentence, and just replacing the second comma with a semi-colon doesn't fix it.

Segue to second misuse: at the beginning of a sentence (or after a semi-colon):

> However, Gross Negligence or Wilful Misconduct does not include . . .

Perhaps not incorrect, but inelegant. Doesn't that initial *however* somehow have a Valley Girl's rising intonation to it? Not quite what you want in your client piece (or your contract, for that matter).

However, properly used, is what is called a post-positive; it needs to rely on a previous statement, like so:

> Mention was made, however, of a continued intention to implement . . .

Be careful, however, not to place it too early. It would be a bit weird to phrase that last example as *Mention, however, was made . . .*

6) *Said, Same, Such*

a) *Said*

I think you'll agree that *said* (as in *the said party* when you've previously referred to that party) is a little fusty-sounding, and has no place in your jazzy client-focused blog post or article. Even in contractual drafting, it sounds more than a little antiquated. *Said* is an unnecessary archaism: be done with it.

b) *Same*

More persistent is *same*. To use an example already used (but with emphasis added):

> A recent case from the ONSC clarifies the law on whether municipalities can regulate boathouses and whether the *Building Code Act* applies to ***same***, finding that (i) municipalities have jurisdiction to zone Ontario lakes and apply zoning by-laws to lakes, regulating construction of boathouses and other structures; and (ii) the *Building Code Act* applies to such structures, where not otherwise prohibited by the by-laws and the *Public Lands Act*.

Do we actually talk this way? Of course not. You would just say something like "whether municipalities can regulate boathouses and whether the *Building Code Act* applies to them."

Ross Guberman has this to say about *same* in this context: "archaic and awkward — a parody of legalese."[14] The *OED* agrees, suggesting that the word can usually be replaced with a simple personal pronoun (*he*, *she*, *it*, *they*).

c) *Such*

Such is another one in this category, also used in the boathouse example, where it's used in the same way as *said*. Wouldn't a normal (that is, non-lawyer) person simply say "these structures" or "structures like this"?

I agree with Bryan Garner that formulations like *we never received such* are barbarous and to be avoided.[15]

And then there is the dreaded phrase, *as such*. Dreaded (by me, anyway) because it's so often misused as mere filler, rather than as a link to antecedent material. Correctly used, it means "in the capacity just specified."

Here is a nice little explanation from Judith Fischer, retired Word Aficionado (great job title) at the Louis D Brandeis School of Law in Louisville, Kentucky:

> The phrase *as such* is sometimes misused as an all-purpose (but grammatically incorrect) transitional phrase. *Such* is a pronoun that must have an identifiable antecedent. If it doesn't have one, its use is incorrect.
>
> EXAMPLE 1 (CORRECT):
> *She is the board president. As such, she is responsible for scheduling the meetings.*
>
> Explanation: Here, the antecedent of *such* is *president*. It can replace *such*: *She is the board president. As president, she is responsible for scheduling the meetings.*
>
> EXAMPLE 2 (INCORRECT):
> *Congress intended to provide an exhaustive list of examples, and it did not mention websites. As such, the statute does not cover websites.*

14 *Ibid* at 18.

15 Bryan Garner, "Garner's Usage Tip of the Day: Such" *LawProse*, online: www.lawprose.org/garners-usage-tip-of-the-day-such.

Explanation: *Such* has no antecedent here; it cannot be replaced with *list* or any other word in the first sentence. The writer of example 2 incorrectly used *as such* as a generic transitional phrase. The word *therefore* would be a better choice.

The following examples illustrate the above points.

EXAMPLE 3
A plaintiff must prove damages in order to recover, but Smith has not done so here. As such, she has no claim.

EXAMPLE 4
This is a question of law. As such, it is subject to de novo *review.*

Explanation: Example 3 is incorrect, because *such* has no antecedent. Replace *as such* with *therefore*. But in Example 4, *question of law* can replace *such*, so the sentence is grammatically correct.

Advice: If you are in doubt about whether *as such* is correct, you may want to choose other phrasing. The transitional terms *therefore*, *thus*, and *as a result* are often suitable replacements for an incorrect *as such*.[16]

All three — *said*, *same*, and *such* — are useless lawyerisms, even when correctly deployed. Avoid them (even when you can use them properly).

7) *Shall, Will, Should, Would, May, Might, Must*

This is more of a contractual drafting or opinions point than a general legal writing tip, but it bears some examination.

a) *Shall, Will,* and *Must*

The difference is to a large extent idiomatic — that is, subject more to instinct and feel than to hard-and-fast grammatical rules. Usage has also changed over the centuries, and varies between North America and Britain. What follows is a distillation, as best I can manage. Or perhaps that's as best I *might*.

16 Quoted with the kind permission of Professor Fischer.

In classic usage, *shall* is used in the first person (*I*, *we*) to indicate a mere wish or to express simple futurity.[17] To say *I will* or *we will* signals an element of stronger intention, volition, or choice. So, *I shall probably be there*, but *I will never do that.*

In North America, *I shall* and *we shall* are less commonly heard for simple futurity, leaving *will* to perform both that function and to express stronger intention. This gives rise to ambiguity, because we lose the potential distinction between *will* and *shall*. (And *shall* sometimes performs for us the classic *will* function, as in *We shall overcome* — perhaps because *shall* is less commonly used in North America and therefore sounds more formal?)[18]

In the second person (*you*) and the third (*he*, *she*, *it*, *they*), *shall* takes on the function of command, menace, or refusal: *You shall repent!* or *He shall never have any, if I have anything to do with it.* Also, *Thou shalt not steal*, to use the old singular second person (equivalent of *tu* in French or *du* in German, as opposed to the plural [or formal singular] *vous* and *Sie*.)

In legal drafting, *shall* is usually used to express a third party's positive or negative obligations: *The Purchaser shall assume all liabilities.* Here, *shall* is synonymous with "is obliged to" or "has a duty to" — command or menace at work. There are arguments that *will*, if used consistently, would also work: it's hard to see much of a difference if you said *The Purchaser will assume all liabilities* — except that *shall* sounds a bit bossier. But convention (and traditional grammar) are on the side of *shall* here.

In common parlance *must* is close to *shall* in meaning: *you must not hit your brother*, *you shall do this or that.* And yet they are not synonymous; in contractual drafting, for example, *must* often takes on a conditional character: *The Borrower must satisfy the following . . .* — that is, must do so in order to do something else, but need not.

17 *Fowler's*, 2d ed, above note 4 at 549; *Fowler's*, 3d ed, above note 4 at 706–7.

18 That *shall* appears to have been changed from the original *will* by Pete Seeger: see Eriq Gardner, "Effort to Free Civil Rights Anthem May Hinge on Difference between 'Will' and 'Shall'" (7 August 2017), *Hollywood Reporter*, online: www.hollywoodreporter.com/amp/thr-esq/effort-free-civil-rights-anthem-may-hinge-difference-between-will-1027137.

b) *Should* and *Would*

Should is the conditional form of *shall*. Its use in the first person has all but disappeared from North American usage, but it is classically correct to say *I should like to go* as a mere expression of desire, and as distinct from the imperative *would* (*I would go, but I can't*).

When used in relation to other people, *should* is less bossy than *shall*; it means "ought to," as in *you should wash your hands after travelling on the subway*. Not dictatorial, if perhaps a bit passive-aggressive.[19]

Should, in opinion-writing, is seen as more qualified than *would* (*this should work* as opposed to *this would work*). Wilfred Estey suggests, however, in his book on legal opinions, that it's unfair to place the burden on a client to figure out the shades of meaning between the two (and all the other ways we lawyers hedge our own bets).[20] Fair point?

There is also *should* in this type of construction: *Should you wish to leave a message, please do so after the tone*. Not incorrect, but fusty — or perhaps fancy for the sake of being fancy. *If* can always replace *should* in these instances. Better yet: *Please leave a message*.

A few more words about *would*. *Would* is, of course, the conditional form of *will*. It's used to express a potential (or non-existent) rather than a certain future state of being.

So it's *I will have the memo for you today* but *I would like to give you the memo today, but I've been asked to work on a big due diligence project instead*.

Relatively straightforward, one would think — but one would be wrong.

c) *Would Of*

Ugh. But I certainly hear and sometimes even see *would of*. In spoken English, *would have* can sound like the contracted form

19 Is this what New Zealand legislators have in mind when they say things like "a trust should be administered in a way that is consistent with its terms and objectives?" See *Trusts Bill* 290-1, online: www.legislation.govt.nz/bill/government/2017/0290/latest/whole.html#DLM7382822l. (Thanks to Angela Swan for this reference.)

20 Wilfred M Estey, *Legal Opinions in Commercial Transactions*, 3d ed (Markham, ON: LexisNexis Canada, 2013) at 17–18.

would've, which has led some astray into thinking that it's actually *would of*.

Of course it's not.

Ever.

d) *May* and *Might*

These can mean the same (or almost the same) when they express possibility: *I may go to the party, I might go to the party.*

May also expresses permission: *"You may not go to the party," the parent told her teenager.*

Because of this dual use of *may*, caution is advised. Avoid using it for negative obligations, since *may not* could mean either "is not permitted to" or "might not." Better: *shall not*. In contractual drafting, confine *may* to the meaning "reserves the right to."

e) Tense Accord

No, not a strained agreement, but the proper alignment of various verb tenses.

I would be a rich man if I had a dollar for every time I've seen something like this:

> I *would have* started on your memo earlier if I *would have* known that the big due diligence project was about to land on me.

Wrong, so wrong. That second *would have* needs to be *had.*

Getting technical with talk of the pluperfect and the conditional perfect (aka past conditional) is likely to confuse, so just remember that it's never correct to have two *would have* constructions in succession like this.

f) Journalistic Conditional

Happily, there isn't too much of this in legal writing, but open the newspapers and it abounds (especially in the obituaries). By way of example (emphasis added):

> He *would* go on to write one of the defining Canadian novels of the twentieth century.

That *would go* should just be a simple *went* (or just say *he later wrote*).

g) Journalistic Subjunctive

One of the *Financial Times*'s readers has noted the fungus-like proliferation of *would* as a subjunctive, in phrases like *Since such-and-such has occurred ... it is less likely that whatever-else-it-is* would *come to pass*. A simple *will* would suffice.[21] (See also Chapter 3, Section A(19), "The Subjunctive.")

8) *And/Or, And, Or*

a) *And/Or*

The construction *and/or* is criticized by grammarians, prose stylists, and many legal drafters (both contractual and statutory). There are good reasons for this.

HW Fowler found *and/or* distasteful.[22] It looks as though you couldn't take the time to think things through and express yourself other than by way of a fairly crude (if expedient) short form. *And/or* also has an air of the commercial purchase order to it. Less than ideal — even inelegant.[23]

There are other reasons to avoid *and/or*, and they relate to the meaning (and ambiguity) of words.

b) Disjunctive *and*, Conjunctive *or*

We usually think of *and* as being conjunctive — that is, grouping things together — rather than disjunctive (separating things or presenting alternatives). Similarly, *or* is usually disjunctive. This is largely true, but not always.

Consider these examples:

> *The minister of finance may do X and Y.* [She can do both X and Y, but she is also free to do only one of them or neither — so *and* is not only conjunctive but also potentially disjunctive.]

21 Michael Carter, "Subjunctive Fungus Infects Predictive Statement," Letter to the Editor, *Financial Times* (26 May 2017), online: www.ft.com/content/004682ac-4200-11e7-9d56-25f963e998b2.

22 *Fowler's*, 2d ed, above note 4 at 29.

23 *Fowler's*, 3d ed, above note 4 at 53. See also Marius Potgieter, "The 'Bastard Conjunction' — 'And/Or'" *Lexology* (4 April 2018), online: www.lexology.com/library/detail.aspx?g=7120ed74-24ca-453b-90cf-85f65314c8c3&l=7YV4MA2.

> *The minister of justice may do X or Y.* [Here again, he could do either one or neither, but he could also do both — a conjunctive *or* is one possible interpretation.][24]

To avoid confusion, you are better to say one of the following:

* *both A and B*
* *A or B, but not both*
* *either A or B*
* *A or B, or both*

Otherwise, your fate may be like that of the New Jersey judge whose repeated use of *and/or* rendered her jury instructions so "hopelessly ambiguous" that a new trial was ordered by the appeal court.[25]

In contractual (and legislative) drafting, you probably want to avoid any ambiguity that might arise from *and/or*; in other kinds of legal writing, *and/or* just isn't pretty.

9) *Only*, the Lonely

I wish people would think about the placement of the single word *only*. Where it falls in your sentence can have a crucial effect on meaning. *Only* feels lonely because it's often in the wrong place at the wrong time, misused and misunderstood.

Consider these examples (devised by James Forrest, emeritus professor, Department of English, University of Alberta):

* He ***only*** told her that he loved her
* He told ***only*** her that he loved her
* He told her ***only*** that he loved her
* He told her that ***only*** he loved her
* He told her that he ***only*** loved her
* He told her that he loved ***only*** her
* He told her that he loved her ***only***[26]

---

24 As that excellent (and legally trained) writer Renata Adler observes, "And I've found, I think, the strongest 'or' in language anywhere. It's the lawyers' phrase: as he then well knew or ought to have known. The strongest or." See Renata Adler, *Speedboat* (New York: NYRB Classics, 2013) at 126–27.

25 *State of New Jersey v Gonzalez*, 130 A3d 1250 (NJ Super Ct App Div 2016).

26 Thanks to Joan Bilsland of Bennett Jones LLP, Calgary, for sharing them.

In speech and casual writing, we don't always place *only* so carefully. In more formal writing — and certainly in transactional drafting — misplacement can lead to ambiguity and confusion. For this reason, Richard Wydick calls *only* a "notorious troublemaker."

To avoid problems with *only*, place it immediately before the word you want to modify (as in the Forrest examples), or isolate it at the end or beginning of a sentence. Examples include:

* Ambiguous: *The lessee shall use the vessel only for recreation*
* Clear: *The lessee must use the vessel for recreation only*
* Ambiguous: *Shares are sold to the public only by the parent corporation*
* Clear: *Only the parent corporation sells shares to the public*[27]

Where contractual certainty is not at stake, you can be a bit less careful (and HW Fowler warns in *Modern English Usage* against excessive pedantry on this point), but you still run the risk of conveying a slightly different meaning than intended.[28]

10) *Who* and *Whom*

You knew this would come up sooner or later.

The simple rule is that *who* is a subject (*Who said that?*), *whom* is an object (*To whom is that letter addressed?*). The verb *to be*, you will remember, takes a subjective completion (*who*) rather than an object (*whom*). So it's not *Who's whom* but *Who's who*.

But it's a bit more complicated than that.

First, *who* has largely displaced *whom* in common usage, to the point where the *OED* admits that it is "no longer current in everyday speech." As a result, one usually hears *It's not what you know, it's* who *you know*. That really should be *whom you know* (of course), because you need an object for *you know*. If Theresa May had asked UK voters ***Whom*** *do you trust to have the strong and stable leadership to get on with that job . . . ?*, instead of *Who do you trust*, perhaps the 2017 election might have gone differently.

27 Adapted from Wydick & Sloan, above note 1 at 48.

28 *Fowler's*, 2d ed, above note 4 at 418–19; *Fowler's*, 3d ed, above note 4 at 551–53.

To whom it may concern persistently survives in reference letters, but we could dispense with it as archaic (if grammatically correct). The reader of the letter will either be the appropriate person or will pass it on as necessary. If you don't have the name of a specific recipient, you can just put the company address or even just the name of the subject of the reference as a heading, with no address or salutation.

Whomst has recently surfaced on Twitter and other social media, "For times when you want to ask 'who or whom,' but need a fancier connotation."[29] This misguided advice is perhaps suggested by *whilst*, a slightly old-fashioned/UK version of *while*. *Whilst* is fine, but do not succumb to the temptation of *whomst*, other than in a jocular post.

If *whom* has largely fallen by the wayside, people do sometimes use it, incorrectly, because they think it sounds classier: I've actually heard *May I ask whom is calling?* from someone on the other end of the telephone. And those of a certain vintage may know a similar error in a line by The Clash. Great song, terrible grammar.

Who and *whom* can also be what's called relative pronouns: *the man who mistook his wife for a hat* but *the lawyer whom time forgot*. Here again, the subject-object distinction governs.

Another complicating point is that whether it's *who* or *whom* may depend on the surrounding words. It's correct to say *I'll talk to whomever* but not *I'll talk to whomever will listen*. In the second example, that *whomever* is wrong because you need a subject for the *will listen* bit — and that has to be *whoever*. Similarly, it's *Whomever we hire will work hard* rather than *Whoever* because you need an object for *we hire*.[30]

Confused? Take comfort in the fact that Shakespeare got it wrong in the line *Young Ferdinand, whom they say is drowned* — as did the King James translators of the Bible with *But whom say ye that I am?* These examples can be readily fixed if you prune the excess words to get at the core of the sentence: in the example from *The Tempest*, *they say* is merely a parenthetical remark, the core being *Ferdinand*,

29 See Urban Dictionary, online: www.urbandictionary.com/define.php?term=whomst.

30 *Fowler's*, 2d ed, above note 4 at 708–9.

who is drowned; and the verse from Matthew is, essentially, *But who am I?*[31]

And while we're on the subject, don't confuse *who's* and *whose*. *Who's* is short for *who is*, as in *Who's who? Whose*, on the other hand, is a relative pronoun: *Whose book is this?*

11) All *Well* and *Good*

If I had a dollar for every time I've heard *Good, thanks — and you?* in response to *How are you?*, I'd be writing this from a villa in Tuscany. (Or not writing it at all, just sipping Negronis on a deck-chair by the pool.)

The grammatically correct response to *how are you* is *well*, not *good*. *Good* traditionally refers to a moral, not a physical or mental, state. *I'm good* really ought to be confined to situations where you mean you are virtuous, good at something, or well-behaved. (And not as a way of saying "No, thank you" to an offer of food or drink.)

Well is both an adjective and an adverb; *good* is only ever an adjective (or a noun), and therefore it can't modify a verb. So, *We did good* means we effected works of charity and the like, rather than we did a good job. For that, you mean *We did well*.[32] But this appears to be a losing battle: pass me another Negroni.

The battle is entirely lost with the verb *to look*. Classically, one would have said *That colour looks well on you* — but you would attract uncomprehending looks if you said that now.

There is still time to win the adverbial battle with constructions like *Travel safe* or *drive clean*. *Safely* and *cleanly*, please: it's how you travel or drive, which demands an adverb to modify the verb. (Although *drive clean* is possibly justifiable if you mean *clean* as an adjective that describes a drug-free driver.)

31 *Ibid.*

32 And see Bryan Garner, "LawProse Lesson #136: Is 'Good' Becoming an Adverb? Are We Losing 'Well' as an Adverb?" (1 October 2013), *LawProse*, online: www.lawprose.org/lawprose-lesson-136-is-good-becoming-an-adverb-are-we-losing-well-as-an-adverb; Robert Hartwell Fiske, *Robert Hartwell Fiske's Dictionary of Unendurable English: A Compendium of Mistakes in Grammar, Usage, and Spelling with Commentary on Lexicographers and Linguists* (New York, NY: Scribner, 2011) at 196.

Sometimes *good* is the right choice, however—with *taste* and *smell*, for example (where *good* isn't so much an adverb as an adjective describing whatever is being sampled). You would use *well* if you were referring, though, to an expert wine-taster's skill at sniffing and sipping.

Feel is trickier. Many insist that it's OK to say *I felt bad about having to fire her*, but traditionally it's *badly*. James Brown may have felt *good* in his famous song (and I wouldn't change that line for all the Negronis in the world), but grammatically it should be *well* (even if that could also mean skill in groping). We still say *I don't feel well* when we're ill; we could usefully revive the Jane Austen-ish construction *It was done very ill.*

While we're on the subject, a few words about *best*. There are many reasons to pity Melania Trump (although maybe she knew what she was signing up for and got what she deserved—hard to say, really).

Mrs T got into some linguistic hot water with the slogan for her campaign for children's health and happiness, launched in May 2018: *Be Best.*[33]

One can *be good* and one can *be better*, but one really ought to *be the best*, not just *best*. That said, it would be idiomatic (and correct) to say *It would be best not to do that.*

The origin of Melania's little solecism? Her not always grammatically correct husband, perhaps. Or a desire to outdo, with a superlative, Michelle Obama's exhortation in 2016 for men to *be better*. Or possibly a staffer's subtle mockery of the First Lady's somewhat shaky command of English and its use of definite articles (which are foreign to her native Slovene).

Not, by any means, the greatest failing of the reign of Trump, but worth noting.

33 See Tim Hill, "'Be Best': Does Melania Trump's Oddly Named Initiative Break the Laws of Grammar?" *The Guardian* (8 May 2018), online: www.theguardian.com/us-news/2018/may/08/be-best-melania-trump-initiative-grammatical-flaw.

12) *Respect* and *Regard*

Feeling respect and regard for your readers is important, but I'm more concerned here about words and phrases derived from *respect* and *regard.*

a) *Regard* and Derivatives

First, *regards* as opposed to *regard.*

Regards are what you express, typically at the end of a letter or email, in order to sound friendly; but as we've seen earlier, you could usefully dispense with them altogether — they add nothing (see Chapter 1, Section E(3), "Beginnings and Endings"). In any event, do NOT say *with regards to* or *in regards to.* Here, the correct word is *regard* (singular). Better yet, just say *about* or *on.*

Irregardless is not a word (or at least not in the standard English you want to be using); you mean *regardless* (or perhaps *irrespective*).[34]

b) *Respect* and Derivatives

Respect can be used like *regards*, to express esteem for another person. In professional writing, this may sound a bit too Ali G ("*Massive respect . . .*").

When you disagree with someone, you should also avoid that leaden opener *With respect*, which usually indicates that the writer has anything but respectful thoughts about the recipient.

The adverb *respectfully* is just as bad, if not worse. Use it in a factum if you must, but don't lard the thing with it, as John Laskin, formerly of the Ontario Court of Appeal, has written in his excellent "Forget the Wind-Up and Make the Pitch." He advises: "Avoid using the phrase 'it is respectfully submitted' more than twice in your factum. . . . Repeated too often, this phrase disrupts the force and flow of your argument."[35] It also sounds pompous and old-fashioned.

---

34 But see "The Shadowland" *The Economist* (25 July 2020), online: www.economist.com/books-and-arts/2020/07/25/the-shadowlands-of-language.

35 Justice John I Laskin, "Forget the Wind-Up and Make the Pitch: Some Suggestions for Writing More Persuasive Factums" (1999), Court of Appeal for Ontario, online: www.ontariocourts.ca/coa/en/ps/speeches/forget.htm.

In a legal setting, try to confine *respect* to these two phrases: *with respect to* and *in respect of*. But here again, you're better off going with a simpler construction entirely, like good old *about*. And to say *respecting* in this sense looks like you're writing with a quill pen.

Respectively is frequently misused. It needs to connect items in one list with their counterparts in a second list in the same sentence. *Fowler's Modern English Usage* entertainingly lists five types of incorrect use, but space doesn't permit full discussion here.

This is wrong: *X, Y, and Z respectively guarantee Z's obligations.*

This is correct: *X, Y, and Z shall not make capital expenditures in any fiscal year in excess of $5 million, $3 million, and $1 million, respectively.*[36]

13) *Between* and *Among*

This one may surprise you.

Purists often say that *between* must — MUST! — refer only to a relationship involving two parties or things, and no more. The –*tween* bit does have the same origin as the number *two*, after all.

Among, the purists say, is to be used when the relationship involves three or more persons or things.

The purists are too pure. The *OED* and *Fowler's Modern English Usage* have long warned that this supposed distinction between *between* and *among* is merely superstitious.[37]

According to *OED*, "*between* has been, from its earliest appearance [at least as far back as the year 931], extended to more than two" — and "it is still the *only* [emphasis added] word to express the relation of a thing to many surrounding things severally and individually; *among* expresses a relation to them collectively and vaguely."

One would therefore correctly say:

- *The grassy area lying between the three trees*
- *An agreement between three parties*

36 Examples adapted from Ross Guberman & Gary Karl, *Deal Struck: The World's Best Drafting Tips* (Legal Writing Pro Press, 2014) at 72.

37 *Fowler's*, 2d ed, above note 4 at 57, citing *OED*; *Fowler's*, 3d ed, above note 4 at 106.

* *A difficult choice between three candidates*
* *You are among friends*
* *Among many choices, he took the easiest option*
* *She is a keen tennis-player, among other things*

In contractual drafting, however, you may be better off saying *The agreement among X, Y, and Z* — if only to keep the (misguided) purists at bay. As Ross Guberman observes, debating the point with them is probably "not constructive."[38]

And while we're on the subject . . . never *between you and I*. Always *between you and me*.

14) Noun Fatigue

Nouns can be used in ways that tire the reader. Here are some things to watch for.

a) Noun Chains

Long chains of nouns used as adjectives don't make for vigorous prose.[39] (But see Chapter 3, Section A(15), "Hyphens and Dashes," for the contrasting German approach, which is fine with noun-accumulation.)

Writers of headlines in a certain kind of newspaper love noun chains:

CORONAVIRUS HEALTH CRISIS WARNING

DEATH CRASH POLICE OFFICER RELEASE

HOLLYWOOD STARLET DRUG SCANDAL SHOCKER

NAZI MYSTERY GOLD TRAIN DISCOVERY HOAX

So (perhaps oddly) do drafters of legislation and other bureaucrats: a glance at federal regulations beginning with A yields (among other gems) the *Animals of the Sub-family Bovinae and Their Products*

38 Guberman & Karl, above note 36 at 70.
39 Wydick & Sloan, above note 1 at 50.

Importation Prohibition Regulations and the *Alberta Sex Offender Information Registration Regulations*.

This is OK in the interests of concision on the front page or in a legislative table, but in other kinds of writing the effect is deadening or downright confusing. Example: *business process outsourcing strategy*.

Remove some nouns, insert some verbs — make a sentence, not a verbal car crash.

b) Noun Phrases (aka Nominalizations)

Here, noun combines with verb (and some other stuff) in order to make what could usually be a straightforward verb. Another way to describe it is with the awful noun *nominalization* (making a noun out of something else, basically).

Examples (with their preferable, simple verb alternatives in parenthesis):

- *make a recommendation* (*recommend*)
- *provide assistance to* (*help* or *assist*)
- *make a decision* (*decide*)
- *provide advice to* (*advise*)
- *this is to acknowledge receipt of* (*we received*)

Etc., etc. — you get the drift. The problem with these constructions is that they make your sentences longer, flabbier, and less direct. Surely you'd rather be concise, toned, and vigorous (in your prose, at the very least)?

c) Weak Verbs from Nouns

Another tendency of dull legal prose is to use verbs that are derived from nouns (like *nominalize*). Other examples: *facilitate*, *operationalize*, *utilize*. Why not the simpler (and livelier) *help*, *launch*, and *use*?

Also resist turning a verb into a noun (*action*, *credential*, *reference*, *task*, and others of this misbegotten brood).

Gift

One verb-from-noun that may be OK is *gift*.

It doesn't mean anything that *give* doesn't, so arguably there is no real need for it, but some lawyers like to use it for things like donations. Does *gift* sound more formal and legal/technical than plain old *give*? Perhaps, but that's not good reason to use it.

Gift as a verb does have a fairly long history, going back to the sixteenth century. And it is natural to talk about someone as being *gifted* with some sort of skill or talent.

In the gift-bestowing, present-making sense, the *OED* suggests the verb is mainly Scottish, and most of the examples of usage are in fact from Scots legal sources.

Use *gift* as a verb if you must, but you might be better just to *give*.

Summons

Less good is summons as a verb. Summons is one of those odd nouns that ends in –s in its singular form; so the plural is summonses.

Odder still is the use of *summons* as a verb, meaning to command someone's appearance in a court of law by way of a summons. Verbs don't typically end in –*s* either.

Not everyone is happy with this state of affairs: Glanville Williams wrote in *Learning the Law*, 11th ed (1982), that "the horrible expression 'summonsed for an offence' (turning the noun 'summons' into a verb) has now become accepted usage, but 'summoned' remains not only allowable but preferable."

A little digging in the dictionary (the *OED*, of course) shows, however, that *summons* is older than Williams suggests — if not entirely reputable.

The usage citations in *OED* go back as far as 1780, with a quotation from Martin Madan's *Thelyphthora*: "A woman had but to summons her seducer before the judges." Madan (1726–1790) was a barrister (and a clergyman), but a controversial one; *Thelyphthora* scandalized its readers in advocating polygamy as a remedy for the "female ruin" brought about by what he called whoredom, fornication, and adultery. Perhaps not the *best* authority, then?

Next in the citations comes a line from Dickens's *Nicholas Nickleby* (1828), where the sadistic schoolmaster Whackford Squeers (oh, those Dickensian names!) ejaculates, "Say another word and I'll summons you for having a broken winder.'" The dialectical *winder* may suggest that *summons* too, is non-standard.

And a further example is from the novels of Marie Corelli, a forerunner of Barbara Cartland and EL James (so not exactly an exemplar of great literature): "You can summons me ... if you feel so inclined" (*God's Good Man* (1904)).

All in all, not an impeccable pedigree for the verb *summons*, but it isn't as newfangled a word as Glanville Williams suggests. I agree, though, that *to summon* is the better way to go.

d) Weak Nouns from Verbs

Avoid the temptation to turn verbs into nouns, especially when there are perfectly serviceable nouns already. I am so sick of hearing about *the disconnect*! Please say *communication failure, disconnection, disjuncture, failure* (not *fail*), *gap* — anything but *the disconnect.*

Other examples (with their better, existing nouns): *ask* (*request*), *build* (*construction*), *consult* (*consultation*), *spend* (*expenditure, cost*), *value-add* (*benefit, advantage*). *Commute* as a noun to describe your journey to and from work now seems unavoidable.

15) Phrases We Love to Misuse

For all intensive purposes

A friend suggested I include this, but I didn't think people actually said it — until I heard it recently at a meeting. Cringe.

A malapropism for *for all* ***intents and*** *purposes*, of course.

Hell hath no fury

Completed by most with *like a woman scorned*, but this is a misquotation. The original (from William Congreve's *Mourning Bride* (1697)):

> Heav'n has no Rage like Love to Hatred turn'd,
> Nor Hell a Fury like a Woman scorn'd.

But that brings us to a more important point. The "scorned woman" business is more than a bit sexist, and most of the other phrases in this section are decidedly shopworn. You'd be better to avoid hackneyed expressions and tired old proverbs in favour of wording that is direct and original.

Out of pocket

I didn't realize people misused this until I went to a meeting at an accounting firm (where management-consulting-speak is much in evidence).

The person at the meeting used it to mean "unavailable, out of the office, out of the picture, inaccessible." What it actually means is to have disbursed money from one's actual or metaphorical pocket: *I am out of pocket by about twenty bucks because I paid for everyone's coffee.*

Sooner than later

This is now frequently heard (thank you, Drake). While it does make some sense, it lacks the elegance and completeness of thought of the original phrasing: *sooner* ***rather*** *than later.*

Is confusion with *sooner or later* at work?

The devil is in the details

Misused if you take the view that it's a later variant of the original *God is in the details.*

They both mean the same thing: you cannot fully understand or appreciate something unless you look at the inner workings, the fine print, the subtleties. In the one version, those details will send you to perdition if overlooked; in the other, they are sublime.

Often attributed to the architect Ludwig Mies van der Rohe (1886–1969), but probably older.

The proof is in the pudding

This kind of makes sense, especially if you grew up in a culture where it is common to put a coin or other prize in a festive dessert (like the English at Christmas or the French on the *jour des Rois*). But that isn't the origin of the phrase. In its full, correct form, it's *the proof of the pudding is in the eating.*

In other words, you don't know what the thing is going to taste like until you actually sample it. Also applied metaphorically to any situation or thing that needs to be tested before you can say it worked.

This begs the question

Often used by someone who wants to say, "This raises another issue . . ." — but it's not quite what the phrase means. To trot out some Latin (never to be used again), the original expression is *petitio principii*, a rhetorical term for a statement containing circular reasoning. That is, a statement that offers, as proof of its truth, another statement that itself requires proof: for example, "God is great because He is the Supreme Being."

16) Just How Frequently Is That?

a) *Bi–*

HW Fowler draws attention in *Modern English Usage* to the *bi–* words that are used to describe the frequency of intervals: *biannual*, *bi-monthly*, *bi-weekly*, and the like.[40] The problem with them is that they are ambiguous: *bi-weekly*, for example, can mean either twice a week or every two weeks. At least a *biennial* (like the *Biennale* art exhibition held in Venice) is always held every two years, not twice in one.

Careful drafters of contracts will obviously want to make things perfectly clear, especially when dealing with dates of payment obligations and the like. And even non-contractual writers may wish to avoid uncertainty.

There are some options to avoid the ambiguity of *bi–*. *Semimonthly* is clearer than *bi-monthly*, if you want to say that something is to occur twice in any given month. But both words are unattractive hybrids. *Fortnightly* is an option, if you're OK with sounding very British. Or you could just say *twice monthly*, *every two weeks*, or *every other week*. *Fowler's* proposal to adopt *half-monthly* doesn't appear to have gained much traction, but you could try it — and you wouldn't be misunderstood.

b) Centuries

If you're old enough, you'll remember Canada's *centennial* in 1967 and the *bicentennial* of US independence in 1976. In the United

40 *Fowler's*, 2d ed, above note 4 at 58.

Kingdom, these would have been *centenary* (pronounced *cen-TEEN-er-ee*) and *bicentenary* (*bye-cen-TEEN-er-ee*).

When Toronto celebrated the 150th anniversary of its incorporation back in 1984, someone dredged up *sesquicentennial*, a word that doesn't appear to be used all that much. It did engender a twee squirrel mascot called Seskwee (although it wasn't black like the characteristic Toronto rodent).

The federal government, wisely, did not try to figure out the Latinate term for the 125th anniversary of Confederation when that occurred in 1992. (The unwieldy *quasquicentennial* has been suggested.) Instead, the feds opted for *Canada 125*, universally called *Canada one two five* (perhaps a deliberate echo of the colloquial term for a case of beer). *Canada 125* made up in clarity what it lacked in imagination — and, predictably, we have now had what was officially called *Canada 150*.

But perhaps we still have the *dodransbicentennial*, *dodrabicentennial*, or possibly *dequabicentennial* of Confederation to look forward to in 2042 — with Dodra or Dequa the beaver as mascot?

c) *Millennial*

Once every thousand years. Also, now, used to refer to the much-maligned generation that came of age around the dawn of the new millennium — although *millennial* is often used for anyone born somewhere between the early 1980s and the early 2000s.

Note: spell *millennial* and *millennium* with two Ls and two Ns. Millennia (and centuries) begin in years ending in 1 (2001, not 2000), by the bye; there was no year 0.

17) Numbers and Dates

This is in response to a number (hah!) of queries.

a) Is There a Preferred Format for Dates?

Depends on your preference.

If you're American, *12/11/17* means December 11, 2017; to a Brit, it would be 12 November 2017.

Better to avoid ambiguity by spelling things out? Or use the format *YYYY-MM-DD*.

b) What About Times of the Day?

I have never quite seen the point of the colon in *8:30*. A period would work, no? The British do it that way.

I also like the clarity of the twenty-four-hour clock: there is no doubt about what time is meant by *1730*. But *5.30 p.m.* is also clear enough — just don't say *5.30 p.m. in the afternoon.*

c) Is There a More Inclusive Way to Express Dates than AD or BC?

Yes. In academic publications, these abbreviations are often replaced by *CE* and *BCE*.

The *CE* bit is an abbreviation for "common era," a term in use since the seventeenth century as a translation of the Latin *vulgaris æræ*. ("Vulgar" not meaning "rude" here but "popular," as opposed to the regnal years used in official legal dates.) *BCE* is "before common era," obviously.

The numbers won't be different, just the letters: *2017 CE* is the same as *AD 2017*.

d) Do I Need to Write "Fifteen (15) Days"?

No, this is unnecessary, even in contractual drafting.

There is nothing ambiguous about "fifteen" — although there could well be disagreement about what a "day" means and when you start counting them.

e) Microsoft Always Wants to Make Superscripts When I Type Things Like "4th" — Is That OK?

Personally, I find it annoying when Microsoft does this with ordinal numbers.

And, technically, superscripted forms like *4th* are incorrect in legal citations. But it's annoying to have to go back and remove them too. At least Microsoft doesn't recognize *2d* and *3d*, which are the usual forms in legal citations, as ordinals.

f) When Do I Write a Number Out in Words and When Do I Use Numerals?

The convention is that numbers under 10 should be written out (*We saw eight episodes but gave up on the series when it grew boring*), numerals after that (*The thought of watching all 24 episodes was simply too much*). It isn't a hard-and-fast rule, however, and style guides differ about this.

One often writes out single-word numbers: *I've read that book at least twenty times*; *If I've told you once, I've told you a thousand times*. Approximations can be a hybrid: *Dinosaurs became extinct about 66 million years ago, but scientists debate the precise causes.*

It is unusual to begin a sentence with a number expressed in numerals, although just possible when talking about a year (or the novel *1984*). Generally, spell out the number: *Twenty-three hours is a long time to wait for a plumber*. With years, you might want to recast the sentence: *The 2000 vintage was exceptional in Bordeaux*; *The year 2020 is one I'd rather forget.*

Traditional/British usage is to insert *and* in the spelled-out (and pronounced) forms of numbers like 101 and 1,397: *a hundred and one*; *one thousand, three hundred and ninety-seven*. Americans drop the *and*.

g) Miscellaneous Points

A couple of things but *a dozen things*.

Hyphens in compounds like *fifty-seven* and *thirty-two*.

A six-year-old girl and *A six-year-old could have painted that* (although usually she couldn't), but *She is six years old.*

C. WORDS THAT DON'T (OR MAY NOT) MEAN WHAT YOU THINK THEY DO

The English language is (unlike the US Constitution, apparently) a living tree: meanings change over time, with usage — even when that is at odds with a traditional meaning or with etymology.

A good example is *meticulous*, a quality legal employers often seek in relation to their professionals' attention to detail. But originally, this was not a positive attribute: it meant overcareful about mintutiae; only later did it come to be seen in a more positive light as "careful" or "scrupulous" (or the dreaded "detail-oriented" of job postings). Similarly, few would now use *decimate* to mean to reduce in number by a tenth; today, it suggests more drastic measures.

1) Misused Words, Confusing Pairs, and Troublesome Triplets

Word	Meaning	
a priori	**Doesn't mean:** in advance	**Does mean:** based on theory rather than experiment
adverse	unfavourable (***adverse*** *weather conditions*); opposite (***adverse*** *in interest*)	
avert *advert*	one ***averts*** one's gaze from something unpleasant; one ***adverts*** (turns one's attention) to other matters; the two have been confused since the Middle Ages	
averse	opposed to (*I'm not* ***averse*** *to trying this out*); you are *risk-averse*, not *risk-adverse* (but you are ***adverse*** in interest to someone)	
alternate	as a verb, ***alternate*** means to follow one another in alternation (*The two speakers alternated in answering questions from the audience*); as a noun, a substitute (*I can't attend the conference, but we're allowed to send an alternate*); as an adjective, happening in turns (*The cake consists of alternate layers of cake, whipped cream, and fruit filling*)	
alternative	***alternative*** involves a choice between two options: *A healthier alternative to cake is fresh fruit*	
affect	to influence (*This legislative change* ***affects*** *all mutual fund companies*); also a noun meaning a feeling, response to stimulus, emotion or mood	
effect	(NOUN) the result of (*This legislative amendment has the* ***effect*** *of requiring all mutual fund companies to . . .*) (VERB) to cause something to happen (*This legislative amendment* ***effects*** *radical reform to mutual fund regulation*)	
amuse	entertain (*Some lawyers were not* ***amused*** *by the students' light-hearted and satirical holiday-party video*)	
bemuse	confuse or baffle (*The students were* ***bemused*** *by the reaction of some lawyers to their otherwise popular video*)	

Word	Meaning
appraise	to value (*She took her jewellery to be* ***appraised*** *before offering it for sale on eBay*)
apprise	to inform (*She did not* ***apprise*** *her partner of her decision to sell her jewellery on eBay*)
assure	to enter into an agreement for the payment of money on the occurrence of an event, typically death, or loss or damage to property (chiefly UK); to make sure (*He* ***assured*** *me that he knew what he was doing, but I had my doubts*)*
ensure	to make something happen (*Her prompt intervention* ***ensured*** *that nothing was damaged*)*
insure	to enter into an agreement for the payment of money on the occurrence of an event, typically death, or loss or damage to property (North America and UK) (*It turned out he didn't know what he was doing, but happily he was* ***insured*** *against injuries caused to third parties*)* * These are the most common modern senses; over the centuries, the three words have to some extent been used interchangeably.
back story	the fabricated biography that a spy is given as a cover, to be used when interrogated by someone hostile
background	the more prosaic underlying information about something (don't use ***back story*** when all you mean is ***background***)
born	produced through birth (*I was* ***born*** *this way*)
borne	carried, supported (*That theory is* ***borne*** *out by the scientific evidence*)
broach	You ***broach*** a subject when you raise it with someone (*The partner broached the issue of missed deadlines with the hapless associate*)
brooch	A ***brooch*** is a piece of jewellery typically pinned to the upper breast (*The Queen always wears a large diamond brooch on her coat or dress, but her ancestor James I preferred to pin one to his hat*); the two words are pronounced in the same way (like *broach*)
canvas/ canvass	In modern usage, *canvas* is a noun that refers to the cloth used for sails and tents, and as the surface of oil-paintings (*The novice painter failed to prime the* ***canvas*** *properly, which is why the painting is now in poor condition*); *canvass* is a verb that means to solicit or ascertain support (*The candidate went door to door, to* ***canvass*** *the level of support for her party in the constituency*)

Word	Meaning
	Historically, the spellings were interchangeable. The verb sense derives from tossing a person in a canvas sheet, for fun or punishment — and, by extension, tossing ideas around.
categorize	to classify (*European settlers in Australia weren't sure whether to* ***categorize*** *the platypus as a mammal or a reptile; it has characteristics of both*)
characterize	to identify defining or typical attributes (*The platypus is* ***characterized*** *by its duck's bill and laying of eggs*)
chronic	**Doesn't mean:** severe **Does mean:** long-term
classic *classical*	Over time, these have been used interchangeably to some extent, but they are now best kept separate and more or less as follows: ★ ***Classic*** refers to something of recognized quality and enduring value (*Mozart's four greatest operas are* ***classics*** *of the repertoire*); it can also mean something like "typical" or "characteristic" (*The politician's answer was a* ***classic*** *example of evasion and obfuscation*) ★ ***Classical*** is generally used in relation to ancient Greece and Rome (***Classical*** *mythology is filled with tales of rape, incest, and murder*) or to music of the kind played by a symphony orchestra (in particular, material from the late eighteenth century to the early nineteenth): *Mozart is among the greatest of the* ***classical*** *composers.*
complement	(NOUN) number or thing that completes a whole (*With the addition of four new students, we have a full* ***complement*** *for articling*)
compliment	(NOUN) polite thing to say (*She paid him a* ***compliment*** *by saying he was intelligent, but did he deserve it?*)
complementary	that which completes something else (*The Act and the regulations form a* ***complementary*** *whole*)
complimentary	worthy of praise; free of charge (*The partner was less than* complimentary *about your performance; The associate received a* complimentary *gym membership as a benefit*)
complex *complicated*	These are interchangeable, both meaning (1) involved or intricate and (2) made up of different elements, compound. We tend, I think, to say ***complex*** *proteins* and ***complex*** *litigation* but a ***complicated*** *problem.*

Word	Meaning	
compose/ comprise/ consist	similar in meaning (and more than a pair), but often used incorrectly: properly, a group is ***composed of*** or ***consists of*** six people but it ***comprises*** six people	
concerning	**Doesn't mean:** troubling, disturbing, of concern	**Does mean:** about, regarding
contemptuous	showing contempt (***Contemptuous*** *damages are awarded when a judge believes the successful plaintiff should never have brought the action in the first place*)	
contemptible	worthy of contempt (*Were the presidential candidate's words and actions* ***contemptible****? No, they were beneath contempt*)	
continual	constantly occurring or recurring at short intervals, apparently without end (*If you try to do your work on the flight, you will have to put up with* ***continual*** *distractions from the cabin crew and other travellers*)	
continuous	occurring over a defined period without pause (*If a fire is detected, you will hear a* ***continuous*** *ringing over the PA system until the situation is under control*)	
credible	believable (*Inconsistencies in the witness's testimony led to the conclusion she was not* ***credible***)	
creditable	reputable, bringing credit to (*Irwin Law is a highly* ***creditable*** *publisher of legal titles*)	
cue/queue	You ***cue*** up a meeting (think of an actor's *cue*; it's all about timing); you ***queue*** *up in a line to get in somewhere*	
defuse	to remove the fuse (of an explosive); to render less dangerous (*The lawyer* ***defused*** *the tense situation in the boardroom*)	
diffuse	(VERB) to spread widely (*The pesticide was* ***diffused*** *over a large cultivated area*) [the S is pronounced like a Z] (ADJECTIVE) evenly spread, indirect (*The* ***diffuse*** *lighting did not help the associate in reading the fine print*) [the S is pronounced like SS]	
depose	It depends on the context! One of the best headlines of 2018 was "Stormy Daniels' Attorney Wants to Depose Donald Trump."[41] He's not the only one . . .	

41 See The Associated Press, "Stormy Daniels' Attorney Wants to Depose Donald Trump" CBC News (28 March 2018), online: www.cbc.ca/news/world/daniels-avenatti-trump-deposition-1.4596470.

Word	Meaning
	Of course the headline was using ***depose*** in its US legal sense, which is to examine a witness for the purposes of discovery or a later trial. Many Canadian non-lawyer readers would, however, have interpreted ***depose*** as overthrowing a bad king. In Canada, we would not ***depose*** *a witness* or *take a* ***deposition*** — we would *examine a witness for discovery.*
dependant	most commonly used to describe someone depending on another's support (*He is a single man with no* ***dependants***)
dependent	***Dependent*** is the adjectival form of the noun (*Each* ***dependent*** *child will receive a payment . . .*) *Dependent* also means, more generally, contingent on or owing to something else (*Your success as an articling student is* ***dependent*** *on many factors, some of which may not be apparent to you*). In the United States, *dependant* is almost never seen; Americans use *dependent* for both noun and adjective.
deprecate	to disparage (*It is unprofessional to* ***deprecate*** *other firms or lawyers*)
depreciate	to lower in value (*The property will* ***depreciate*** *if not properly maintained*)
desert	(NOUN) waste place without trees or water (*The explorer found a welcome oasis in the midst of the parching* ***desert***) (NOUN) what one deserves (*The accused received his just* ***deserts*** *in the form of a two-year prison sentence*) (VERB) to abandon (*The office was* ***deserted*** *at 4 o'clock on the Friday before the long weekend*)
dessert	a course served after supper or dinner (in the United Kingdom, fruit but not pudding; in North America, puddings, fruit pies, etc.) (*Life is short: eat* ***dessert*** *first*)
dichotomy	a state where there are two mutually exclusive alternatives (*Most lawyers' understanding of the difference between law and equity may be based on a false, or at least simplistic,* ***dichotomy***)
discrepancy	difference (*There is a* ***discrepancy*** *between the number of hours docketed and the number billed, owing to a write-off of student time*)

Word	Meaning
disburse	to pay out (*The lender will* ***disburse*** *funds once the borrower meets all conditions in the loan agreement*)
disperse	to scatter (*The population of Canada is widely* ***dispersed*** *over its large landmass*)
discreet	careful, acting with discretion (*Lawyers should be* ***discreet*** *in their conversations, especially in public places*)
discrete	self-contained, separate (*This assignment can be broken up into eighteen* ***discrete*** *tasks; I need one student for each*)
disinterested	**Doesn't mean**: displaying a lack of interest, bored (for that, use *uninterested*) **Does mean**: objective, impartial, without an interest in the outcome
e.g.	for example [*exempli gratia*] (*I love many things,* ***e.g.*** *books, wine, and art* — but actually, you're better not to use the Latin, especially if you get it wrong)[42]
i.e.	that is, namely [*id est*] (*There is only one thing that I truly love,* ***i.e.*** *wine* — but same comment as for *e.g.*) (One sometimes still sees *viz.*, often used incorrectly. It's a mediaeval abbreviation for the Latin *videlicet*, and it means "namely" or "to wit." Used to identify something: *The victim received a call from an unwelcome visitor,* ***viz.*** *the accused. Sc.*, short for *scilicet*, is close in meaning, but introduces information that is missing or clarifies ambiguity in the original: *The witness said she had seen him* [***sc.*** *the accused*].) Avoid.

42 See *Speedway Corp v Wilson Real Estate II LLC*, Memorandum Decision 67A01-1709-SC-2089 (Ind CA, 18 April 2018), which considered a contract that made one party responsible for "the periodic repair of damages to said Easement area caused by vehicular traffic (i.e. potholes)." That party argued it was therefore not responsible to repaint lines in the area in question (a parking lot) after normal wear and tear from traffic not causing potholes. The trial court held that potholes were but one example of damage to the parking lot. The Indiana Court of Appeals reversed, taking a typically US literalist view of contract interpretation: *i.e.* means "that is," not "for example," so the responsible party was required to fix potholes, and only potholes. A Canadian court might take a more contextual approach to arrive at the opposite result, but the Indiana case is a useful reminder that you're better off using English if your Latin is rusty (or non-existent).

Word	Meaning
elder/older	Confusing because they mean the same thing, but are used differently. One ought to say *My* **elder** *sister* to describe a sister who is merely older than you are, but *I have an* **older** *sister* to identify an older one your reader or listener may not be aware of, but I doubt this distinction is maintained now — most people will use *older* in both contexts. *Elder* persists as a noun (*The kids just don't respect their* **elders** *these days*) and as an adjective in some stock phrases (**elder** *statesman*; but is there a gender-neutral formulation one could use instead?). Related point: if you have two children, don't refer to the senior one in age as your *eldest* or *oldest*; you mean *elder* or *older.*
elderly/old	*Elderly* is a tricky word. In North America, it's used as a euphemistic — or at least less harsh — way to say old. Example: *The elderly are considered among those at the greatest risk of contracting the coronavirus.* What the threshold age is for that is more difficult to determine. Sixty years is the number generally seen in relation to COVID-19, but otherwise it might be set at sixty-five or higher. Sixty-five is the new fifty-five? But then fifty-five is old enough to qualify for the seniors discount at the drugstore. A further complication is that usage of the word is different in the United Kingdom (and perhaps Australia, New Zealand, and other dominions beyond the seas). There, it is used to mean "not old, but getting up there." The *–ly* suffix operates like *–ish* or *–like*, essentially. So, anywhere from about fifty? North Americans seem not to like referring to harsh realities like old age: a *senior citizen* here would be an *old age pensioner* (or OAP) in the United Kingdom. And heaven forbid that anyone should mention death in Canada or the United States; people now *pass away* or even just *pass*, both dreadful, mealy-mouthed circumlocutions. That happens in the United Kingdom too, of course. It used to be that people who had completed their studies

Word	Meaning	
	at Oxford (*gone down*, in university parlance) were called *old members*, regardless of age. Now they are *alumni*, the American, academic, Latinate, age-neutral term. The cricket and rowing teams for Magdalen College alumni are still called the Withered Lilies, however — a reference to the flowers found, in more flourishing condition, in the college arms. A colleague recently bristled when someone described her as *elderly*, but perhaps the person using the adjective was British, in which case it was accurate. But I didn't point that out.	
enormity	**Doesn't mean**: vastness, large size	**Does mean**: profoundly evil or immoral act
enquire/ enquiry *inquire/ inquiry*	Fowler recommends using the *en–* form as a formal word for ask, *in–* for investigations, e.g., *The journalist* **enquired** *about the judicial inquiry. (Fowler's Modern English Usage*, 2d ed at 287. *Fowler's Modern English Usage*, 3d ed at 252, notes that this has yet to solidify into a rule.)	
every one *everyone*	two words in the "each and every" sense, one where you could substitute *everybody* (*I ate* ***every one*** *of the sandwiches* BUT ***Everyone*** *ate a sandwich*)	
expansive	(of things) expanding in volume; (of people) effusive (*Party balloons are made of highly* ***expansive*** *material*; *After a few drinks, the partner became* ***expansive*** *in his praise of the associate's work*)	
extensive	wide-ranging (*After an* ***extensive*** *search in the case law, I have found precisely nothing on point*)[43]	
expatriate	An *expatriate* (often shortened to *expat*) is a citizen of one country who lives in another. A *patriot* is one who feels love for and pride in a country.	
ex-patriot	And an *ex-patriot*? This may simply be a vulgar error for *expatriate*, although one wonders if there is perhaps a negative judgment at work about people who leave their country of origin for foreign parts — a suggestion that in moving they have somehow betrayed where they came from.	

43 Even the *New York Times* confuses *expansive* and *extensive*: see Choe Sang-Hun, "Park Geun-hye, Ex-South Korean Leader, Gets 25 Years in Prison" *New York Times* (24 August 2018), online: www.nytimes.com/2018/08/24/world/asia/park-geun-hye-sentenced-south-korea.amp.html.

Word	Meaning
	And *ex-patriot* is strangely common: Democrats Abroad used it (with no negative judgment) during the US election campaign of 2016 but have since corrected the error: see DocJess, "Meet the Delegates: Joe Smallhoover — Democrats Abroad" (4 August 2016) *Democratic Convention Watch*, online: www.democraticconventionwatch.com/diary/6012. (For another reader who has remarked upon the increasing use of *ex-patriot* where *expatriate* is meant, see Carol McCabe, "Expatriates and Ex-Patriots", Letter to the Editor, *The Washington Post* (10 June 2012), online: www.washingtonpost.com/opinions/expatriates-and-ex-patriots/2012/06/20/gJQAdio6SV_story.htm.)
famous	celebrated (*Paris Hilton is one of those celebrities who was **famous** for being **famous**, but whose fifteen minutes have since expired*)
infamous	of ill fame (*Hitler's **infamous** crimes will never be forgotten*)
fazed	disturbed (*I wasn't **fazed** by her decision to dye her hair green; I just wish she had chosen a better colour*)
phased	introduced or withdrawn in stages (*IT announced that computer upgrades will be **phased** in over the course of the year*)
flesh out	to provide substance or context (*I **fleshed out** the substance of the agreement based on the barebones precedent you provided*)
flush out	to force from a place of concealment (originally, used in relation to gamebirds) (*On-campus interviews provide an opportunity to **flush out** the less desirable candidates*)
flaunt	to display ostentatiously (*Did the partner really have to **flaunt** that Rolex the size of a dinner plate?*)
flout	to ignore flagrantly (*He **flouted** the firm's dress code by wearing orange Converse running shoes*)
forbear	(VERB; emphasis on second syllable) to refrain from enforcing a right (*The lender decided to **forbear** with the borrower by not insisting on payment of interest and penalties*)
forebear	(NOUN; sometimes spelled *forbear*; emphasis on first syllable) ancestor, usually fairly remote (*A Supreme Court justice and a Father of Confederation are among her distinguished **forebears***)

Word	Meaning
forgo/forgone *forego/ foregone*	Warren Buffet has confused these two: the Sage of Omaha wrote to his followers that "Investing is an activity in which consumption today is foregone in an attempt to allow greater consumption at a later date." A nicely expressed observation, but for the error; Buffet means ***forgone*** ("relinquished," "given up") not ***foregone*** ("preceding" as in *foregone* conclusions or foregoing reasons). Historically, though, the two spellings were more or less interchangeable. Both have nice past tenses one ought to see more of: *for(e)went.*
forceful *forcible*	***forceful*** means "powerful" or "effective"; ***forcible*** is "using force" (*The lawyer made a forceful plea for clemency on behalf of the accused; the complainant alleges that her treatment by the mall's security guards amounted to forcible confinement*)
foreword	introduction, preface (*The chief justice contributed a* ***foreword*** *to the collection of essays by eminent legal scholars*)
forward	(ADJ) onward, (VERB) to send on (*I'll* ***forward*** *the message that we need to move* ***forward*** *with the project*)
fortuitous	by chance (*It was* ***fortuitous*** *that I ran into you in the library, because I know you don't often go there*)
fortunate	lucky (*It was* ***fortunate*** *that you were able to help me out, as I really needed a hand*)
flounder	to flail about ineffectively (*The lawyer* ***floundered*** *in the face of pointed and awkward questions from the judge*)
founder	to sink (literally or figuratively) (*Heenan Blaikie* ***foundered*** *for reasons we don't fully understand*)
fulsome	**Doesn't mean**: full, detailed, in-depth **Does mean**: servilely flattering (as in *That thank-you email was a bit* ***fulsome****, don't you think? All I did was pay for coffee*)

Word	Meaning
guaranty	A *guaranty* is the act of securing, warranting, or guaranteeing something. It also means "security" or "warranty," and, more particularly in law, a party's a written undertaking to be answerable for the payment of a debt or the performance of an obligation by someone else.
guarantee	A *guarantee* is similar: it is (a) a person who provides a guaranty or gives a security, (b) what is given by the person doing that, and (c) a person who receives a guaranty. Clearly there is some overlap, and you'll never go wrong if you use *guarantee* for all senses. *Guaranty* is preferable where you mean the fact that security has been given rather than the security itself or the party providing it — so, "a contract of *guaranty*."* *Guaranty* used to be the verb form; this is now always *guarantee*. * *Fowler's Modern English Usage*, 2d ed, 233.
hanged	(OF PEOPLE) executed by hanging with a rope (*The convicted murderer was* ***hanged*** *by the neck until dead, as was the custom in those barbarous times*)
hung	(OF OBJECTS) suspended (*I* ***hung*** *a new picture on my living-room wall*); (of juries or parliaments) deadlocked (*A* ***hung*** *jury results in a mistrial*; *When there is a* ***hung*** *parliament, the governor-general will ask one of the party leaders to form a government*) — and there is a slang meaning of *hung*, but we won't go there
hesitant *reluctant* *reticent*	These are close in meaning, so any confusion is perhaps to be forgiven. To be ***reticent*** is to be unwilling to speak freely. ***Reluctant*** is a bit broader: it is to be unwilling to do something in general. ***Hesitant*** is like *reluctant*, but suggests the person may get over that momentary unwillingness. While someone who is *reticent* is also *reluctant*, the reverse is not (necessarily) true, so don't say *I am reticent to participate in the meeting.*

Word	Meaning
historical *historic*	These two words used to be used more or less interchangeably, but they have parted company. *Historical* now refers to what is part of the record of the past or in accordance with that record, depicts events from history, or is based on developments over time. For example, *Your memo doesn't need to provide a* historical *account of the law of unjust enrichment since* Moses v Macferlan *(1760); just give me an overview of the current state of Canadian law.* *Historic* is now confined to the sense of "memorable" or "fit to be recorded in history": *On that* historic *day, the Dominion of Canada came into being.* One often sees *an* before these two adjectives ("*an* historic occasion"), but this is unnecessary. The rule is that you use *an* only before a word beginning with a silent H (so it is *an honour*, but *a house*). In front of *historic*, *an* is a hold-over (*an hold-over*?) from the days when *an* was usual before any word with an unaccented syllable beginning with H. We no longer say *an hilarious joke*, so *an historic occasion* can give way to *a historic* one. It's normal to write *an unusual turn of events* or *an upper berth*, but most people now would not use *an* before words beginning with a long U (like *ubiquitous* or *useful*) — although the original version of an obituary in the *New York Times* wrote *an ubiquitous* (since changed to *a ubiquitous*).[44]
homage	***Homage*** (pronounced *HOM-idge*) is what mediaeval knights swore to their lords. Prince Philip paid it to his wife at her coronation in 1953.
hommage	***Hommage***, which is French (pron. *o-mahzh*), is a rather pretentious way in English to express indebtedness or non-feudal tribute (*The director's recent movie is an hommage to the film noir classics of the 1930s and 40s*) Don't confuse the two (or their pronunciations).

44 Bruce Weber, "Buck Henry, Who Helped Create 'Get Smart' and Adapt 'The Graduate,' Dies at 89" *New York Times* (9 January 2020; corrected 10 January 2020), online: www.nytimes.com/2020/01/09/movies/buck-henry-dead.html.

Word	Meaning
home	to converge (*The police* **homed** *in on the suspect*)
hone	to sharpen, literally or figuratively (*After* **honing** *her tools, she* **honed** *her wood-carving skills*)
imply	to suggest to someone (*The partner* ***implied*** *— but without saying so directly — that the associate had been less than helpful*)
infer	to deduce (*The associate* ***inferred*** *from the partner's sarcastic tone that her work hadn't measured up to expectations*)
in spite of *despite*	Actually, no difference in meaning. ***Despite*** (shortened from the earlier *in despite of*) perhaps sounds a little more old-fashioned? *Although* or *even though* would also work.
incredible	unbelievable, amazing (literally and figuratively) (*The articling student's lame excuses for not finishing the work on time were, frankly,* **incredible** *— but apparently she did have an* **incredible** *time at the amusement park instead*)
incredulous	unbelieving (*The articling student's lame excuses left the partner* **incredulous** *that someone could abandon her post on a Wednesday afternoon to go to the amusement park*)
indisputable *undisputed*	The first means "incontrovertible," "not capable of being disputed" (*The attribution of this painting to Picasso is* ***indisputable****; it is signed and dated, there is film footage of Picasso painting it, and its subsequent history is impeccably documented*) The second means just that something hasn't been contested, although perhaps it could be (*The election results are* ***undisputed*** *so far, but that may change if allegations of ballot-tampering come to light*)
inter/intern	Often confused in the death notices in the newspapers. Your late aunt is not going to be *interned* in the cemetery but rather *interred*. People are *interned* in things like prisoner-of-war camps.
lay	to place (and a slang meaning we won't go into), past tense *laid*, past participle *laid* (*Asked to* ***lay*** *the gun on the table, she* ***laid*** *it there; having* ***laid*** *it there, she left the room*)
lie	to recline, past tense *lay*, past participle *lain* (*"I need to* ***lie*** *down," said the associate, so he* ***lay*** *down in the sick room; having* ***lain*** *there for a while, he wondered how often the coverlet was washed*); also, to deceive (*He* ***lies*** *now, he* ***lied*** *in the past, he has always* ***lied***)

Word	Meaning	
lead *led*	The first is the past tense of the verb *to lead* (*She* led *an expedition to the South Pole*); the second, as a verb, is the infinitive form (*to lead*) or the present tense in the first or second person (*I now* lead *the derivatives group at my firm* or *You* lead *and I follow*). Mistaken use of *lead* as the past tense of *to lead* is said to be one of the commonest errors on CVs.[45] Lead is also a noun: when it rhymes with led, it's a metal; with leed, something you put round a dog's neck.	
literally	Used by the unlettered as a mild form of emphasis	**Does mean**: actually, not figuratively
loath	reluctant, unwilling (ADJECTIVE; rhymes with *both*; also spelled *loth*) (*I am* ***loath*** *to admit that you could be right about this*)	
loathe	to detest (VERB; rhymes with *clothe*) (*I don't actually* ***loathe*** *people who misuse words on this list; I just feel sorry for them*)	
lose, loose	Strangely frequent the confusion between these two. Surely the difference needs no explanation?	
militate *mitigate*	The first is to "lend support or give credence to"; the second, to "alleviate or moderate." *The totality of the circumstantial evidence* ***militates*** *in favour of a finding of guilt; The youth of the accused and her lack of a previous criminal record are* ***mitigating*** *factors that should be considered in sentencing her.*	
momentarily	**Doesn't mean**: in a moment, shortly, soon	**Does mean:** for a moment, briefly (so it's actually rather alarming when the flight crew says the plane will be taking off ***momentarily***)
moot	proposed for discussion at a moot; open to argument; uncertain; not capable of being clearly determined; (North America) purely theoretical, academic (*That is a* ***moot*** *point*)	
mute	incapable of speaking (*She was rendered* ***mute*** *by the associate's confusion of "mute" and "moot"*)	

45 See Mark Abadi, "9 Résumé Mistakes That Make You Look Less Qualified, Less Impressive, and Less Intelligent Than You Really Are" *Business Insider* (4 December 2017), online: www.businessinsider.com/common-spelling-mistakes-resume-2017-11.

Word	Meaning
moral(e)	***Morale*** entered the English language at the time of the First World War, when it was first used to describe the collective state of mind of the troops. It seemed like a borrowing from French, and the final *–e* signalled a Gallic pronunciation with the emphasis on the second syllable. This posed a problem for pedants, who pointed out that the equivalent noun wouldn't have a final E in French. And in French *la morale* with a final E means what we would call *morals*. As is often the case, people ignored the language nerds, with the result that in English ***morale*** is usefully distinguishable from ***moral***. Don't confuse them.
mortgagee *mortgagor*	This shouldn't need to be mentioned, but you'd be surprised — shocked, really — by the number of lawyers who have said to me that they sometimes get confused about which is which. One gives a mortgage to a lender, perhaps to the point of being *mortgaged to the hilt*. So, if you like, think of the ***mortgagee*** as the *donee* in this scenario. That is, the bank or some other lender who takes security for the loan (although this person is the giver (*donor*) rather than the recipient of credit). The ***mortgagor***, then, is the giver of the mortgage (but the taker of credit).
nauseating	causing nausea; disgusting (*The cocktail was a* nauseating *concoction of sweet liqueurs, fruit syrups, and food colouring*)
nauseous	suffering from nausea; disgusted; causing nausea (*Drinking the loathsome cocktail left me feeling* nauseous) [And please don't pronounce *nauseous* as though you come from 1950s Brooklyn; it isn't NAW-shuss but NAW-zee-uss]
oral	spoken (*While his* **oral** *French is good, his written skills are weak*)
verbal	in words, either spoken or written (but also used to mean purely spoken communication since at least the early 1600s; as a result, careful drafters would want to avoid the ambiguity of, say, *The Borrower shall provide* **verbal** *assurances that . . .*)

Word	Meaning	
passed, past	These used to be largely interchangeable, but in modern usage *passed* is only ever the past tense or past participle of the verb *pass*; *past* performs various functions, as an adjective, adverb, preposition, or noun. ★ *He **passed** his driving test on the seventh attempt.* ★ *The deadline has **passed**.* ★ ***Past** performance is no guarantee of future results.* ★ *A herd of elephants thundered **past**.* ★ *This cheese is **past** its sell-by date.* ★ *That's all in the **past***	
peak *peek* *pique*	*I took a **peek** through my binoculars at the distant **peak** of the mountain; this **piqued** my interest to travel across the valley to climb it.*	
pedal *peddle*	You ***pedal*** your bicycle; Donald Trump ***peddles*** more fake news than the so-called Fake News he decries. Someone who *pedals* is a *pedaller* (if you're American, *pedaler*); who *peddles*, a *pedlar*.	
penultimate	**Doesn't mean**: a fancy word for "the last"	**Does mean:** the next to last (*Elizabeth I was the last of the Tudors; her elder half-sister Mary was the **penultimate***)
perquisite	fringe benefit (often abbreviated *perq*) (*Among the **perquisites** offered to associates and students are Friday evening drinks and gym memberships*)	
prerequisite	requirement, condition (*Biz Org I is a **prerequisite** for Biz Org II*)	
perspicacious	penetrating, perceptive, discerning (*A **perspicacious** associate will readily grasp the point*)	
perspicuous	easily understood, clearly expressed, lucid (*His **perspicuous** explanation of a difficult area of the law was very helpful*)	
pore	to examine carefully (*The associate **pored** over the prospectus and provided comments that were both perspicuous and perspicacious*)	
pour	to dispense a substance, usually a liquid (*The associate accidentally **poured** coffee all over the prospectus*)	

Word	Meaning	
practicable	capable of being done (*Your solution to the problem just isn't **practicable**; it can't be implemented with existing technology*)	
practical	suitable for actual use (*His legal advice is **practical** because it reflects the client's current financial state*) As *Fowler's Modern English Usage* notes, however, these two words often overlap in meaning: "the practicable is often practical, and . . . the practical is nearly always practicable; but a very practical plan may prove impracticable owing to change of circumstances, and a practicable policy may be thoroughly unpractical.* * *Fowler's Modern English Usage*, 2d ed at 469.	
prescribed	required, mandated (*The borrower will pay interest at a **prescribed** rate of 2.4 percent*)	
proscribed	prohibited (*Under the* Criminal Code, *interest at a rate of more than 60 percent per year is **proscribed***)	
presently	**Doesn't mean:** at present, now	**Does mean:** by and by, in the fullness of time (*presently* originally meant "immediately" but over time came to mean "in an unspecified but probably long-ish time," as in *Lord X will be with you **presently*** or *I shall send payment **presently***)
presumptive	based on inference, providing reasonable grounds to believe (*Seeing his tax returns might provide **presumptive** evidence of collusion with Russia*)[46]	
presumptuous	unduly confident, impertinent (*It was **presumptuous** of the associate to think he knew better*)	

46 *Presumptive* also has a technical meaning in reference to an heir or heiress whose rights will be displaced by the birth of a nearer heir: *During the lifetime of her father, the Queen was only heiress **presumptive** (not heir apparent) because it was always theoretically possible that her mother might give birth to a son (male primogeniture then being the rule of succession).*

Word	Meaning
principal	(NOUN) person in authority, supervisor (*Your articling* ***principal*** *will be assigned to you once you start at the firm*) (ADJ) main, chief (*The* ***principal*** *source of the Canadian legal system is English common law*)
principle	(NOUN) guiding concept (*In* ***principle****, there is no reason to get this wrong; in practice, many people do*)
prostate, prostrate	The first is a gland that men have (***Prostate*** *cancer can be treated effectively if detected early*). The second means "to throw oneself to the ground in reverence or submission," "to knock down," "to overcome, to reduce to helplessness," "to reduce to extreme physical weakness or exhaustion" (*OED*). As in *That combination of intense heat and humidity will* ***prostrate*** *those who attempt overly vigorous physical activity*. *Prostrate* is occasionally used for the gland, but this is "non-standard" (which is to say, wrong).
ravage ravish	Not a common pair, but I've seen them confused. To ***ravage*** is to cause destruction (*The Amazonian rainforest has been* ***ravaged*** *by fires, clear-cutting and bull-dozers*) ***Ravish***, on the other hand, originally meant to seize and carry away a person, usually a woman and often with sexual intent. And since we're on the subject, ***rape*** was also originally just the act of seizing and carrying off, with what probably followed being inferred. The related word ***raptor*** is a bird (or, apparently thanks to a 1990 book by Michael Crichton, a dinosaur) that snatches its prey; but another obsolete meaning is ***rapist***, which the owners of a professional basketball team in Toronto may not have known. But back to ***ravish***, which can also mean to transport a person in a figurative and non-sexual/non-aggressive sense, frequently as a result of ecstasy or delight (*She lost herself in the* ***ravishing*** *melodies of Mozart's opera*)
rational(e)	I've seen these mixed up recently, which surprised me. ***Rational*** (ADJECTIVE) means "reasonable" or "logical"; ***rationale*** (NOUN) is the underlying reasoning for something. We get ***rationale*** (like *locale*) from French (and without the misapprehension we've seen with *morale*).

Word	Meaning
repel	to resist; to drive away (literally and figuratively) (*I was* **repelled** *by the stuffy atmosphere of some of the downtown firms; The army's advance was* **repelled** *by a concerted counter-attack*)
repulse	to drive away (literally and figuratively); to cause disgust (*The army's advance was* **repulsed** *by a concerted counter-attack; I was* **repulsed** *by the truly disgusting conditions in some of the hostels on my backpacking holiday*)
shear	to remove by cutting (*A summer in the Australian outback taught her how to* ***shear*** *the wool off a sheep*)
sheer	(ADJ) diaphanous (of cloth); unmitigated; very steep (of rock-faces, etc.) (VERB) to swerve, change course (*She had the* ***sheer*** *effrontery to wear a* ***sheer*** *top to the funeral; The inexperienced climber faced the* ***sheer*** *cliff-face with* ***sheer*** *terror; The lawyer's argument* ***sheered****, like a ship heading unexpectedly off-course, in pursuit of a tangential point*)
stationary	not moving (*It is not a good idea to jump off the bus before it is* ***stationary***)
stationery	writing supplies (*The firm buys much less* ***stationery*** *than it did in the 1980s, but it would be a gross exaggeration to say we've gone paperless*)
straight	***Straight*** as an adjective is straightforward; and even if your circumstances are *straitened*, you can *straighten* something that is at an angle. A *straight* is, in common parlance, a non-LGBTQ2S+ person.
strait	One is in *straitened circumstances* or *dire straits* if things are going badly. If things are going really badly, you might be put in a *straitjacket*. These expressions derive from ***strait***, meaning "tight," "narrow," or "confined."[47]

47 See *Cavendish Square Holding BV v El Makdessi*, [2015] UKSC 67 at para 225, where Lord Hodge refers (incorrectly) to "the *straightjacket* into which the law risked being placed by an over-rigorous emphasis on a dichotomy between a genuine pre-estimate of damages on the one hand and a penalty on the other" (emphasis added). (A regrettably large number of other instances may be found through quick searches of CanLII and BaiLII.)

Word	Meaning
	Hence also ***strait*** in the maritime sense, used to describe a narrow and perhaps difficult passage between land masses: the *Strait of Gibraltar,* the *Strait of Georgia* (although the Vancouver newspaper is *The Georgia Straight*, presumably because it conveys the straight goods to people on either side of the strait). It used to be that one was on (or off) the *strait and narrow*, but this is now spelled *straight and narrow*.
substantial/ substantive	a tricky one, because their meanings overlap (and they have been used interchangeably at least since 1768); best to use *substantial* where you mean solid, sturdy, weighty (literally or figuratively) and to confine *substantive* to matters that relate to legal rights and duties (as opposed to *procedural*) — and in terms of pronunciation it's *subSTANtial* but *SUBstantive*
systemic	related to a system (*The forensic accountant's work revealed a* ***systemic*** *lack of financial controls at the company, from the CEO down*)
systematic	organized according to a system; methodical; deliberate (*Our* ***systematic*** *approach to fact-gathering allowed her to make a* ***systematic*** *attack on the opposing side's credibility*)
tenant *tenet*	I didn't think I had seen these confused, only heard. I have now. Another bubble. A ***tenet*** is a doctrine or principle; a ***tenant*** is a renter of property.
than	conjunction used in comparing two things (*Your eyes were bigger* than *your stomach, weren't they?*)
then	adverb indicating sequence, consequence (*I used to think seeing "then" for "than" was just a typo, but* then *I realized it's too common to be just that*)
therefor/ therefore	The first, pronounced with the emphasis on the second syllable, means "for a specified thing" (*Shares and any and all substitutions* ***therefor***). The second, with the emphasis on the first syllable, means "in consequence, as a result" (*This opportunity will not be available for long; it is* ***therefore*** *imperative to act quickly*).

Word	Meaning	
	Let's confine *therefor* to the scrapheap of lawyerly archaisms: it just sounds so 1770, and you may come across like you're trying to be a clever-clogs for knowing the difference between it and *therefore.* Say *Shares and any substitutions* ***for them*** (please, not *substitutions* ***for same***). *Any and all* in the example is a redundancy too; *any* on its own does the job.	
their	third-person plural pronoun (*The neighbours should not let* ***their*** *dog bite people*)	
there	adverb indicative of location (*That wretched dog bit me* ***there****, on the ankle*)	
they're	contraction of *they are* (***They're*** *going to hear from me if they don't restrain that dog of theirs*)	
tomb	grave (rhymes with *whom*)	
tome	book, volume (usually long and tedious; rhymes with *Rome* not *tomb*)	
trooper *trouper*	If you see someone described as a *real trooper*, it's probably meant as a compliment — but it's also probably a terminological error. A ***trooper*** is a soldier, probably enlisted rather than an officer in a *troop. Trooper* is an actual rank in some Commonwealth regiments, at the bottom of the hierarchy. When you are saying someone is a team player who really goes the distance, it's ***trouper*** you mean — that is, the member of a theatrical *troupe* (borrowed from French) who steps in at the last minute to save the show when somebody else is ill or who takes on a horrible role without complaint.	
ultimate	**Doesn't mean**: the best	**Does mean:** the last (but maybe people assume that the latest thing is always the best; not always a safe assumption in these degenerate times)

Word	Meaning
upmost *utmost*	To do one's utmost is to make the maximum possible effort: *We will do our utmost to meet the deadline imposed by the regulator.* What one sometimes sees (or, more often, hears) is *upmost* instead of *utmost*. Close, but no cigar. ***Upmost*** is a legitimate word, but it's obsolescent in its correct sense. It refers to something that occupies the highest place or most important position. The more common word for that is now *uppermost*. As in, *The reader's convenience was not uppermost in the mind of the drafter of these complicated regulations.* Or, *The book was on the uppermost shelf in the library.*[48] Most of the ninety-two cases in CanLII that use *upmost* get it wrong (*upmost good faith*, etc.): *utmost* would be correct. In only a handful of those ninety-two is there a judicial "[*sic*]" to indicate that the error occurs in quoted material. Avoid *upmost* entirely — especially when *utmost* would be correct. Use *uppermost* when you mean something like "chief in importance" rather than "best efforts." For those, utmost is the way to go.
vary *very*	I've yet to see something like *vary good* — but I have come across *to very* when the meaning is intended to be to "alter" or "amend." *Vary* is correct there, obvi. Could be a typo, but long and sad experience suggests otherwise.
ware	*Wares* (usually used only in the plural) are articles of merchandise or manufacture: *Local hippies displayed their hideous* wares *in the market on the music festival grounds.* *Ware* in the singular is less common, except where a descriptive word is tacked on: *earthenware*, *glassware*, *hardware*, *silverware*, *software*, *tableware*.

48 An example of the correct use of *upmost* is found in Decision No 2399/14 2015 ONWSIAT 3, which refers to the "upmost flexion" of the distal phalangeal joint (at para 8). See also *Re Loblaw Groceterias Co Ltd and Minister of Highways* 1963 CanLII 222, [1964] 1 OR 271 (CA) (the "upmost round" of a ladder).

Word	Meaning
wear	*Wear*, as a noun, can be what you wear, as in *men's wear* (often now compressed to *menswear*, not entirely properly). *Outerwear* and *underwear* are well-established, but there are less attractive coinages: *beachwear*, *eyewear* (can we not just say *(eye)glasses* or *specs*?), *innerwear* (used for *underwear*, but illogically; you don't wear this stuff inside you, you wear it under other garments), *knitwear* (how about *woollens*? Although technically I suppose that could include synthetics, if that's your thing), *nightwear*, *sleepwear*, *swimwear* (OK, I can't think of better one-word terms for the last three, but they're still icky).
weary/wary	To be ***wary*** is to be cautious; ***weary*** just means tired. Surprisingly, these get confused, although more in speech than in writing.
who's	contraction of *who is* (*Hark,* ***who's*** *there?*)
whose	interrogative or relative pronoun (**Whose** *book is this?*, *She is a lawyer* **whose** *time has come*)
your	possessive pronoun (**Your** *dog just bit me*)
you're	contraction of *you are* (**You're** *going to have to keep that dog on a leash*)

2) Some Contractual Points

This is not primarily a book about contractual drafting, but let's mix things up a bit.

Definitions

Two lawyers at my firm asked which formulation I preferred:

> *"Notice" has the meaning ascribed to it in Section 9.1.*
>
> *"Notice" has the meaning ascribed in Section 9.1.*
>
> *"Notice" has the meaning ascribed thereto in Section 9.1.*

Being a dangerous radical, I opted for the second one. It's the simplest. *Thereto* is to be avoided at all costs, and *to it* in the first possibility really doesn't add anything.

The more senior of the two lawyers made a good point, though: opposing counsel will probably want to add the *to it*, so leaving it out would only occasion more of a mark-up and more work for you. Sometimes it is better to give people what they expect, rather than what you know is better drafting.

Another possibility would be to say *assigned* instead of *ascribed* (and the more senior lawyer sent a neat chart depicting the gradual decline of *ascribed* since 1800, from Google Books).[49]

Other possibilities:

> *"Notice" has the meaning given to it in Section 9.1.*

> *"Notice" has the meaning given it in Section 9.1.* [But North Americans tend not to use *give* this way; *Give it me* would strike them as alien, and it is (while perfectly normal in the United Kingdom).]

> *"Notice" is defined in Section 9.1.*

> *"Notice", as defined in section 9.1, . . .*

Or just say *Notice* (with an upper-case N) and assume your reader can Control+F to find section 9.1. The point is that there are lots of ways to express something, some better (and plainer) than others. Go with what you think your audience will want — unless you can clearly show why your rendition is superior.

Depositary *and* depository

Depositary in US contracts has always seemed wrong to me. Shouldn't it be *depository*?

No, in fact. The two words, while often confused, mean different things.

A *depositary* is a person or entity with whom something is placed in trust, committed or confided, or a bailee of personal property.

A *depository*, on the other hand, is the place or receptacle where things are deposited or placed for safe keeping.

49 See online: https://books.google.com/ngrams/interactive_chart?year_end=2008&content=ascribed&corpus=15&year_start=1800&case_insensitive=on&direct_url=t1%3B%2Cascribed%3B%2Cc0t1&smoothing=7#t1%3B%2Cascribed%3B%2Cc0.

So a *depositary* must be a person (including an artificial one at law) who holds onto things for you, while a *depository* must be a place or thing where or in which you put things. I take some comfort, however, from the knowledge that *depository* could be used of people too (but not since about 1878).

Enforceable as against

Drop the *as*. Better, just rephrase it to say *so-and-so is obliged* [or *bound*] *to* ... (or *shall* ...).

Indemnitor *and* indemnitee

Please, no. These are recent American coinages, and not attractive ones. Just say *indemnifier* and *indemnified* (or *indemnified party*). There is no need for the *faux* neo-Latin and the clunky *–ee* back-formation.

It could be worse, however: the *OED* lists *indemnificator* — but says it's rare (only one example of usage, from 1827).

Whereas *and* witnesseth

I agree with Ross Guberman that these terms in contractual recitals are "substantively harmless," but unless you're drafting on parchment with a goose-quill, don't use 'em.[50]

3) Problematic Pasts

Not things you did as a teenager that you'd rather forget about, but past tenses of verbs that continue to cause people trouble.

Dive

The past tense of this verb is not *dove*. That's a bird, mispronounced. The past tense is *dived* (or should be — the Yanks differ on this one).

50 Guberman & Karl, above note 36 at 51. See also Shawn Burton, "The Case for Plain-Language Contracts" *Harvard Business Review* (January–February 2018), online: https://hbr.org/2018/01/the-case-for-plain-language-contracts.

Lead

As in *lead me astray*. The past tense (and past participle) is *led*. Similarly, *mislead* and *misled*.

Confusion may arise because these two don't follow the same pattern as *read*, which is the same in the past and present tenses: *I read the last chapter of the book last night; I always read in bed before I go to sleep.*

Apparently, *lead* for *led* is one of the most common errors that recruiters see in CVs (*lead a team of 15 . . .*).

And, as stated earlier, lead is also a noun: when it rhymes with led, it's a metal; with leed, something you put round a dog's neck.

Plead

American usage to the contrary, the past tense is not *pled* or *plead*: it's *pleaded*. Always.

Shrink

Honey, you *shrank* the kids! Now that they have *shrunk* they will need new clothes in smaller sizes for their *shrunken* bodies.

And it's *drink, drank, drunk(en)*; *sink, sank, sunk(en)*; *spring, sprang, sprung*; *stink, stank, stunk* (although in colloquial speech one hears *stunk* as the past tense as well as the past participle; there's that song about the Grinch).

It isn't *think, thank, thunk*, though — except in the jocular *Who'd have thunk?*

Sneak

The past tense is not *snuck* but *sneaked*. I have taken the *Financial Times* (which ought to know better) to task for this.[51]

Spit

The past isn't *spit* — it's *spat*. Same deal if you replace the *p* with an *h*.

51 Neil Guthrie, "Don't Sneak in Any More Snucks" Letter to the Editor, *Financial Times* (8 September 2012), online: www.ft.com/content/808d2b2e-f5d3-11e1-bf76-00144feabdc0.

D. MISCELLANEOUS THINGS THAT ANNOY ME

Oh, so many of these — but I'll mention just a few.

Air on the side of caution

Uh, no. It's *err*. But, as the poet said, to err is human, to forgive divine.

Alright

No, you are thinking of *almost*. It's *all right* — two words, always.

And *a while* and *a lot*.

Any questions, please contact X

We've all seen this, and we all know what it is intended to mean (and *Please contact myself* is worse). Interpreted literally, it means the questions themselves are being directed to contact X.

It should be either *If you have any questions, please . . .* or *Any questions? Please . . .*

Anyways

A word that used to be used to mean "in any way." Witness the *Book of Common Prayer* (1560): "all those who are *anyways* afflicted, or distressed, in mind, body, or estate" (by the way, English prose doesn't get much better than the BCP).

More recently, *anyways* has come to mean "in any case" or "in any event" — but in usage that may variously be described as "informal," "colloquial," "dialectical," or (ahem) "illiterate."

The better way, in both speech and writing, is *anyway*.

Around

Overuse of *around* is rapidly becoming an epidemic, and it's one that needs to be contained.

Of late, *around* has been taking the place of better and clearer words like *on, about*, or *related to. Surrounding* is also seen in this context, but should not be.

These have all been seen or heard recently:

- *conversations around A*
- *discussions around B*

- *research around C*
- *a point around D*
- *rules around E*
- *allegations around F* [*of* would be better here, rather than *on* or *about*]
- *charges around G* [ditto]
- *issues around H*
- *a piece around I*
- *a profile around J*
- *questions around K*
- *legislation around L*
- *opinions around M*
- *transparency around N*
- *concerns around O*
- *conferences around P*
- *research around Q*
- *papers around R*
- *programmes around S*
- *decisions around T*
- *language around U*
- *advice around V*
- *your point around W*

Stop the *around* insanity! It is, admittedly, a bit less awful than *regarding* or *concerning* (stuffy lawyerisms, both), but not much.

Basis, based

Basis is, basically, bad. Why, you ask? It's one of those words that lawyers love to use, but one that renders their prose flabby and verbose. Instead of *on a temporary/permanent/daily/whatever basis*, just write *temporarily*, *permanently*, *daily*, etc. While adverbs are not a hallmark of vigorous prose, a single word is better than four.

A related word is *based*: *Where are you based?*, people ask; *I'm based in Toronto*. Doesn't this sound affected? Why can't it just be *live*? Perhaps *based* sounds more cosmopolitan and jet-setty (put another way, pretentious)?

More along the lines of *basis* are *manner* and *fashion*. Only a lawyer would ask for a memo to be delivered in *a timely manner* (*promptly* or even *soon* would be plainer and better). And *in an orderly fashion*? Please trim the fat and just say something like *in order, neatly, regularly* . . .

Behaviours

I was going to rant about current usage of this plural form to describe modes of conduct, on the grounds that *behaviour* covers every way in which one conducts oneself and needs no plural, but a quick check in the *OED* held me back: the dictionary points to usage of the plural as far back as 1563, as well as in the works of Shakespeare ("Which giue some soyle (perhaps) to my *Behauiours*," *Julius Caesar*, i.ii.44 (1623)).

But I still don't like its use by HR types; it always sounds to me as if they want to make it sound as though they know more about your various *behaviours*, and have a longer list of them, than in fact they do.

British case

There is no such thing in law. You mean an *English* case (or perhaps a Scottish one).

(Great) Britain, which came into being when James VI of Scotland inherited the English throne on the death of Elizabeth I in 1603, consists of England (and Wales) plus Scotland. England and Scotland have separate legal systems and courts, so there can never be a *British case*: it's either English or Scottish, but not both; *British* is not synonymous with *English*. (And it's *Great* Britain to distinguish it from that lesser Britain, Brittany in France.)

I suppose there could be a *UK case*, since the United Kingdom Supreme Court hears appeals from all the constituent parts of the United Kingdom (Great Britain plus Northern Ireland), and the law lords make it clear when a judgment is applicable to all parts (as in *Donoghue v Stevenson*, a Scottish case the House of Lords did not confine to Scots law). But it's purer to describe cases by their jurisdiction of origin.

All of this may unravel in the wake of Brexit, however.

Can not

No. It has been one word in English since the Middle Ages: *cannot.* And when you say it, the emphasis is generally on the first syllable.

Caselaw

This always suggests coleslaw to me.[52]

It isn't *commonlaw*, *customarylaw*, or *statutelaw*, so why would it be *caselaw*?

It's *case law* (add a hyphen to make that an adjective: *case-law research*).[53]

Chomping at the bit

Purists often say that really should be *champing* (and they're not wrong). But *champ* and *chomp* mean the same thing: to chew vigorously, to munch, to bite at something hard like a horse's bit.

Chomp is the US variant, *champ* the English (in the United Kingdom *chomp* is regarded as "dialectical," which is code for non-standard or *déclassé*) — so take your pick.

Avoid the phrase in any event; it's a cliché.

Co–

This prefix is overused.

Certainly, as mentioned in Section B(1)(a), "Redundancy" in this chapter, in *co-conspirator*, where it is unnecessary, as *co–* and *con–* both import the notion of joint action. That doesn't stop US legislators from perpetuating the redundancy, however: see, for example, Rule 801 of the *Federal Rules of Evidence* (where — strike two! — it is spelt without a hyphen).

Co– also appears a lot in modern job titles: *She is co-head of the financial services practice group* or *The firm appointed two new co-managing partners*. This isn't wrong, but somehow it's not

52 The origin of the name of the blog Slaw is intended in part to suggest this because it offers a *mélange* that is like a shredded cabbage salad with added bits, but also a contraction of "It's law, you'll see." See online: www.slaw.ca/about-us.

53 See also United States Department of Justice: Office of the Solicitor General, *The Solicitor General's Style Guide*, 2d ed by Jack Metzler (Washington, DC: interAlias Press, 2015) at 87.

pretty — especially where the shared position has two elements like *vice-president* or *managing partner*.

Joint would be a more elegant substitute.

Conflicted

To conflict is to be incompatible, at variance, with someone or something else.

Lawyers must avoid situations that involve *conflicting* interests, but should also avoid the lazy shorthand of *conflicted* when they mean *in a conflict of interest*.

Consider it to be X/find it to be X

This isn't wrong, but it's inelegant.

Better just to *find something X*. *I find him boring* has a better ring than *I find him to be boring*, no?

Convicted of eight counts

Properly, *on* eight counts.

Countless

If this word appears in your bio, please remove it immediately. (Search the website of a major Canadian law firm for the word and you'll probably come across a silly example.)

It's unlikely that *Bob has authored countless case comments and articles*. We could count them (if we wanted to).

And, while we're at it, let's change *authored* to *written* and admit that articling students did most of the work.

A couple things

Wrong! It must be *a couple of things* (even though you would correctly say *a few things* — who said English was regular?).

Did you want milk or cream?

I did want milk, and I still do. Or maybe I've changed my mind.

Or maybe you should use the conditional (*Would you like milk or cream?*) or the present tense (*Do you want . . .*) instead of this weird, incorrect use of the past tense.

Due to

Riders of the subway in Toronto will be familiar with announcements along these lines: *Due to signal problems at Eglinton station, you can expect longer than normal travel times.* You know all too well what this means, but it isn't quite grammatical.

Due to, usually but not always following some form of the verb *to be*, properly means "attributable to." It needs to be attached to a noun, rather than the vaguer concept of expecting (in the subway example). *Due to* is frequently misused as a substitute for "because of" or "as a result of."

So, your longer-than-expected subway experience is *due to* signal problems; but *because of* signal problems, you are spending more time on the subway than you were expecting. Admittedly, the shade in meaning between "attributable to" and "because of" may be slight, and no real confusion will result from a misuse that most people won't even notice.

Due to the fact that should give way to *because*.

Firstly, lastly

These have a ring of *circa* 1875 to them: you'd be better not to use them.

One of the oddities of traditional English style is enumerating as follows: *First, Secondly, Thirdly, … Last. Firstly* appears, in fact, to be a nineteenth-century invention that has always sounded fussy.

In modern writing, you could even go with *second* and the like over the *–ly* form, which would have the advantage of being consistent with both *first* and *last*.

Forfeiture

A small point, but let's not confuse this with *seizure*.

It's incorrect to say (as the title of an article in the *New York Law Journal* did), *Why the Feds Cannot Forfeit Jeffrey Epstein's Mansion*.

The horrible Mr Epstein would have been the one doing the forfeiting, not the authorities. They would have been *seizing* his assets.[54]

54 See Evan T Barr, "Why the Feds Cannot Forfeit Jeffrey Epstein's Mansion" *New York Law Journal* (6 September 2019), online: www.law.com/newyorklawjournal/2019/09/06/why-the-feds-cannot-forfeit-jeffrey-epsteins-mansion/?slreturn=20200626115151.

Fulfill

Take off the final L. And it's *fulfilment*. Only two Ls in *skilful* and *wilful* too (except in the United States, where there would be two Ls before the second F).

Fulsome

We've covered this one elsewhere in this chapter (C. Words That Don't (or Many Not) Mean What You Think They Do)), but it bears repeating. *Fulsome* properly means "servilely flattering" (*The guest speaker was visibly embarrassed by her host's fulsome introduction*), **not** "full, complete, detailed, ample."

That *Securities Act* disclosure was not likely therefore to have been *fulsome*.

As pointed out before, however, insisting on the correct meaning appears to be yet another losing battle: a writer in the *Financial Times* wrote about Picasso's "gloriously well-rounded and fulsome life" (20 March 2018), while someone in the *Globe and Mail* referred to "a fulsome garbage bag" (16 August 2018).[55]

Shouldn't newspaper editors know better?

Grab

This is frequently used in more casual email correspondence (and in speech): *Let's grab lunch/drinks/coffee.*

Isn't it impolite to be grabby? *Have* or *meet for* would be nicer. And I get very annoyed when the barista asks me, *Can I grab your name?* No, but you may have it.

Heads up!

The origins of this phrase are a little obscure, but appear to be from the exhortation of sports coaches or more senior people in the army for the players/troops to look up from whatever is distracting them from the game/drill/war. (Their mobile devices, perhaps?)

55 Jo Ellison, "Why Can't We Be as Productive as Picasso?" Financial Times (28 March 2018), online: www.ft.com/content/f975f05a-2ec3-11e8-9b4b-bc4b9f08f381; Emira Tufo, "Summertime Blackouts Make Me Think of Sarajevo, and Kaurma" *Globe and Mail* (16 August 2018), online: www.theglobeandmail.com/life/first-person/article-summertime-blackouts-make-me-think-of-sarajevo-and-kaurma.

Be on the alert or on the *qui vive*, in other words. There may also originally have been an element of *buck up!* to it. Fair enough. But at some point, people in business and government started talking about giving their underlings *a heads-up* [note the hyphen for the noun] — to the point now where it has become one of the most tiresome clichés.

I cringe whenever some passive-aggressive person says, *Just wanted to give you the heads-up . . .*

The expression also causes spelling issues for people: either they omit the hyphen in forming the noun (a no-no) or they insert apostrophes in strange places. To avoid orthographical anxiety — and to keep me from cringeing — please stop using this expression.

And on the subject of *cringeing*, it's better to spell that with an *e* so the soft g is clearly preserved; otherwise, you might be tempted to pronounce it to rhyme with *singing* (compare *singeing*). Same goes for *bingeing* on Netflix.

Honour role

Seen in more than one student application letter or CV.

Yikes. It's *honour roll*.

Impressed

The partner was impressed by the associate's memo. OK, but was the impression favourable or unfavourable? We generally mean *impressed* in a positive way, but if you think about it the word means that something elicited a reaction, whether negative or positive.

That said, *She was not impressed* would never be taken to mean neutrality or lack of response. Avoid anyway, not least because it's a journalistic/Wikipedia-entry kind of word.

Just desserts

Those who grew up in Toronto in the 1980s may remember a restaurant of this name, which served nothing but cakes and fruit pies. The moniker was a play on the phrase *just deserts*, which (with the emphasis on the second syllable of *deserts*) means getting the reward one merits.

With the emphasis on the first syllable of *deserts*, the phrase would mean "solely arid wastelands."

Licensure

This is becoming more common in regulatory law in Canada, but it's unnecessary. It's fairly old — *OED* gives citations going back to the mid-nineteenth century. The word is listed there as an Americanism.

The Law Society of Ontario has begun to use it (emphasis added): "*Licensure* is the official recognition by the Law Society that a candidate has met all the qualifications specified by the Law Society and is, therefore, approved to practise as a lawyer in Ontario." The more usual *licensing* (which the LSO also uses) would do perfectly well. (And I'd prefer to see *practise* for the verb and *practice* for the noun, which the LSO does use above.)

I wonder if *licensure* was coined to make the process of getting a licence to do something sound fancier and somehow more legalistic. As lawyers, we should try to get away from words and phrases that our non-lawyer readers (and listeners) wouldn't normally use, much less understand — especially when there is a non-lawyer way of saying things that they'll actually get.

Like

Don't even get me started on its annoying use as meaningless filler in speech, particularly by those under thirty.

What I hate in a written context is *like in the past, like in the movies, like in the recent decision, like I said, like I do*. What you mean is *as* not *like*. Reserve *like* for *like me, like a virgin*, and the like (*like* plus noun or pronoun without a verb attached, or an adverb like *so*).

Me thinks

One sees this occasionally as a jocular archaism.

Those familiar with *Hamlet* will know it should be one word, not two: *Methinks the lady doth protest too much.*

It would be nice to see the past tense *methought* now and then (*Methought I was done for!*).

Mid

This doesn't always have a hyphen after it.

It's *mid-year review*, because you're making a compound adjective out of *mid* and *year*; but it's *I'll see you in mid March* (no hyphen). You don't write *I'll see you in early-March* or *I'll see you in late-March*. Ergo.

Most basic, most fundamental
Something can't be more or less *basic* (or *fundamental*); once you're at the base (or foundation), that's as far as you can go.

No-one
This is seen, but it's better to write *no one*, in part to prevent the inevitable drift from *no-one* to *noone* (which looks like an Elizabethan spelling of *noon*).

Of (the awful extra variety)
Please don't say *outside of* or *inside of*. The *of* is both unnecessary and incorrect in each case.

So just this: *outside the house*, *outside Canada*, *outside the realm of possibility*, etc. Same goes for *inside*. *Of* creeps in elsewhere where it should not. As in the shudder-inducing *off of*, Please, just *off*. Or perhaps *from* (*I got it from the internet*, not *off of*).

Or as in *It's not that big of a deal*. You mean *It's not that big a deal* (although *not much of a big deal*). Where you should be using *of* is with the verb *enamoured*: you are *enamoured of* (not *with*) someone if you are in love with that person (*enamoured by* the person if you are loved back).

On to, Onto
These are different, but people lose sight of that. *Built onto the roof was an illegal structure that* ... but *Counsel went on to argue that* ...

In to and *into* work in the same way. It is likely that the person who tweeted about *turning the leakers into the FBI* actually meant *in to*.[56]

56 See online: https://twitter.com/joshtpm/status/1171612181366001664 (10 September 2019).

Pre-

Why do people tack on this prefix where it really isn't necessary?

Please don't *preheat* your oven, just *heat* it — this requires prior action before you can cook, so *pre-* is redundant.

Similarly, *pre-approve*, *pre-arrange*, *pre-book*, *pre-build*, *pre-chilled*, *pre-cooked*, *pre-existing*, *pre-owned* (just say *used* or *second-hand*), *pre-plan*, *pre-prepare* (an absurdity of the first order), *pre-qualify*, *pre-select*, and *pre-set* can all lose the pesky prefix and suffer no loss in meaning. The concept of priority is built into all of them.

To *pre-pay* a mortgage is well-established, but also fails the logic test (in a way that *pay early* or *pay in advance* would not).

Pre-drinking as a concept has its uses, however.

Prior

As in, *Should we meet prior?*

A construction I'm hearing a lot, and one that is irritating me. *Prior* here needs to be followed by *to* and something more (*We met on the night prior to his arrest*); not *We met the night prior.* If you're tempted to use *prior* on its own like that, substitute *earlier*, *before*, or *previous(ly)*.

As an adjective, *prior* is fine (*prior testimony*), but remember that good old rule of thumb that a word with Anglo-Saxon roots (like *earlier* or *before*) is more forceful and direct than one that comes to us through Latin or French (like *prior* or *previous*).

To give you an example, compare the fancy, Latinate words *copulate* and *defecate* with their one-syllable Anglo-Saxon equivalents. The latter certainly pack more of a punch.

Re- plus back

In the space of two days I saw both *return back* and *reply back*. The *back* is redundant, as it's built into the *re–* prefix already.

The reason is because ...

No! The reason is *that* ... Always, always, always. And never *The reason why is because ...*

Renumeration

This is heard fairly often and seen as well, but it's an error for *remuneration*, if the meaning is intended to be "compensation" or "payment" rather than "renumbering." It's a very old and persistent error, however: the *OED* cites examples from the early fifteenth century to the present. It probably arose as a typo or, in speech, as an example of what's called *metathesis*.

That's a fancy word for transposing the initial letters of two words or syllables (*e.g.*, *Cake Blassels* for *Blake Cassels*). A colloquial name for this is a *spoonerism*, named after the Revd William Archibald Spooner (1841–1930), an Oxford cleric who was apparently apt to metathesize in sermons, with unintentionally comic effect. (Most of the examples attributed to him are probably apocryphal, however; concocting spoonerisms became something of a late Victorian parlour game.)

Shut down, shutdown

Don't confuse these. You *shut down* your computer in anticipation of the firmwide *shutdown* (originally, *shut-down*) by the IT department. On a similar footing, *log in* and *log-in*.

Situation

If something isn't a *conversation* these days, it's a *situation*. An *extreme weather situation*. Or, on public transport in Toronto, any number of the following in service announcements (all from ttc.ca): an *emergency situation*, a *power-off situation*, a *flooding situation*, even a *full-throttle situation*.

All can be recast without the *situation* bit: *extreme weather*, *an emergency*, *a power-outage*, *a flood* — although admittedly a substitute for the *full-throttle* thing doesn't come readily to mind. I'd even avoid *situation* on its own, as there are less tired expressions: *incident*, *circumstance*, *event*, *occurrence* ...

Worse, though, than any of these *situations* is a *win-win situation*. This expression is done to death! In contract negotiations, NAFTA negotiations, M&A deals ...

Why not just say a *good outcome*, a *positive result for everyone*, or *a good compromise*? It's unlikely everyone got everything they wanted without making any concessions, so *win-win* probably overstates the case in any event.

Sometime

Spell-check thinks this always has to be one word. It doesn't.

As a single word, it means "former" or "erstwhile": *Bob Sharpe, sometime dean of law at U of T, was appointed to the Ontario Court of Appeal.* But *Let's have coffee some time, Do you have some time for me?* and *At some time in the future, we'll see ...* I acknowledge, however, that current usage may be against me on this.

It definitely seems to be against me with respect to my preference for *in the mean time* over *in the meantime*: the third edition of Fowler tells me I'm living in the nineteenth century.[57] I'm OK with that.

Stating the perfectly obvious

You really, really don't need to write *Gurpreet Singh ("Singh")* if he's the only Singh you mention in your client update or blog post. This isn't contractual drafting.

Similarly, there is no need to say *two (2) months* (or whatever unit you're talking about). Everyone knows what *two* means, and no amount of "for greater certainty" is necessary. Even in contractual drafting.

Surveil

This is like the awful *liaise*.

Surveil is a misguided back-formation from *surveillance*, but an ugly and unnecessary one; just say *watch* or *follow*.

The below

For the love of all that is beautiful and true, no!

Please see above (or *below*) or *the paragraph above* (or *below*) would be fine, but *the below* in reference to something set out lower down is inelegant.

57 *Fowler's*, 3d ed, above note 4 at 726, says there is variation in how both forms get used. On *meantime*, see: *Fowler's*, 3d ed, above note 4 at 487.

The both of you/us

Never *the both of us* (*pace* Adele in "Hello"). It is *both of you* and *both of us*, with no definite article — not even when it's from the other side.

'Til

Please, no.

There are two English words that mean the same thing: *until* and *till*. *'Til*, an unnecessary modern variant of the latter, must (like *caselaw*) be exterminated. I have seen *'til* (with a single quotation mark rather than an apostrophe) in a book published by an Ivy League university press, but forbear to name and shame its author and editorial staff.

A ways to go

Mike Pompeo, the US Secretary of State in the Trump administration, said at one point that negotiations for the nuclear disarmament of North Korea had *a long ways to go*. In colloquial US English, this is a normal thing to say (if something of an understatement in reference to progress with Pyongyang).

In correctly written English, use the singular *way*.

Well wishes

Where on earth did this expression come from? You *wish someone well*, but send *good wishes*. *Well wishes* awkwardly places an adverb where only an adjective should go.

Having said that, *OED* has examples of *well wishes*, *well-wishing*, and *well-wisher* going back to the late sixteenth century. I take comfort in the fact it is described as now less common than forms using *best* or *good*.

Whistleblower

In law and business, this now means an employee who snitches on bad practices by co-workers (especially the higher-ups) but who is protected from recrimination by legislative provisions like s 27 of the federal *Digital Privacy Act* and s 66.1 of the *Competition Act*, or, in the US, s 922 of *Dodd-Frank*.

Think Edward Snowden, but without the subsequent need to live as a fugitive. All well and good (unless you're Edward Snowden), but I'm weary of the word. And it's imprecise: in a sporting match, the whistle is blown not by a player, but by the referee — so by a neutral third party rather than someone in the scrum (or what have you). Or, if the word derives from policing, the blower of the whistle is a cop, not someone directly involved in the activity giving rise to the calling of a foul.

Whistleblower does have the advantage of sounding positive, in a way that alternatives like *informant* or *informer* probably do not (much less, *snitch* or *rat*). And it's certainly shorter than statutory formulations like "Any person who has reasonable grounds to believe that a person has contravened or intends to contravene a provision of . . ."

But it's still shopworn.

E. TERMS FOR LAWYERS

Counsel

Counsel is an ancient term for one's legal advisers as a body (*The accused did not have the benefit of counsel when he was interrogated*) or for a single legal adviser (*Maria acted as counsel to the federal government, for which she was made Queen's Counsel*).

A judge will address a Canadian barrister as *Counsel* (if not by name); in the United States, it would more usually be *counselor* (with a single American L).

The *OED* says *counsel* is rarely pluralised; should never be, in my view (and Fowler's), but one sees it. As a job title, *legal counsel* is a redundancy. Just *counsel* (although *investment counsel* might disagree).

In US firms, many (typically grey-haired) professionals are described as *of counsel* — that is, still practising, but no longer a partner and too senior to be an associate. As a description, that's fine, but as a job title it is not (*How many Of Counsels does your firm have?* Yuck.).

Counsel and *council* were historically to some extent interchangeable; over time, *council* came to mean a board or assembly and its members *councillors* (*Privy Councillors, municipal councillors*)—although the members of such a group could also be one's *counsellors* if they offered advice, whether legal or general.

Juniors in general

"Why can't we just use *sponsee*?" This question came up in a recent discussion forum for professional development people at law firms. The subject was terminology to describe law students and recently minted lawyers in need of guidance from more senior members of the profession.

The reason we can't use *sponsee* is that it is an ugly neologism (as bad as *attendee, evaluatee,* or *secondee*), see Chapter 3, Section B(2)(a), "This, That, or the Other Thing?"

Other equally icky suggestions that came up:

* *aspirant*
* *disciple*
* *fosterling*
* *protégé(e)*
* *ward*

And, of course, the dreaded *mentee*—which must be rejected because there is no verb *ment* (a *mentor* is called that after *Mentor*, who took charge of Telemachus, the young son of Odysseus (Ulysses), during the latter's absence during the Trojan War), see Chapter 3, Section B(2)(a), "This, That, or the Other Thing?"

Budding English advocates undergo a *pupillage*, but *pupil* may seem a bit old-fashioned in North America. And, like *articling student, articled clerk*, or *articled student*, it describes only someone who is not yet a lawyer. A more recent UK term is *NQ*, for *newly qualified* [*lawyer*], which would work—but only for those who have passed out of the student phase.

Why not something simple like *junior*, which is inclusive and has both the sanction of time and the advantage of simplicity?

Dickens uses it in *Pickwick Papers* (1837): "Mr. Sergeant Buzfuz . . . leads on the other side. That gentleman behind him, is Mr. Skimpin, his junior." (A *sergeant* or *serjeant* was a senior barrister in the old Court of Common Pleas.)

Terms for associates who won't make partner but who are allowed to stick around

The old Darwinian rule for associates was "up or out," meaning that if you weren't going to be asked to join the partnership, you'd be more or less politely shown the door. Some firms still do it that way, but not all. Terminology varies, but the most common term in my neck of the woods for someone who'll never have a corner office is *Senior Associate*.

Counsel is also used for associates not on the partner track, but also for lawyers past retirement age but still profitable or prestigious enough to keep on board. *Counsel* is also used for senior lateral hires who are not immediately made partners, although that often follows a sort of probationary period. (And see the discussion of the bastard noun *Of Counsel* in the previous section.)

In the United States, there is a wider variety of nomenclature. For associates who aren't on the partner track, these titles are apparently seen on US business cards:

* *Agile Counsel*
* *Career Associate*
* *Department Attorney*
* *Innovative Staffing Attorney*
* *Permanent Associate*
* *Practice Group Attorney*
* *Staff Attorney*
* *Team Attorney*

Agile Counsel and *Innovative Staffing Attorney* sound especially bizarre: don't you want *all* your lawyers to be agile, at least mentally? And is every other job assignment unimaginative? *Career Associate* and *Permanent Associate* are descriptive but a bit tragic (career-limited, stuck in a rut) — and *Permanent* may imply a level of job security that no associate should expect. *Staff Attorney* suggests in-house counsel to me, but maybe that's the idea. The others have a Knowledge Management feel to them, but that may accurately reflect the work this type of lawyer ends up doing. In the United Kingdom, this would be a *Professional Support Lawyer* or *PSL*, in Canada a *KM Lawyer* (if not a *Senior Associate*). In light of that KM-ish category, *Agile*

Counsel may refer to *Agile*, the project-management process, rather than *agile* (the normal adjective). That makes a bit more sense, but as a job description it would baffle all but initiates.

Law students

A friend, who is originally from the United Kingdom and not a lawyer, asked me why we call our trainees *articling students*.

The *articling* element comes from the *articles* (provisions, clauses) of the agreement by which a mediaeval apprentice was bound to his (it would have been his in the Middle Ages) principal.

In full, it was always *articles of clerkship* for would-be lawyers, *clerk* being an old word for anything kind of scribe-y. My late, very old-school father would refer to *articled clerks* (and pronounce the second word to rhyme with *larks* not *lurks*).

In British Columbia, the technical term is *articled student*; in Ontario and other provinces, it is the rather unlovely *articling student*, which I suspect dates from the 1960s.

Both come from the verb *to article*, meaning to be in a formal legal apprenticeship under the supervision of a lawyer.

In England, trainee accountants also *article* — and there, one is generally *articled <u>to</u>* someone specific. In Canada, one just *articles* in a general way, as the first Canadian usage listed in *OED* suggests: *He articled as a student-at-law in September of 1912* (from the *Manitoba Free Press*, 1918).

The *at-law* bit is an old fashioned way of saying "in relation to the activity of law"; one is also *at the bar* or a *barrister-at-law* once called *to the bar*.

The *bar* being the railing or other physical barrier surrounding the judge in a courtroom, not one of the cocktail variety — although lawyers are often no strangers to those. By extension, the practice of advocacy itself.

Most of this would baffle an American legal practitioner, who typically does a brief stint as a *summer associate* (what we would call a *summer student*), then writes the *bar exam*, and immediately becomes *an attorney* (in a firm, with the title of *associate*, as here).

F. FRENCH

1) Fractured French

There is a distinct love-hate relationship between the English and French languages. We've borrowed a lot from the French over the years, with mixed results. All of this goes back a long way (1066 and all that), but shows no sign of abating.

French words we've more or less naturalized

There are some borrowings from French that we don't even think about, because they've become fully anglicized, sometimes with changes in spelling: *apartment, baton, hotel, parliament.*

Sometimes we try to make anglicized French words more French again, for example when we pronounce *niche* like NEESH, instead of the acclimatized (and perfectly correct) pronunciation NITCH.[58]

Other French words are still in transition, although it appears to be a losing battle to keep the final French *–me* in *program(me)*. There may be hope yet for *manoeuvre* against the tide of *maneuver* (but I doubt it).

Accents disappear readily, but not always. A good example is the French-derived word for *CV*: is it *résumé* (which would be the correct spelling in French) or *resumé* (which is common in English)? The pedant in me prefers the former, even though that runs the risk of looking ... well ... pedantic. So I avoid the issue and just say *CV*.

Debris is also neither fully English nor French: the E has generally lost its accent, but (as in French) we don't pronounce the final S. (English Canadians treat the S in *Métis* as silent; in French it is not.)

French expressions that don't really have an exact English equivalent

Can you come up with pithy English equivalents for *après-ski, je ne sais quoi, joie de vivre, sang-froid,* and *savoir-faire*?

58 And see Dot Wordsworth's article on the subject: "Niche: An English Word That Turned into a French One" *The Spectator* (24 September 2016), online: www.spectator.co.uk/2016/09/niche-an-english-word-that-turned-into-a-french-one.

Keeping one's cool, perhaps; but *know-how* isn't quite the same as *savoir-faire* — it lacks that *certain something*?

French expressions that will make you sound pretentious

Basically anything that already has a serviceable and well-established English equivalent.

French expressions that the French don't really use

And then there is that category of words and phrases used in English and ostensibly derived from French, but that the French don't really, actually use. At all. Ever. Some examples follow.

AU JUS

I have yet to see this on a menu in France. (And please, don't say ***with** au jus*; *au* means "with.")

AU NATUREL

This just means "plain, unadorned" to the French. They say *nu* ("naked") when they mean "naked."

BRUNETTE

A woman with brown hair is *brune* or *une brune*.

DÉCOLLETAGE

One would talk about a woman's *décolleté* in French (if one mentioned it at all).

DOUBLE ENTENDRE

A French person would say *double entente* or *sous-entendu*.

DUVET

To a French speaker, this is just the down that fills the quilt, not the quilt itself — which is a *couette*.

ENCORE

The French don't shout this after particularly good performances: they call out *bis!* ("repeat").

ENSUITE

This doesn't mean an adjoining bathroom to a French person; it just means "then." For the room, say something like *salle de bain attenante*.

MÉNAGE À TROIS

The French do use this, but not to describe a casual or occasional sexual encounter involving three people; a *ménage* is a household, so this expression connotes a longer-term arrangement.

The one-off variety is *un plan à trois* or (in Quebec) *un trip à trois*. The terms *l'amour à trois* and *le triolisme* would be appropriate for any kind of three-way action.

RAPPORT

In French, "a connection" with someone, whether good or bad; to convey the positive sense this word has in English it would be necessary to say *un bon rapport*.

RÉSUMÉ

The French use this, but only to mean "summary"; the biographical document is a *curriculum vitae*.

RISQUÉ

Merely "risky" to the French. For "slightly daring or scandalous," you'd want to say *osé*.

★★★★★

This is not to suggest that you ought to use the genuinely French versions of these now-English expressions, however, because the versions we use are so entrenched that you'd attract funny looks for trying to be more authentically Gallic. (See "French expressions that will make you sound pretentious," above.)

If it's any consolation, the French use "English" words that look nothing short of outlandish to us, like *le people* (celebrities, the *beau monde*) or even *un people* (a celebrity); *un brushing* (blow-dry); *un pressing* (dry-cleaning); *un relooking* (make-over) and *se faire relooker* (to get a make-over); *un basket* (sports shoe); *talkie-walkie* (walkie-talkie) — amongst many others.[59]

59 For more on this, see Cristiano Furiassi & Henrik Gottlieb, eds, *Pseudo-English: Studies in False Anglicisms in Europe* (Berlin: De Gruyter, 2015).

2) Law French

Law French — or perhaps more accurately, Law "French" — is a strangely persistent medieval hold-over. After the Normans conquered England in 1066, their form of French became the language of the aristocracy, the government, and the law courts. It was used in reports of cases until the end of the seventeenth century, although in a much-debased and anglicized version.

The classic example from the period of Law French's degeneracy is this famous passage:

> [The prisoner] sudenment throwe ove grand violence un great stone al heade del dit Seignior Rychardson quel per le mercy del Dieu did come close to his hatt et missed him et auxi le Seignior George que sitt prochin a luy, et le stone hitt the wanescott behind them and gave a great rebound, quel si ceo stone had hitt le dit Seignior Rychardson il voet have killed him.[60]

It's easy enough to get the gist (accused throws rock at counsel), but mercifully the court reporters switched to current (if jargon-filled) English soon after.

Law French isn't dead, however. There are some survivals, especially in the fields of equity (estates and trusts, in particular) and the criminal law. Examples:

* *autrefois acquit*
* *cestui que trust*
* *chattel*
* *chose in action*
* *cy-près*
* *estoppel*
* *force majeure*
* *laches*
* *profit à prendre*
* *replevin*
* *voir dire*

60 Mr Justice Hutton's Report, Cambridge University Library, MS Add 6863, fo 57 (1631).

Among lawyers, these can offer a useful shorthand, but your client (especially if he or she is a defendant in a low-level criminal trial) may be mystified by them. Try to think of an equivalent in modern English, even if that means having to explain that where a bequest in a will gets the name of a charity wrong, it will be necessary to get a judge to allow the gift to be made to the closest thing in name and purpose. A bit long-winded, but clear, at least, and you'll have to explain things like this and *estoppel* to a layperson anyway. Contractual drafters may be reluctant to stop using *force majeure*, but still feel the need to define it with a detailed list of qualifying occurrences — so perhaps the term itself can be replaced with a modern English expression like "unforeseeable event."

Chattel is a funny one, sometimes used by non-lawyers as a plural or collective noun, and in a pejorative way (*He treated them like chattel*). This perhaps arises from the belief that *chattel* is a fancy legal word for *cattle*. In fact, this isn't off the mark: *chattel* and *cattle* are both derived from the Latin *capitale*, "principal, property, goods." In the Middle Ages, when the size of one's herd was a significant and often definitive indication of personal wealth, the words were interchangeable and synonymous with livestock. Now, we use *cattle* purely for bovines. *A chattel* (singular) or *chattels* (plural) came to be used by lawyers to describe personal property of any kind that is both movable and physical — but you're better to say just that or *tangible personal property*.

chapter three

Grammar and Punctuation

A. COMMON GRAMMAR ISSUES

1) Avoid the Adverb

The novelist Graham Greene — a master of lean, mean prose — called adverbs "beastly."[1] (In spite of the *–ly* ending, that's an adjective.) Think of the adverb *quite*, which is either ambiguous or weak: *quite good* can mean "better than expected," "something a bit less than good," "actually good," "very good." In any case, it lacks oomph.

Or indeed *very*, which the nineteenth-century newspaper editor William Allen White called "the weakest word in the English language."[2] By way of example is the cautionary note that circulated by email at my firm that *This matter is very confidential* (in red, boldface type!). Some matters may be more sensitive or interesting or salacious or newsworthy than others, but as a matter of law and legal

1 *Ways of Escape* (Toronto, ON: Lester & Orpen Dennys, 1980) at 225.

2 See The Guardian and Observer Style Guide, "V" (5 November 2015), *The Guardian*, online: www.theguardian.com/guardian-observer-style-guide-v. See also Christian Lorentzen, "Could We Just Lose the Adverb (Already)?" *New York* (18 May 2016), online: www.vulture.com/2016/05/could-we-just-lose-the-adverb-already.html; Ross Guberman, "Adverbs on Trial: Innocent on Two Counts, but Guilty on Three More" *Legal Writing Pro* (13 November 2014), online: http://legalwritingpro.com/blog/adverbs-on-trial-innocent-on-two-counts-but-guilty-on-three-more; Jacob Gershman, "Why Adverbs, Maligned by Many, Flourish in the American Legal System" *The Wall Street Journal* (8 October 2014), online: www.wsj.com/articles/why-adverbs-maligned-by-many-flourish-in-the-american-legal-system-1412735402.

ethics they can't be more (or less) confidential. As lawyers, we owe the same duty of confidentiality to each client, and the standard is as high as it gets.

As a matter of English grammar, the *very confidential* warning is as bad as it gets. It's like saying something is *very unique*. It's unique (or confidential) or it isn't. These adjectives are absolutes. (Some readers have suggested that *highly confidential* has its uses, in signalling a particularly sensitive matter, but I'm not buying it.) Or, as a partner once said to me of a research task, "This is *somewhat urgent*." I was about to reply, "Oh, so it isn't urgent," but anticipating a sense-of-humour failure, kept quiet and just got on with the job.

In legal writing, adverbs are often used as qualifiers or fillers. I'm thinking of words like *generally*, *clearly*, *unfortunately*. In opinions, *generally* may have a valid place as a signal of potential uncertainty in the law (although even there it can be overused when it's a substitute for actual analysis). In an article or blog, try to eliminate *generally*. You're not writing an opinion (and there will be a boilerplate disclaimer saying that your piece is not to be taken as legal advice anyway), so all it does is soften your impact.

If you must say *clearly*, odds are the point isn't clear at all. The word is just padding — or an attempt to make the best of a bad job. Even worse is *unfortunately*, which I see a lot in student memos (*Unfortunately, there appears to be no case law on point*...). It's not unfortunate, it just is.

Kindly, used as synonym for *please*, is limp (or passive-aggressive).

Another weak one is *strictly*, which is meant to sound tough but isn't. Think of *strictly prohibited*, which is frequently seen in toothless email notices: "This email message is privileged and confidential. Any unauthorized use or disclosure is *strictly prohibited*." By what? Sender, the horse is out of the barn door.

Strictly prohibited seems to be especially popular in the regulations of Nova Scotia. Some choice excerpts from the *Boxing Authority Regulations*, NS Reg 155/2002, for example (emphasis added):

> **184** It is *strictly prohibited* for boxers to practice "blood boosting", the intravenous administration of blood or blood products to enhance the boxer's performance, for non-medical or recreational purposes.

> **185**(1) The administering or use of drugs or stimulants, including smelling salts or ammonia, either before or during a boxing match, to or by a boxer is *strictly prohibited.*
>
> **187** The use of iron-based coagulants such as "Monsel's Solution" or any of its derivatives is *strictly prohibited* and the use of any such coagulant is cause for immediate disqualification.

As opposed to *loosely prohibited, somewhat prohibited, only a little bit prohibited*? Just say something is *prohibited* and set out the penalty for violating that.

As bad is *strictly forbidden*, often seen in warnings not to reproduce or download material — and in the English versions of Quebec regulations:

> A common drinking-cup is strictly forbidden. [*Regulation respecting sanitary conditions in industrial or other camps*, CQLR c S-2.1, r.5.1, s 11]

Adding *strictly* runs the risk of exposing your threat as empty if you can't back it up. Just who is policing shared use of cups in the industrial camps of Quebec anyway?

And please don't misuse *literally* as a mild form of emphasis. It means "as opposed to figuratively." It would be correct to say *I have literally got to run* if the starting gun for your ten-kilometre race is about to go off; incorrect if all you mean is "I must go."

Another adverb that is often weak is *even*. It can be used effectively to indicate a special or unusual case (*This is a question that even a first-year law student could answer*) but it is often employed to add an air of the special where there is none, or not much: *The sequel is even better than the first in the series*; *She liked the quotation from Lord Denning so much she even had it tattooed on her back*; *Articling students are offered taxi chits, gym memberships, and even iPads.*

The adverb is unavoidable when you want to modify an adjective. Our American friends notwithstanding, it is wrong to say *real good*; it must be *really good* — but always think whether the adverb adds anything, or just weakens the effect. As linguistics prof Geoffrey Nunberg puts it, "Adverbs tend to show people at their worst — posturing, embellishing, apologizing, or just being mealy-mouthed."[3]

Bad Transitional Adverbs

In an op-ed piece prompted by the Ontario government's threatened invocation of the *Charter*'s "notwithstanding" clause (s 33) back in 2018, Professor Lissa Paul of Brock University mused about the prevalence of similar "useless adverbs" in student writing.[4]

Wise words. The "infestation" of so-called transition words in undergraduate essays is also a weakness found in legal writing, which is replete with adverbs "feigning the existence of non-existent connections." Odds are, if you're using words like *additionally*, *furthermore*, *moreover*, and *nevertheless* to connect sentences, paragraphs, or sections of your piece, you're labouring to establish a logical or rhetorical connection that may well be absent.

It is more effective to create the connection organically, through the (judicious) repetition of a central concept or term. Think about building your argument rather than hitching disparate elements together with so-called transitional adverbs, which may signal the opposite of what you intend.

But Do Use an Adverb When You Should

The data analytics unit at one of what we used to call the Big Four accounting firms exhorts us to *Think different. Do different. Be different.*

Be different is fine (grammatically and as a matter of practice), but the other two? Oh, dear. They really should be *Think differently* and *Do differently*, as those verbs need adverbs (typically ending in *–ly*) rather than adjectives like *different*. The copywriters wanted something that would catch the eye, of course — even if that meant resorting to a grammatical solecism.

3 See Geoffrey Nunberg, *Going Nucular: Language, Politics, and Culture in Confrontational Times* (New York, NY: Public Affairs, 2004) at 280, copyright © 2004. Reprinted by permission of PublicAffairs, an imprint of Hachette Book Group, Inc.

4 Lissa Paul, "'Notwithstanding' and the Transition Word Epidemic" *Globe and Mail* (21 September 2018), online: www.theglobeandmail.com/opinion/article-notwithstanding-and-the-transition-word-epidemic.

What these phrases mean is "Think [or do] that which is different" — but that would be too much of a mouthful (or eyeful). So, there is a logic to the construction, but it's still a stretch grammatically.

Sometimes an adverb is not required: *Think big, Think pink, Think victory*. But with *different*, let's just say it's different. And besides, the whole verb + *different* formulation is a bit of a cliché: Apple is famous for *Think different* back in the late 90s, and CBC Radio has recently used *Hear different* in exactly the same way.

2) Apostrophe Catastrophes

In many ways, we'd be better off without the apostrophe, judging by the frequency with which it's incorrectly used, its functions misunderstood. Mixing up *its* and *it's* is one of the most common errors out there, compounded in typing or texting by the insistence of the auto-correct function (about which, more elsewhere) that you must mean the incorrect one.

Here's a handy guide.[5]

a) Possessive

Singular possessor: *John's book.*

Singular possessor ending in S: *James's* is preferable to *James'*, but both are OK (although the *Chicago Manual* prefers the former); and the possessive form of many biblical and classical names traditionally leaves out the additional S (*Jesus'*, *Claudius'*), although, again, this may vary by style guide.

Plural possessors: *the Singhs' house is next to the Joneses' house* [*not the Jones' house* — or, heaven forfend, *the Jone's* — but *the Jones house* (non-possessive) would be fine. A reference to *The Bill Davis' legacy* on LinkedIn was distressing. (See "Is It Plural or Possessive?" below.)].

5 See also HW Fowler, *Fowler's Modern English Usage*, 2d ed, revised by Sir Ernest Gowers (Oxford, UK: Oxford University Press, 1983) at 466–67 [*Fowler's*, 2d ed]; RW Burchfield, *Fowler's Modern English Usage*, 3d ed, revised (Oxford, UK: Oxford University Press, 2004) at 58–59 [*Fowler's*, 3d ed]; Simon Griffin, *Fucking Apostrophes: A Guide to Show You Where You Can Stick Them* (London, UK: Icon Books, 2016); and Neil Guthrie, "Lawyers and Greengrocers" (2007) 25 *Advocates' Society Journal* 11 [Guthrie, "Lawyers and Greengrocers"].

So it's *Queen's College, Oxford* (named after one queen, Philippa of Hainault, the wife of Edward III) but *Queens' College, Cambridge* (named after Margaret of Anjou (Henry VI) and Elizabeth Woodville (Edward IV) — although until the early nineteenth century, the apostrophes were all over the place or not used at all.

No apostrophe: possessive pronouns (*his*, *hers*, *ours*, *yours*, *their*, *theirs*, *whose*, and the sometimes troublesome *its*, not to mention *mine*). *Their's* is very common, but it's awful.

Is it *Amber and Veronica's children* or *Amber's and Veronica's children*? It could be either, depending on what is meant. The first refers to the children Amber and Veronica parent together; the second to two sets of children, separately parented. So, you would say *Amber and Veronica's children are in regular contact with their biological father* but *Amber's and Veronica's children went on the school outing, travelling in separate cars.*

Things are different when you combine a noun and pronoun in the same sentence, however.

This is correct: *Angela's and my view is that* ... I have seen *So-and-so and mine's* ... and *So-and-so and I's*, which are not correct at all. (Thanks to Ross Guberman for suggesting this topic and pointing out where Justice Kagan of the US Supreme Court gets it wrong.)[6]

The possessive forms of *women*, *children*, and *men* also seem to cause problems, because they take *'s* (which is more usually attached to a singular noun, not a plural one). As a result, *women's hockey*, *children's toys*, and *men's room.*

The compounds *menswear*, *womenswear*, and *childrenswear* are rather ugly compressed versions of two-word forms with proper apostrophes (*men's wear*, etc.), but a trip to a local department store will probably confirm that one-word, apostrophe-less compounds have become the norm. (Although on the computer screen, only *menswear* appears without a squiggly red line of warning under it.)

6 Justice Kagan gets it wrong in *Kelly v United States* (7 May 2020) at 8, online: www.supremecourt.gov/opinions/19pdf/18-1059_e2p3.pdf (as Ross Guberman has pointed out, online: www.linkedin.com/posts/ross-guberman-1303915_interesting-grammar-glitch-in-kagans-kelly-activity-6664505556759298049-uP3B).

You keep something or someone *at arm's length* in order to ensure independence or impartiality. Note that apostrophe (and its placement; *arms' length* is justifiable but not preferred). If you want to turn the phrase into an adjective, you'll need to add a hyphen (even if you think that looks a bit over-punctuated): *an arm's-length transaction.* (A French-Canadian boss of mine always pronounced it *harm's length*, which had a certain unintended logic to it.)

It's *New Year's Eve*, but you express wishes for the *New Year* (whether happy or otherwise). *Happy New Year!* not *Happy New Years!* (You could omit the capitals where the reference is general, not specific to the first day of January, or in a greeting: *I'll see you in the new year.*)

b) Contraction

Here, the apostrophe stands for letters that have been omitted, either for the sake of brevity or to make a written form replicate how it comes across in speech (*fo'c's'le* being the classic example — it's short for *forecastle* but traditionally pronounced like the version with apostrophes).

Examples: *it's* (short for *it is*); also *what's up*, *let's* (a contraction of *let us*, so it can't be *lets* or the truly bizarre *lets'* that I have seen), *who's who* (but *whose book?*), *don't*, *takin' care of business*, *you're*, *we'll* (short for *we shall* or *we will*), *you'd.*

It was (almost) certainly a one-off, or at least an idiosyncratic error, but I've encountered *'though.* No: it's *though* or *although.*

Rock 'n' roll is a tricky one: spellcheck may turn that first apostrophe into a single quotation mark, and many writers will omit the second one — or even render it *rock'n roll.* A better solution would be *rock & roll*, but no one does that. There is no reason at all to write *fish 'n' chips* (but they are unlikely to come up in legal writing anyway).

You're merits special attention. It is short for *you are*, never to be confused with the possessive *your. Your welcome* is distressingly common nevertheless: my welcome what?

Note, however, that some contractions conventionally take a period (*Mr.*, *St.* (for "Saint")) — although they could usefully lose that, as they have in the United Kingdom. British usage (and the *McGill Guide*) would have us drop the periods in initials (*H W Fowler*) and other abbreviations (*the Hon Bertha Wilson*). I'm OK with that, but it may look odd to a North American reader.

Over time, apostrophes can disappear: one seldom now sees *'flu*, and *'phone* never; *Hallowe'en* is increasingly rare (the apostrophe stands in for a *v*).

Avoid contractions like *it's* and *don't* in more formal legal writing; write them out in full.

c) Plural

Don't go here! But people do. A major Toronto law firm used *franchisee's* for *franchisees* in a publication that came my way. It wasn't a typo, judging by the number of times it was intended in a non-possessive, clearly plural sense. I have also seen *firm's* where *firms* was clearly correct. This is the dreaded "greengrocer's apostrophe" (*tomato's*, *bean's* . . .).[7] Left unchecked, it will lead to things like *Euro's*.

It is traditional, however, to pluralize some things with an apostrophe (*dot your i's and cross your t's*), but it would be better to use capitals and drop the apostrophe altogether (*cross your Ts*; *MPs voted on the bill yesterday*). Go with *how-tos* and *dos and don'ts*.[8] This may help you avoid the temptation to use an apostrophe when you absolutely must not (see that *franchisee's* howler).

d) Is It Plural or Possessive?

Some things could go either way: *British Bankers' Association* (possessive) and *Canadian Bankers Association* (plural, adjectival noun) are both correct; similarly, *shareholders' agreement/shareholders agreement*.

7 *Fowler's*, 2d ed, above note 5 at 467. Bravo to the "grammar vigilante" who patrols the streets of Bristol in southwestern England to correct egregious apostrophes in signage: see Thu-Huong Ha, "A Grammar Vigilante Sneaks Around at Night Fixing an Infuriatingly Common Error on Public Signs" *Quartz* (3 April 2017), online: https://qz.com/948496/a-grammar-vigilante-sneaks-around-at-night-fixing-a-common-error-on-public-signs. But see Tim Baker, "Apostrophe Society Shuts Down Because 'Ignorance and Laziness Have Won'" *Evening Standard* (1 December 2019), online: www.standard.co.uk/news/uk/apostrophe-society-shuts-down-because-ignorance-has-won-a4301391.html.

8 *Fowler's*, 3d ed, above note 5 at 232.

Some things probably could not go either way: *Keep out, police dog's working* (Fowler's example).[9] Inexplicable is the hair salon near my office, *Razors Edge's*.

e) Past Tenses

It is usual to insert an apostrophe for certain past tenses of verbs formed from abbreviations: *She OK'd the document before we sent it to the client; The boxer KO'd his opponent; The singer OD'd after the concert.*

For verbs ending in vowels, let caution be your guide: *He ski'd down the mountain* looks odd, but so does *He skied*. Would she have *blue-skyed* an idea, or *blue-sky'd* it? I'm not sure which. In any event, *ski'd* is probably better for the alpine thing, even though it will attract wavy red underlining on your computer screen (as do both *sky'd* and *skyed*).[10]

Fowler's 3d says, however, to go with the *–ed* form as a rule, even where this results in odd-looking constructions like *shanghaied, shampooed*, and (more to the point in a book on legal writing) *subpoenaed*.[11] I am of two minds: these look weird (especially *subpoenaed*), but if adding the E keeps people away from atrocities like the non-possessive *franchisee's*, fine.

f) Do I Have to Add an Apostrophe to "Five Years Imprisonment"?

The better view is yes.

Either it's a possessive form, in which case the apostrophe is mandatory (and goes after the S in *years*); or, you could treat *five years* as an adjectival noun, in which case there is no apostrophe.

But regarding this kind of construction as possessive is preferable, because that's consistent with *one year's imprisonment*, which can *only* be possessive (*one years* being just plain wrong).

g) Law Firm Names

Apostrophes have been creeping in (e.g., *Gilbert's LLP*, which to me has the somewhat unfortunate ring of "Gilbert's very own little LLP").

9 *Fowler's*, 2d ed, above note 5 at 467.
10 *Ibid* at 144; *Fowler's*, 3d ed, above note 5 at 245.
11 *Fowler's*, 3d ed, *ibid*.

Edition three of *Fowler's Modern English Usage* remarks on the gradual disappearance of the apostrophe in business names — although we seem to be stuck with the inexplicable *Lands' End*, as Lynne Truss has pointed out.[12]

Is confusion with the plural at work here? But be careful with that too: *Torys* is correct (two Torys founded it), *Stikemans* is not (only one Stikeman).[13]

h) RIP Apostrophe Protection Society

In December 2019, John Richards, the founder of the Apostrophe Protection Society, decided to call it quits after eighteen years of fighting for the correct use of the troublesome punctuation mark. Part of the reason was that Richards, a retired journalist, felt that at the age of ninety-six he needed to scale back his activities. But he also concluded that "ignorance and laziness have won," his efforts over the years having proved so much tilting at windmills.[14]

He may have a point: my phone's auto-correct feature assumes that *its* must always be *it's*, and I routinely encounter things like *keeping up with the Jones'* and *Closed Monday's*. One apostrophe error in an isolated tweet could just be a typo, but when the managing partner of a Toronto firm (which shall remain nameless) tweets these within the space of twenty-four hours, there is clearly a larger issue:

> *Lets roll even higher in 2020*
> *Hat's off to the workers*
> *Hows this one . . .*

With John Richards's retirement, the apostrophe lacks the protection it clearly needs. Does this matter? It can.

12 Lynne Truss, *Eats, Shoots & Leaves: The Zero*[-]*Tolerance Approach to Punctuation* (London, UK: Profile Books, 2003) at 50.

13 For more on this, see Guthrie, "Lawyers and Greengrocers," above note 5 at 11.

14 See Tim Baker, "Apostrophe Society Shuts Down Because 'Ignorance and Laziness Have Won'" *London Evening Standard* (1 December 2019), online: www.standard.co.uk/news/uk/apostrophe-society-shuts-down-because-ignorance-has-won-a4301391.html.

There was heated debate in Ghana in early 2020 over the name of a new holiday celebrating the country's path to independence. Was it to be *Founder's Day* or *Founders' Day*? The first would have focused attention on Ghana's first post-colonial leader, Kwame Nkrumah; the second, on the broader movement that brought about independence.[15]

One small mark has the power, if used correctly, to honour an entire generation.

3) Take a Pass on the Passive

Does the subject of your sentence do something (*She said that*), or is something done to the subject (*That was said by her*)? The first is an active construction; the second, a passive one.

The active voice is much more effective. It tends to be shorter and simpler, more natural and direct, more engaging. Lawyers, who are often accused of being verbose and overly complicated, unnatural, indirect, and anything but engaging, favour passive constructions.

Which is more forceful? *I love you* (active) or *You are loved by me* (passive)? *We recommend the chocolate mousse* (active) or *The chocolate mousse is recommended by us* (passive)? No points for getting the right answer: it's too obvious. With good reason, Theodore Blumberg calls passive constructions the first deadly sin of legal writing.[16]

There are some occasions when the passive is the better choice, but not many:

* the responsible party is unimportant or unknown (*The summons was served.*)
* the result is more important than the responsible party (*Mission accomplished.*)
* you want to deflect blame (*Mistakes were made,* as opposed to *Our client made mistakes.*)

15 Holly Honderich, "Do Apostrophes Still Matter?" *BBC News* (9 December 2019), online: www.bbc.com/news/world-us-canada-50692797.

16 Theodore L Blumberg, *Seven Deadly Sins of Legal Writing* (Baltimore, MD: Owlworks, 2008) at 3.

* for emphasis (*He was shot.*) — although it's easy to deaden rather than heighten effect with the passive
* to improve flow between two sentences (*Bupinder is a model associate. He is consistently praised by partners.*)
* to vary sentence structure? (Trust me, though [note the active voice there], the passive rarely works.)
* sounds better? (Doubtful; see the examples about love and mousse above.)
* to create ambiguity and uninteresting prose? (For sure.)[17]

4) Get Your Pronouns Right

a) Common Pronoun Problems

It's astonishing how many people have trouble with personal pronouns.

Perhaps like Lorelei Lee in *Gentlemen Prefer Blondes*, they think it's somehow inelegant to say *me* — so the heroine of that classic book says *A girl like I*. But (between you and me) that's wrong: it should be *A girl like me*, of course.[18]

Others, faced with the awful choice between *I* and *me*, opt for what they think is the safer ground of *myself*. This is less wrong (if that's possible), but not ideal — and it leads to weird constructions like *Mohammed and myself went to the meeting. Myself* is best used reflexively (*I asked myself*) or for emphasis (*I did it myself*).

Things can go awry when people use even slightly complicated sentence structure. The venerable *New York Times*, usually a stickler for grammar (of an American variety), initially published this:

> *More familiar to we of the social media era is a type of . . .*

17 For a differing view that I hesitate to publicize, see George D Gopen, "Why the Passive Voice Should Be Used and Appreciated — Not Avoided" (Winter 2014) 40 *Litigation* 1–2. The Johnson column in *The Economist* has pointed out that the passive and the active can both be used as the "evasive" voice: see "The Weasel Voice in Journalism" *The Economist* (26 May 2018), online: www.economist.com/books-and-arts/2018/05/26/the-weasel-voice-in-journalism.

18 This did not prevent a law prof and Liberal parliamentary candidate from tweeting this in May 2019: *Last night we gathered with a group of Liberal supporters who*, like I, *care about combatting climate change . . .*

This has since been corrected, changing that *we* to *us* (no doubt after readers harrumphed at the error).[19] You need an object for the preposition *to*, not a subject. It would be correct, of course, to write *We of the social media era are more familiar with . . .*

To refresh, *I*, *you*, *he*, *she*, *we*, and *they* are **subjects**; *me*, *you*, *him*, *her*, *us*, and *them* are **objects**.

Example: *She did that to me* **not** *Her did that to I.*

So, how to get it right every time? Five simple rules:

1) After a preposition
   * After *at*, *between*, *from*, *in*, *of*, *on*, etc., the pronoun will always be an object (*me, him, her, us, them* not *I, she, him, we, they*).
   * *You* is easy — it's both a subject and an object, so you'll never get that one wrong.
   * So between you and me, it's *a girl like me.*
2) Take out the extra person
   * When in doubt, take out the extra person.
   * If you think it might be *She invited Jacques and I to the meeting*, remove Jacques from the picture, and you're left with *She invited I to the meeting*, which obviously can't be right.
3) Add missing words
   * Is it *She is older than him*?
   * No. What you're saying is *She is older than* ***he is***, so it's actually *older than he* (although in colloquial speech, *him* would be just about acceptable).
4) Subject is always "I" (not "me")
   * The subject of a sentence can never be *me, him, her*, etc.
   * People routinely say *Mary and her went to the meeting* or *Me and him went fishing*, but they are wrong, wrong, wrong. Rule 2 will help you here too (*her* didn't go, did she?).
5) "To be" takes "I" (technically)
   * If you're a purist, the verb *to be* should always take *I* (subjective completion) not *me* (object).

19 See Elizabeth Bruenig, "Michael Bloomberg and the Long History of Misogyny Toward Mothers" *New York Times* (28 February 2020), online: www.nytimes.com/2020/02/28/opinion/mike-bloomberg-women-discrimination.html.

- This may sound a bit archaic in conversation, however, and I wouldn't wince if you say, *Hi, it's me*. On the other hand, *It is I* or *This is she* can have a satisfyingly forbidding effect on cold callers who ask to speak to you by name.

To recapitulate:

1) Preposition + *me*
2) Take out the extra person
3) Add the extra words
4) Subject is always *I* not *me*
5) *To be* takes *I* (except when it sounds fussy)

b) Let's Get Personal

With pronouns, that is.

A pronoun is a word that stands for a noun. Example: *The **guy*** [NOUN] *I was talking to is a third-year associate; **he*** [PRONOUN] *works in the corporate department.*

That *and* Who

These pronouns have distinct uses: *that* refers to things and *who* to people.

So don't write this: *Thanks to all **that** came to the event*. It's *all **who** came to the event* (unless they were robots).

An Entity Is an It

Not a *they*. Thus, *The bank was subject to a class action alleging that **it** had overcharged its customers for foreign-exchange transactions*. In the United Kingdom, however, one would normally say *Lloyds Bank announced changes to their fees for foreign-exchange transactions*.

Either way you do it, an entity is a *that* or a *which*, not a *who*. And be consistent with the number you're using, unlike the Saïd Business School at Oxford, which posted on LinkedIn that *It's fantastic that Oxford* are *doing this with* its *MBA students*.

They

See "Go Gender-Neutral" and "The Problem with Pronouns" (Chapter 1, Section D(5)(a) and (b)).

Whose

This is what's called a relative pronoun, which tells us more about the noun it relates to ("a lawyer *whose* time has come") or asks a question about it ("*Whose* book is this?").

Ideally, *whose* should be used only in reference to a person, not a thing; *of which* is the logical construction for the inanimate. So, "the *Securities Act*, the purpose *of which* is to regulate ..." rather than "the *Securities Act*, *whose* purpose is to regulate ..." Fowler says that where *of which* would lead to an artificial and clumsy sentence, you can relax a bit — but don't get too casual.[20]

5) Split Infinitives; or, *Star Trek*, You Have a Lot to Answer For

The infinitive of a verb is the form with "to" in front of it. As in, *to be or not to be*.

A split infinitive is a verb in this form, but with something stuck between *to* and the main bit: *to not be*, by way of example. People (OK, grammar nerds) have been getting their knickers in a twist about split infinitives for ages.

Writing back in 1926, HW Fowler divided the world into (1) those who neither know nor care about split infinitives, (2) those who don't really know what they are, but think they're bad, (3) those who know and condemn them, and (4) those who know and distinguish.[21]

Ever since *to boldly go* flashed across people's TVs screens in the 1960s, the world has largely fallen into category (1).

Herewith (not a word you should use, by the bye), a plea to put yourself in category (4).

To give Gene Roddenberry his due, *to boldly go where no man has ever gone before* does have a good ring to it (apart from the gendered terminology). *To really understand* is also fine, and sounds less stilted (at least today) than the classically correct *really to understand*. A reader of *The Economist* recently took that newspaper to task for choosing a similarly awkward and unnatural construction out of

20 *Fowler's*, 2d ed, above note 5 at 712; *Fowler's*, 3d ed, above note 5 at 849–50.
21 *Fowler's*, 2d ed, above note 5 at 579.

some doctrinaire refusal to split the infinitive.[22] On the other hand, *to function fully* is better than either *to fully function* or *fully to function.*

Routine splitting of infinitives can have a deadening effect. Compare:

> I told you to not do it.
> I told you not to do it.

> She resolved to never do it again.
> She resolved never to do it again.

In each case, the un-split infinitive is stronger; there is a kind of built-in pause for effect. Hamlet didn't say *to be or to not be*, with good reason.

Think as well about what you actually intend to say (Fowler's examples): *our objective is to further cement* and *our objective is further to cement* have slightly different meanings (the first, more cementing; the second, more objectives). A subtle distinction, but we're lawyers — people pay us to make these.

6) Comma Conundrums

The humble comma seems to confuse many people. Space doesn't permit full discussion of the subject (you may be relieved to hear), but here are some pointers.[23]

a) Pauses

If you've ever read a contract or a will drafted by an English solicitor, you'll have noticed the complete lack of commas (omitted because they can be the source of ambiguity or error, as the cases attest).[24]

---

22 Geoffrey Pullum, "Defending the Split Infinitive" Letter to the Editor, *The Economist* (21 January 2017), online: www.economist.com/news/letters/21714965-letters-editor; and see "The Ban on Split Infinitives Is an Idea Whose Time Never Came" *The Economist* (28 April 2018), online: www.economist.com/news/books-and-arts/21741127-boldly-go-where-grammarians-have-feared-tread-ban-split-infinitives.

23 See also Ross Guberman, "Avoid the Most Common Comma Crimes Committed by Counsel" (March 2016) 95 *Michigan Bar Journal* 40–41.

24 See *Austin v Bell Canada*, 2019 ONSC 4757, rev'd 2020 ONCA 142; *Vitol E&P Ltd v New Age (African Global Energy) Ltd*, [2018] EWHC 1580 (Comm);

Read that English document aloud, and you'll be left breathless: no pauses.

The basic principle is that a comma should be inserted wherever there is a natural pause for the reader, although this is by no means a hard-and-fast rule. Don't overdo it, though: too many commas make things choppy. Lawyerly writing definitely suffers from excessive use of commas. The modern tendency is to lighten up on them. You don't always need one around *therefore*, for example, which will be a struggle for lawyers: *The judge was therefore unwilling to grant the order requested.*

O'Connor v Oakhurst Dairy, No 16-1901 (1st Cir 2017); *Osmium Shipping Corp v Cargill International SA*, [2012] EWHC 571 (Comm); *Coyote Portable Storage LLC v PODS Enterprises Inc* (2011), 85 Fed R Ev Serv 459, 2011 WL 1870593; *Chartbrook Ltd v Persimmon Homes Ltd*, [2009] UKHL 38; *Hamilton v Nerbas*, 2008 ABQB 674; Telecom Decision CRTC 2006-45, 2006 LNCRTCE 43, var'd Telecom Decision CRTC 2007-75, 2007 LNCRTCE 67; *AMJ Campbell Inc v Kord Products Inc* (2003), 63 OR (3d) 375 (SCJ). See also Sarah Lyall, "A Literary Battle That May Hang by a Comma" (16 March 2002) *New York Times*, online: www.nytimes.com/2002/03/16/books/a-literary-battle-that-may-hang-by-a-comma.html; Carrington Coleman, "'Eats, Shoots & Leaves' Applied: Commas Matter" *Lexology* (15 April 2016), online: www.lexology.com/library/detail.aspx?g=0b3baa49-1d52-414f-8d5d-5444ceec7409&l=7R550EA; "Comma Comeuppance: When Rogue Punctuation Proves Costly" (17 March 2017), *BBC News*, online: www.bbc.com/news/business-39300432 (not exclusively comma cases); Mary Norris, "A Few Words About That Ten-Million-Dollar Serial Comma" (17 March 2017) *New Yorker*, online: www.newyorker.com/culture/culture-desk/a-few-words-about-that-ten-million-dollar-serial-comma; Thu-Huong Ha, "Willingly Flawed: The Common Grammar Mistakes in Wills That Have Landed Families in Court" *Quartz* (18 April 2017), online: https://qz.com/957196/serial-comma-and-semicolons-in-wills-keep-leading-to-lawsuits (serial commas and semi-colons); Chris Stokel-Walker, "The Commas That Cost Companies Millions" BBC Capital (23 July 2018), online: www.bbc.com/capital/story/20180723-the-commas-that-cost-companies-millionssynd_digg. See also Sam Anderson, "New Sentences: From 'Reticent Sonnet,' by Anne Carson" (21 March 2017) *New York Times*, online: www.nytimes.com/2017/03/21/magazine/new-sentences-from-reticent-sonnet-by-anne-carson.html; Omar Ha-Redeye, "A Legally Induced Comma" *Slaw* (25 August 2019), online: www.slaw.ca/2019/08/25/a-legally-induced-comma; Ken Adams, "More Comma Confusion: The Opinion of the Ontario Superior Court of Justice in Austin v. Bell Canada" (26 August 2019), online: www.adamsdrafting.com/more-comma-confusion-austin-v-bell-canada.

b) Clauses

Use a comma to separate independent clauses joined by a conjunction (*and*, *but*, *for*, *or*, *nor*, *so*, *yet*): *The plaintiff was severely injured in the accident, but the limitation period has now expired.*

c) Bracketing

Use a comma to set off information that is useful but non-essential or in some way extra (it could be removed and the sentence would still make sense):

> The comma is, of course, a useful thing.
>
> The plaintiff, who has suffered multiple injuries, is unable to perform basic tasks.

d) Lists

Separate items in a list with a comma (or a semi-colon, if individual items within the list contain internal commas).

But, you ask, is there a comma (sometimes called a "serial" or "Oxford" comma) before the *and* (or *or*) preceding the final item in the list? In the United States and Canada, generally; in the United Kingdom, generally not.[25] Take your pick, but I tend (as in most things) to go with the Brits. That final comma looks fussy and a bit cluttered. The publishers of this book disagree with me, but in the interest of receiving royalties I have acquiesced to house style.

Sometimes a serial comma is essential, though. This sentence could use a second comma, methinks: *This book is dedicated to my parents, Margaret Thatcher and God.*[26] Ambiguities could also arise where a list is longer and more complicated.

25 See also John Hightower, "Observations on the Oxford Comma" *Legal Writing Editor* (22 March 2017), online: https://legalwritingeditor.com/2017/03/22/observations-on-the-oxford-comma/#.XQzjT5WotHe.

26 Former prime minster Stephen Harper tweeted this on International Women's Day in 2019: *Special mention to @LaureenHarper, my mother and daughter*. An extra comma (or maybe a *my* before *daughter*) would help (unless, of course, there is some weirdness going on in the Harper family that we didn't previously know about). Another example comes from the copy editor (!) who posted this on LinkedIn: *My husband,* [X] *and I are relocating to Canada in April* (all three of you?).

Further Thoughts on the Oxford Comma

When people hear I've published a book on writing, many of them ask for my views on the "Oxford" or "serial" comma, in that intense "please confirm my own view" sort of way.

The Oxford comma, so called because the University Press has long insisted on it, is used in lists: *A, B, and C.* Whether one needs the comma before the *and* is apparently one of the great punctuation controversies of our time.

Clinging to the Oxford comma seems to be a badge of honour for some, a beacon of erudition in a barbarous age. I've even seen it mentioned in online dating and Twitter profiles, presumably as an indication of moral rectitude and lofty personal standards. "Oxford Comma" is also the title of a 2008 pop song by Vampire Weekend, but the band's intention seems to be gentle mockery of the Students for the Preservation of the Oxford Comma (SPOC), a Columbia University student group.

Those, like the SPOC, with a weird attachment to the Oxford comma are usually disappointed when I say I don't care about it one way or the other, and don't think it necessary. (I do use Oxford commas in this book, because that's my publisher's house style; I'd prefer to dispense with them.)

I hadn't given the necessity point much thought until recently — but I now think I can justify what has hitherto been an off-hand comment.

In a list of two items, no commas are necessary if you use *and* to connect the items: *A and B.* Where you have more things to list, you need something to separate them: a comma or the word *and.* Otherwise, you might run into confusion: *A B and C* just isn't the way we do things, especially where *A B* might seem like one thing, not two. You could do *A and B and C,* but it's more usual, with longer lists in particular, to separate items with a comma. The *and* that precedes the final item in the list is therefore a replacement for the commas that separate the preceding items. As a result, I think one can say you need either a comma or *and* — but not both.

Use the Oxford comma before the final item if it makes you feel traditional or superior or particular, but it doesn't add anything useful because you already have *and* separating the two final things in your list. Right?

e) Descriptions

The comma defines and limits: *I asked my brother Ed for help* and *I asked my brother, Ed, for help* have different implications. The first means I have brothers other than Ed; the second, only one brother, and he's called Ed.

Headlines get this wrong so often: *Singer, Adele, wins . . .*

These are also wrong (but based on real examples): *Partner, Alfredo Garcia, will speak about . . .* ; *My colleagues, Suresh and Amy, will . . .*

The framing commas in the Adele and law firm examples need to come out (unless Suresh and Amy are your *only* colleagues).

In contrast, these two sentences are punctuationally perfect: *Will smith Will Smith smith? Smith Will Smith will smith* (*smith* being a verb as well as a noun).

Placement of the comma also defines in this kind of sentence: *Can you help John?* means John needs your help; but *Can you help, John?* is a request to John for his assistance.

Commas are also used to separate multiple adjectives describing a noun: *She drove a little, red Corvette.*

The comma drops out in descriptions, however, if the final adjective is an integral part of the noun that follows: *The birdwatcher spotted a beautiful bald eagle* (unless it was lovely, had no feathers on its head, and was not the species of bird found in the badge of the United States of America). If you could insert *and* between the adjectives in the string, you need a comma.

f) Inseparables

Don't separate what should not be separated — like subject and verb, or verb and object/complement.

This is wrong: *The thing is, that . . .* [worse: adding another *is* before *that*].

And so is this: *Many Somalis have termed the 2015 election, historic* (the comma must go).[27] As is this slogan seen at a Toronto grocery: *Life is too short, not to eat well.*

27 Alinoor Moulid Bosh, "Canada Voted in Its First Somali-Born Member of Parliament" *Quartz* (25 October 2015), online: https://qz.com/532606/the-

Other examples that have crossed the screen:

How to make working from home, work for you.

Make culture, part of your Performance Management.

It is my hope, with the current modernization efforts that are being implemented, this tradition of exemplary customer service, will blossom and flourish for generations to come!

The Canadian Bar Association, recommended that . . .

Moses will be supporting, Jennifer and Eli in the corporate group.

I have said elsewhere (see Section A(1), "Avoid the Adverb," above) that *kindly* as a synonym for *please* is limp, but whatever you do, don't put a comma after it (*Kindly, return all books to the library*).

g) Connector

The comma does connect, but beware the run-on sentence, which (incorrectly) splices two independent sentences with a comma.

Don't do this: *I am sending you this article, I thought you would find it interesting.*

Instead of that comma, you need a semi-colon, a period, or a word like *because*. (See also "The Dreaded Comma Splice," Section 7(a) below.)

h) Quotations

This is correct: *He said, "I disagree," and then went on to add, "but I won't argue the point with you."* Use a comma before quoted speech (or a colon, although that wouldn't work in the example just given because of the structure of the remaining part of the sentence).

Put punctuation outside the quotation marks unless it's part of the actual quotation (the final period is, the comma after *disagree* may or may not be). In the United States, I am told (by no less an authority than Ross Guberman) that it is usual to place commas and periods inside the quotation marks (whether they are part of the

---

first-somali-born-canadian-voted-into-parliament-signals-a-change-for-its-community.

quoted material or not), but not semi-colons or colons, and question marks only when the quotation is itself a question.[28] This seems too confusing to be desirable, although it is house style at Irwin Law.

i) Vocatives

LinkedIn helpfully provides ready-made comments on the updates that your connections post there. If your colleague Luisa has a new job, you can just click on a button below her update to post an immediate *Congrats Luisa*.

That should be *Congrats, Luisa*, however. To get technical, this is a vocative construction that traditionally requires a comma before the name of the person being addressed. Similarly, it should be *Thanks, Denis* and *Hello, Yolanda*.

In modern professional correspondence by email (or LinkedIn posting), the vocative comma is rarely seen. I suppose I can live with that in the era of *Hi Neil* as a salutation (and I am one who drops the (non-vocative) comma after *Dear Sir or Madam* and *Yours truly* — even in a formal letter).

On a related point, there is some ambiguity in placing the sign-off *Thanks, John* all on one line; only when the name appears below the *Thanks* is it clear that it means *With thanks from John* rather than *Thank you to you, John* (although actual confusion may not arise in practice).

7) Comma Problems

a) The Dreaded Comma Splice

What exactly is a comma splice, you ask? The use of a comma to connect what should be two independent sentences or clauses.

Example: *I won't be able to give you the memo on time, my dog was sick, I had to take her to the vet.* (Two commas, two splices.)

And why dreaded? Grammar nerds frown on comma splices (and other kinds of run-on sentences) because they lack the logical link

28 Ross Guberman (11 December 2016 at 1:31 p.m.), online: http://tips.slaw.ca/2016/research/comma-conundrums/#comment-720678, comment on Neil Guthrie, "A Research Tip: Comma Conundrums" *Slaw* (23 November 2016), online: http://tips.slaw.ca/2016/research/comma-conundrums.

that a mere comma cannot provide — and because they are associated with immature or semi-literate writers. The effect is often weak and unconvincing, as in the above example.

But not always. Lynne Truss, author of the somewhat annoying (and not always correct) *Eats, Shoots & Leaves*, points out (correctly) that many famous writers have used comma splices in ways that are "effective, poetic, dashing."[29]

No one would doubt the effective, poetic dash of Julius Caesar's famous line: *I came, I saw, I conquered.* Short, similar elements like this will not offend the purists, but unless you are very sure of your literary genius, avoid the comma splice.

How does one do that?

* With some punctuation that is stronger than a comma (a semi-colon, a colon, a dash, a period),
* with a "co-ordinating" conjunction (*and, but, for, nor, or, so, yet*), or
* by recasting the sentence in some other way (for example, *I won't be able to give you the memo on time because my dog was sick . . .*).

What does **not** work is throwing in *however* between the two conjoined clauses: *however* is not a proper co-ordinating conjunction but merely a conjunctive adverb (see Chapter 2, Section B(5), "*However*").

b) Dangling Participles

Comma splices bring the dangling (or hanging, unattached, or misrelated) participle to mind. You've both seen and done this.

But let's back up. A participle is a form of a verb: in the present, it will invariably end in *–ing* (*being, seeing*, etc.); in the past, the most common ending is *–ed* or just *–d*, but there are variations and lots of irregular verbs.

Writers (and speakers) often run into trouble when they begin a sentence with a participle and then lose sight of who is doing (or being) what. The modifying participle needs to relate logically to what follows.

29 Truss, above note 12 at 88.

Consider:

> Being an excellent lawyer, I will give her the credit she deserves.

What this is (probably) intended to mean is that *She is an excellent lawyer and deserves credit for it from me*. What it means is *Because I am an excellent lawyer, I will give her credit.*

The same ambiguity (or lack of connection between the participle bit and the main part of the sentence) can arise with other kinds of non-participle modifiers: *At age thirty-five, his health is vigorous*. This isn't quite right, is it? *His health* isn't thirty-five years old, *he is*.

Sometimes, however, the dangling participle is OK, when there is a clearer sense of who is the actual subject of the sentence: *Judging by her hesitation, she seems not to have prepared for this. She* isn't doing the judging, but there isn't the confusion (or presumably unintended boastfulness) of the *excellent lawyer* example.

Good rule of thumb: every time you start a sentence with a short modifying bit followed by a comma, think about who or what is doing what.

8) Colons and Semi-colons

Herewith, a full colonic! Sorry, couldn't resist that.

Actually, full treatment of this subject might take up more space than it may be worth, but here are some basics.

a) The Colon (:)

The colon is most frequently used to introduce a list of items, but it can often be omitted. There is no need for a colon in the following sentence:

> The syndicate of lenders consists of: Bank of Montreal, Bank of Nova Scotia, and TD.

The colon is correctly used after the word "sentence" just before the example; it introduces what is to follow, where that doesn't just flow naturally from the earlier part of the sentence.[30]

30 See *Fowler's*, 2d ed, above note 5 at 589.

The colon can also be used to great effect in pithy contrasts. For example: *Man proposes: God disposes*. Do this sparingly: over-use dulls the effect.

The colon can also be used to introduce a quotation, generally where the context is not conversational (*The witness stated: "Blah blah blah."*).

b) The Semi-colon (;)

Also used with lists, but to separate items that have internal commas. Like so (assuming for the moment that we're still using 1990s law-firm names and punctuation):

> The following firms were represented: Osler, Hoskin and Harcourt; Stikeman, Elliott; and Blake, Cassels and Graydon.

Confusion might arise if the semi-colons were absent (and you didn't know which names went with which). Note the effective use of a "serial" or "Oxford" semi-colon before *and*; but where this isn't necessary in the interests of clarity, I'd omit it.[31]

The semi-colon can also be used to break up long, convoluted sentences that contain lots of subordinate clauses and commas — but it's doubtful that you want to write in a prose style reminiscent of a nineteenth-century novelist, right?

A good use of the semi-colon is to connect two units which could be separate sentences, but which are logically linked. Using a comma would make this a run-on sentence (which is bad):

> I couldn't think of a single thing to say; situations like that leave me at a loss for words.

The bit after the semi-colon doesn't so much complete the thought in the first part as explain or describe it. The semi-colon offers a softer and less abrupt break than a colon; it's only half a colon, after all.

If you find you use a lot of semi-colons, there's a good chance your sentences are too long. Break things into smaller units, especially for readers using a small screen.

31 See Ha, "Willingly Flawed," above note 24.

Semi-colons can be useful in lists where the enumerated items are clauses with internal commas, so you know what goes with what. Parentheses could help, but a thicket of round brackets (or any kind of brackets, really) is hard on the eye (as my friend and colleague Angela Swan points out). In those situations, it might be easier for your reader to put the items in a bulleted or numbered list. In my view, you can dispense with the semi-colon at the end of each line.

Do not place a semi-colon in the salutation of a letter: *Dear Ms Ali;* is just weird. A colon or comma would do. Or you can dispense with punctuation altogether; the white space after the salutation provides an adequate break. Note the use of a semi-colon in the previous sentence, where it effectively joins a thought that explains a previous one. A comma after *altogether* would be wrong, as you'd end up with a non-grammatical comma splice or run-on sentence. An em-dash could also be used in that sentence — and would add a bit more emphasis. But go easy on dashes. Too many and they lose their punch.

9) Periods

Or, as the Brits would say, *full stops* (to differentiate them from partial stops that pause but do not terminate a sentence).

a) Abbreviations

See Chapter 1, Section C(2)(c), "Acronyms" and Section C(3)(d), "Abbreviations."

b) Ellipsis

There are two principal and related uses of the ellipsis (. . .), both based on its function to indicate that something has been left out (*ellipsis* means "omission" in Greek).

The first is what we might call the technical use. Here, the ellipsis shows that a specific word or larger portion of text has been omitted from a quotation: "I did . . . have sexual relations with that woman . . ." (Bill Clinton, 1998).

Be careful when doing this, as in the Clinton example. There, the second ellipsis marks the missing name "Miss Lewinsky," which probably does not need to be supplied; but the first one radically distorts the (intended) meaning of the original by omitting a crucial *not*. Sometimes it's hard to say whether distortion of meaning through omission is inadvertent or deliberate.

Counsel in a 2017 New York case received a stern reprimand from the judge where the use of an ellipsis looked a lot like making a false statement to the court. The judge threatened the lawyer with a fine for contempt, a public reprimand, and possible suspension or disbarment: see *Colonial Funding Network Inc v Epazz Inc*.[32]

The second use of the ellipsis is what might be called the rhetorical, where the writer includes the three periods and lets the reader fill in the blank, or wishes to indicate a pause in thought, an ambiguity. Use this device sparingly (if at all) in formal legal writing — it may suggest too casual a tone, a failure to think something through, or a meaning you did not intend.

c) How Many Spaces After a Period?

Microsoft has decided that it will officially join the ranks of those who consider it an error to put a double space after the end of a sentence. (Although when I recently typed a sample paragraph in Word with the offending two spaces, no red squiggly line appeared; maybe the change has yet to be implemented, or I need to update my version of Word.)

Double versus single spacing is one of those long-running controversies that get people — not just word nerds — all hot and bothered. There are those who get positively irrational about it, as often happens with things that don't actually matter (like whether or not to use an Oxford comma, in most circumstances). The explanation usually given for moving away from double spacing is the fixed (or monospace) nature of typewriter fonts, which no longer applies in the more flexible digital world, although the people at the *Chicago Manual of Style* suggest that it is a bit more complicated than that.[33]

32 16 Civ 5948 (SDNY, 14 April 2017), Stanton USDJ

33 See John W Simek, "Microsoft Has Ruled — No More Double Spaces Following Punctuation" *Your IT Consultant* (27 March 2020), online: https://youritconsultant.senseient.com/2020/04/microsoft-has-ruled-no-more-double-spaces-following-punctuation.html; but compare Russell Harper, "One Space or Two?" *CMOS Shop Talk* (24 March 2020), online: https://cmosshoptalk.com/2020/03/24/one-space-or-two.

Whatever the history, the first thing most professional editors will do with the piece you have submitted is to use "find and replace" to reduce end-of-sentence spacing from double to single. If you insist on keeping two spaces, Microsoft may still allow you to bypass the new default rule (if you can find where to do that in your settings — I can't seem to), and there some hacks are available to do so.[34]

Better yet, go with the cool kids and use just one space between sentences.[35]

10) Exclamation Marks

A certain orange person to the south of us uses these a lot (*Sad!*).

You would probably never see one in a contract, but you might in a factum — but there only rarely, and, one hopes, judiciously.

Overuse of the exclamation mark is a hallmark of the uneducated or unpractised writer, says Fowler.

Experienced writers will confine them to:

- apostrophes (*You miserable swine!*)
- ellipses and inversions expressing emotion (*If only I could! Fat lot of good you are!*)
- exclamations with *what* or *how* (*What a disaster! How awful!*)
- interjections (*Damn! Heavens! Oh!*)
- wishes (*Convention be damned!*)

Resist the temptation to add an exclamation mark to a mere statement, question or even a command. Save it for a time when it really adds something.

Ross Guberman (in a LinkedIn post I can no longer find) notes twenty-one instances of the exclamation mark in *United States of America v AT&T Inc*,[36] where they variously convey:

34 Brendan Hesse, "Don't Let Microsoft Word Judge You for Using Two Spaces Between Sentences" *lifehacker* (24 April 2020), online: https://lifehacker.com/dont-let-microsoft-word-judge-you-for-using-two-spaces-1843044595.

35 See also Avi Selk, "What's Better: One Space After a Sentence or Two? Science Has the Answer" Toronto Star (5 May 2018), online: www.thestar.com/news/world/2018/05/05/whats-better-one-space-after-a-sentence-or-two-science-has-the-answer.html.

36 DC Cir, 2018.

* "exasperation in a youthful vernacular" (*Please! Go figure!*)
* "judicial modesty" (*That is no easy assignment!*)
* spin-control (*But the temptation . . . should be resisted by all!*)
* "supreme certainty" (*I have concluded that the answer to that question is no!*)
* wonderment, sometimes in a sarcastic way (*Small wonder!*)

Each of the *AT&T* examples could have been as effective with just a period, probably. Adding an exclamation mark may be an admission that your phrasing inadequately conveys the desired tone.

A useful place for the exclamation mark is email, where tone is notoriously difficult to capture. An unadorned *Thanks* may appear terse, even grudging; add the flourish of an exclamation mark and you will seem more clearly enthusiastic. In any event, keep this form of punctuation to a minimum; writing that is peppered with exclamation marks is exhausting for the reader, and you may come across like a teenager rather than seasoned counsel.

That US decision is 172 pages long, so twenty-one exclamation marks may not be overdoing it. More than one in a tweet, however . . .[37]

11) Question Marks

Asking questions that aren't questions

Just because you use a word that can pose a question doesn't mean you're necessarily asking one. The question mark in the title of this blog post is wrong: *When Three Rights Make a Wrong?* This is a statement, not a question.[38] Reframe it as *When* Do *Three Rights* . . . and you can add your question mark.

The problem often arises in student memos: *The first issue is whether a motion for summary judgment would succeed?* Wrong again; statement, not question.

37 Although Professor Jason Pearl has suggested that "The glue of civil society is extra exclamation points — 'Sounds great!!! Looking forward to it!!!' — that maintain a level of enthusiasm no one actually feels" (25 September 2020), online: https://twitter.com/jasoninmia/status/1309493003036352512.

38 Erin Sheley, "When Three Rights Make a Wrong?" *ablawg* (13 May 2016), online: http://ablawg.ca/2016/05/13/when-three-rights-make-a-wrong.

One sees non-questions with question marks a lot in email now (*I'm free at 10? I think she is supposed to be starting on the 10th? Please let me know if you have any experience with So-and-so? Let me know if this makes sense? I don't see an attachment??*). Perhaps the punctuation is meant to make things sound lighter in tone, less peremptory, or to mimic the (annoying) rising intonation of millennial speech, but the effect is not good.

These are not questions, obviously. And not even two question marks will make them so.

12) You Can Quote Me

First off, the verb is *quote* and the noun *quotation* — but I would be fighting a pointless rearguard action in trying to stop people from talking about *a quote*.

a) Single and Double Quotation Marks

In the United Kingdom, single quotation marks (usually called "inverted commas") are the default, with anything quoted within a quotation going in double quotation marks, like so: *She said, 'The bus driver told me, "You can't bring such a large animal onto the bus, madam," but in the end he let me.'*

In the United States and Canada, the position is reversed: double quotation marks to start, single for internal quotations. Writers of American advertising copy often go with single marks initially, however, for a cleaner typographical look. Take your pick, but be consistent. My preference is for single initially, but most Canadian publishers (including mine) adopt the US style.

b) Punctuation

Here again, the Atlantic is the great divide, as we saw in Section 6, above ("Comma Conundrums").

In the United States and to some extent in Canada, all commas and periods are placed inside the quotation marks, whether they form part of the quotation or not; other punctuation marks go outside, unless they form part of the original quotation. In the United

Kingdom, punctuation goes inside only if it is an actual part of the words quoted (see the example in the previous section).

The American rule is not entirely logical (why differentiate between a comma and semi-colon?), so my advice would be to follow the British approach.

c) Quotation Marks for Special Terms

Quotation marks can also be used "to signal that a term is being used in a non[-]standard (or slang), ironic, or in another special sense."[39]

They can, for instance, be a substitute for *so-called*: *For "lunch," we were given some stale crusts and a glass of flat ginger ale.*[40]

Quotation marks are also often used where the term is (or is seen to be) newfangled, a bit slangy. By way of example, *I hear that the young people are "tweeting," whatever that means.*

Do all of this very, very sparingly — and avoid the trap of thinking that metaphors somehow require quotation marks. A colleague wrote *We are heading into "Interview Week."* No, it's just *interview week*; the quotation marks and (probably) the capitals are unnecessary. Similarly, there is no need to write *The judge "pierced the corporate veil."* Even persons of limited intellect will understand that we aren't talking about an actual veil. It might be better, in any event, to educate a non-lawyer about disregarding the separate legal personality of a corporation, but without using insider terminology.

For examples of the overuse of quotation marks, see the highly entertaining *Unnecessary Quotes* blog.[41]

American law reviews seem to think that quotation marks for special terms should be single, to differentiate them from actual quotations (which go in double quotation marks), but I can find no real basis for this. This looks like a case of editors creating rules for the sake of them, and new rules to sell new editions of style guides.

39 The University of Chicago Press, *The Chicago Manual of Style*, 16th ed (Chicago, IL: University of Chicago Press, 2010) at para 7.55.

40 *Ibid* at para 7.56.

41 See online: www.unnecessaryquotes.com.

d) Block Quotations

If your quotation is long (more than, say, forty words), offset it as a centred block of text with wider margins than the main text (so the quoted stuff is narrower than the main bit), and perhaps a smaller font size. Because you have done this, there is no need for quotation marks around the offset block: you've already indicated that it's a quotation.

Don't assume anyone will actually read your long excerpt, however. The tendency is, in fact, to skip over big chunks like this (and, perhaps, for the reader to think you were just too lazy to paraphrase or summarize). You therefore need to explain what is to follow.

And don't end your paragraph or section or piece with a block quotation — it's usually more effective to wrap up in your own words.

e) Square Brackets

Law students quickly learn to do this in 1L, when quoting part of a sentence: "[A]*ctions speak louder than words*" ("actions" not having a capital A in the source, but needing one in the writer's sentence). *Only* lawyers do this, and ninety-nine times out of a hundred it's unnecessary. Especially in a piece intended for non-lawyers.

Square brackets can be useful to make editorial comments ("[*that is, disregard the separate legal personality of a corporation*]"). One of these types of comments, [*sic*], is used when the writer wishes to signal that something is accurately quoted, but used incorrectly in the original. *Sic* is Latin for "thus." Example: "*She was the executive* [*sic*] *of her late father's estate.*" It would be nice to think of an equally pithy English equivalent for *sic* in this instance, but nothing comes to mind — not even *thus* — so keep using *sic* (sparingly, though). Or you could just supply the correct term: [*that is, executrix*] or just [*executrix*].

One can also use square brackets to supply punctuation or words that are missing in the original. Putting "[...]" is not necessary; you can omit the brackets and just use the ellipsis in most instances.[42]

42 For a case where counsel's replacement of crucial words with ellipsis marks in a quotation was found unethical, see *Colonial Funding Network Inc v Epazz Inc*, 16 Civ 5948, Case 1:16-cv-05948-LLS (SDNY, 17 April 2017).

Try not to use square brackets too much; they are hard on the eye and may disrupt the flow.

f) Curly or Straight Quotation Marks?

Straight quotation marks (" ") are a hold-over from the days of the typewriter. Curly ones (“ ”) are both prettier and easier to read as a matter of typography.[43]

Go with the curly variety in a Word document. Your email will default to straight, but that's fine.

g) Titles

In legal writing, quotation marks are used for the titles of articles (“The End of Cash? Bitcoin, the Regulators and the Courts”); italics for book and statute titles (Angela Swan & Jakub Adamski, *Canadian Contract Law*; the *Bank Act*), but the *McGill Guide* says roman type for journal titles in citations ((1996) 27 Ott L Rev 201).

13) Slashed

The *slash* is more correctly called the *solidus*, the *oblique*, or the *virgule*. We see it in URLs all the time. It is much older than the interweb, of course.

If you are old enough, and British enough, you'll remember it as the mark for a shilling: 2/- meant two shillings in pre-decimal currency. It was also used after the number of pounds: £4/5/3½ is “four pounds, five shillings, threepence halfpenny,” that last bit pronounced *thruppence hayp'ny.*

The ½ symbol calls to mind another use of the solidus, in fractions (when the numbers aren't placed vertically, with a straight line between). It is also used to express *per*, as in *100km/h*. These are essentially the same usage, *per* here being the Latin for “by” (1 (divided) by 2, 100 km by the hour).

43 Matthew Butterick, *Typography for Lawyers: Essential Tools for Polished and Persuasive Documents* (Houston, TX: Jones McClure, 2010) at 39.

We also use the slash in colloquial abbreviations where it separates the initial letters of syllables: *A/C* ("air-conditioning"), *b/c* ("because"), *w/e* ("weekend"), *w/o* ("without").

So far so good, but there are some problematic uses of the solidus.

I can never remember which is a *forward slash* and which a *backward* one. Doesn't it depend on which way you're facing?

More significantly, the solidus can mean *or* but it can also stand for *and*. This might cause interpretive difficulties. *He/she* and *s/he* probably mean "he or she" and "she or he," but perhaps now have an element of gender fluidity to them.

In constructions like *and/or*, the solidus clearly means *or*. (But don't use *and/or*, for reasons I've pointed out elsewhere.)

The solidus can also function as *and*, as in a piece from the Law Society of Ontario that describes James Wilson Morrice as "probably the most internationally renowned Ontario lawyer/artist."[44] Better to say *lawyer who was also an artist* or *lawyer-artist*. Why? Because it could be unclear whether your solidus is disjunctive (*or*) or conjunctive (*and*).

The party room and gym in this luxury condominium have state-of-the-art audio/video systems. Hmm, that probably means they have both audio and video, but you can never be too sure ...

Whatever you do, please don't follow the lead of this writer for Slate, who spelled out each solidus as the word *slash*: *President Donald Trump issued a stunning threat-slash-promise-slash-constitutional fantasy*.[45] We might do this in speech, but please — not in writing.[46]

---

44 Law Society of Ontario, "Ontario Lawyer-Artists," online: https://lso.ca/getdoc/db6dcad3-11d4-4752-adaa-d6fd0908c5b5/ontario-lawyer-artists.

45 Dahlia Lithwick, "Donald Trump Threatens to Adjourn Congress in What Could Be Unprecedented Power Grab" *Slate* (15 April 2020), online: https://slate.com/news-and-politics/2020/04/donald-trump-threatens-adjourn-congress-power-grab.html.

46 Thanks to John Hightower of Lanier Ford Shaver & Payne PC in Huntsville, Alabama, for suggesting the topic and directing me to that *Slate* horror. For a good article on the subject, see The Communications Skills Company, "Beware the Slash!" online: www.communicationsskillscompany.com.

14) Accentuating the Negative

a) Multiple Negatives

In grammar, the general rule is that you shouldn't use two negatives. It's incorrect to say *I didn't see no one*, although people will know what you mean. The correct thing is, obviously, *I didn't see anyone.*

Contractual drafters ought to avoid double negatives because they give rise to ambiguity. The concern isn't so much over a sentence like *I didn't see no one*, but rather with the repeated use of *not* or other negatives in a long, complicated sentence where the net effect may be uncertain.

Not all languages are averse to the double negative. Think of French: *ne ... pas, ne ... jamais, ne ... rien.* And in Greek, negation is piled on negation to create a multi-layered expression of dissent, refusal, or denial (something the Greeks have been doing a lot of in recent years).

There are times in English when a double negative can express a subtle shading of doubt or negativity, without outright contradiction. To say *I don't disagree* is a bit less certain than the categorical *I agree*, and that may be a desirable effect. I've always wanted to throw this one into conversation, just to see the reaction: *I'm not sure that I don't disagree with you.* How's that for hedging?

b) Not Enough Negativity

Sometimes people underuse the negative.

A gaffe that grammarians love to point out is *I could care less*, when it's used to express lack of interest in something. If you think about it, it actually means you *do* care about whatever it is, because it would be possible to care to a lesser degree. You should say you *couldn't care less* if you don't care at all.

c) *Nor*

A word or two about *nor* would be in order too. The correct construction is *neither ... nor* (and *either ... or*). By way of example: *It is neither fish* nor *flesh,* nor *good red herring; either you understand this* or *you don't.*

As a general rule, don't use *nor* if your previous negative is just *not* (or *no*). This is wrong: *The Tenant agrees that it will not use* nor *permit the use of any asbestos, polychlorinated biphenyls …* When more words pile up between *not* and what should be *or*, it's easy to lose track and put a misplaced *nor*.

Exception: use *nor* to reinforce a previous negative statement, where *nor* is preceded by some punctuation (comma, semi-colon, colon, dash) and introduces a new clause. Example: *I was not present at the scene of the crime, nor was I even aware that my friends were there.*

★ ★ ★ ★ ★

In short, think about whether — and how — to negate. And remember the words of that immortal bard, Sir Tom Jones: *It's not unusual…*

15) Hyphens and Dashes

The word *hyphen* comes from the Greek for *together*, which reflects the hyphen's function as a connector.

Dash is descriptive: it's a bold stroke of punctuation, which can hive things off from each other as well as connect otherwise disparate elements.

a) The Hyphen as Connector

English, like German, likes to combine two or more words into one.

The Germans just shove them all together, stringing a series of words into one long chain (*Rindfleischetikettierungsüberwachungsaufgabenübertragungsgesetz* apparently being the longest; it means "beef-labelling supervision duties delegation law," formerly in the statute book of the German state of Mecklenburg-Vorpommern, but now since repealed).

In English, the tendency is to hyphenate compounds, at least initially. When people started to talk about holders of shares a lot, it made sense to make a hyphenated compound: *share-holder*. Later (as often happens), the hyphen disappeared and left us with *shareholder*. Back in 1997, one probably wrote, *This is so cool! I'm now doing my banking* ***on line*** and ***On-line*** *banking is easy*, but *online* rapidly took over in both adjectival and non-adjectival use. The battle appears to be lost in trying to keep the hyphen in *week-end* and *email*. You will note that this book's publisher, Irwin Law, has removed the hyphen from *email*. Hyphens are also disappearing from words like *vice-president*, but leaving two words (*vice president*) rather than one. *Fowler's Modern English Usage* says this is OK — but doesn't *vice chair* sound a bit naughty?[47]

The hyphen tends to stay, however, where its disappearance would leave a pile-up of letters that don't naturally go together in English or suggest a weird pronunciation: *security-holder* and *loop-hole* are preferable to their unhyphenated versions. *Co-operative* is better than *cooperative* for that reason, but *unco-operative* does admittedly look a bit odd (and gets a red wavy line under it when typed on the screen — not that one should pay unquestioning heed to that). The *New Yorker* has tried since 1928 to get people to write *coöperative* and *reëvaluate*, but nobody is buying it.[48]

Hyphens are usual in compound adjectives: *20-year-old whisky, end-of-year review, pea-green boat, red-hot chili peppers* (a shame it's too late to educate Anthony Kiedis about the hyphen). It's wrong, then, to say, *You can join this seminar by live webinar or in-person* (but correct to say *an in-person session*). Similarly, *You will need your log-in details to log in and view your account.*

So the assistant was correct to say this in his subject line: *Student required for cheque pick-up and drop-off* (each of these actions being a composite noun). He got things wrong in the body of the email, however, when he asked, *Is anyone available to pick-up and drop-off a cheque this morning?* No hyphens when you're using a

47 *Fowler's*, 2d ed, above note 5 at 256.

48 See Mary Norris, "The Curse of the Diaeresis" (26 April 2012), *New Yorker*, online: www.newyorker.com/culture/culture-desk/the-curse-of-the-diaeresis; Jane Mayer, "The Reclusive Hedge-Fund Tycoon behind the Trump Presidency" *New Yorker* (17 March 2017, online: www.newyorker.com/magazine/2017/03/27/the-reclusive-hedge-fund-tycoon-behind-the-trump-presidency ("reëlection"); John Cassidy, "What Are the Chances of Trump Being Reëlected" *New Yorker* (19 June 2019), online: www.newyorker.com/news/our-columnists/what-are-the-chances-of-trump-being-reelected. See also www.dailywritingtips.com/not-an-umlaut.

simple verb-and-preposition construction.[49] My bank is wrong to tell me I'm *all setup* for touch ID on my mobile: that should be *set up* (although the bank would not be wrong to refer to *the set-up for touch ID is easy*).

Esports are now a thing, as they say. I'm not entirely sure what it all involves, but then I'm not that keen on the non-electronic version of sports. My interest in *esports* is orthographical, naturally. Why no hyphen (*e-sports*)? As noted, the hyphen is routinely dropping out of *email* (which I can live with), and to some extent *e-commerce*, but probably not *e-filing* or *e-discovery*.

Inconsistency on this point suggests that the decision whether to hyphenate is driven by look and sound: *ecommerce* may suggest a pronunciation starting in the same way as *ecology*, with the emphasis on the second syllable. This explains the occasional rendition of the word as *eCommerce*, to make it clear(er) that the emphasis is on the first syllable. An old-fashioned hyphen would achieve that more elegantly. *Esports* is, to me, perilously similar to *escorts*, which has an unfortunate connotation.

The *New York Times* (NYT)— generally a newspaper one admires — has taken to writing things like *monthslong*. The NYT also says *yearslong* and I've seen *decadelong*. Really, *decade-long* would be better.[50] *Monthslong* looks unnatural (can you think of any other English word with the sequence *NTHSL*?) and invites one to say *month-slong* or the more awkward *mon-thslong*.

The NYT may do this, but it's best avoided. Keep the handy hyphen.

Hyphens can also harness phrases together, where they modify something else: *state-of-the-art software*, *end-of-life decisions*. Where the modifier is long, quotation marks may be better, as in this unpunctuated trainwreck: *Actually evaluating the merits of this*

49 In the title of an article in the *Chronicle of Higher Education*, the editors got it wrong with "Why Has Black-Student Enrollment Fallen?" (18 August 2019), online (subscription required): www.chronicle.com/article/why-has-black-student-enrollment-fallen.

50 See, for example, Mary Hui, "After a Dip, Hong Kong Real Estate Again Eyes the Stratosphere" *New York Times* (22 March 2019), online: www.nytimes.com/2019/03/22/realestate/hong-kong-luxury-real-estate-turnaround.html.

no corporate lawyer as judges policy involves more than just theorizing (better as *"no corporate lawyer as judges" policy*, although hyphenating that is possible, if not ideal).[51]

Not using a hyphen can lead to confusion: are you getting *extra marital sex* or *extra-marital sex*? Where the first element in a compound adjective is an adverb, the hyphen sometimes disappears: *a well-deserved vacation* **but** (probably) *a soundly argued factum.* The rules on that last point are murky; be guided by common sense.

I'm of two minds about constructions like *second- and third-hand information. Fowler's Modern English Usage* (the Bible for these things) suggests that the first hyphen can go (and may be better from a stylistic perspective than the alternative *second-hand and third-hand information*).[52] There may be times when you'd want to keep it, though, for the sake of clarity: the meaning changes if you drop the first hyphen in *This book is intended for the ill- and well-educated.*

Another common use of the hyphen is for compound surnames. This used to be a posh thing, where the surname of a wife or relation was added in order to inherit that person's property (the most elaborate example is *Temple-Nugent-Brydges-Chandos-Grenville*, although my cousin Henry Blundell-Hollinshead-Blundell gives that a run for its money). It's now an egalitarian thing, so kids get both their parents' names. Sometimes the hyphen is omitted in these formations, which can lead to confusion: is that a middle name or part of the family name, John Ralston Saul? Compound surnames can be a problem for indexers: traditional indexing principles would list someone with that long aristocratic handle under G for *Grenville*, but modern practice would probably put it under T for *Temple*; as to John R S, I don't know.

b) The Dash

The dash has many uses, and as many — or more — misuses. Chief among the uses is to add a parenthetical phrase in the middle of

51 Adam Feldman, "Justice Filtered: Plans to Manage Diversity in the Federal Judiciary" (30 August 2019), online: https://empiricalscotus.com/2019/08/30/justice-filtered. I am grateful to Brendan M Kenny of Blackwell Burke PA, Minneapolis, MN, for pointing out the trainwreck.

52 *Fowler's*, 2d ed, above note 5 at 257–58.

a sentence, by way of explanation or for emphasis. If you hadn't noticed, there is an example in the opening sentence of this paragraph. You can also do it towards the end of a sentence, for emphasis — as I've just done now. Go easy, though: too much emphasis de-emphasizes.

c) A Bit of Typography

The hyphen is one short stroke, like so: -

There are two types of dash: the "em" dash (—) and the "en" dash (–), so-called by printers because they are the length of the bits of metal type used for printing the letters *m* and *n* respectively. (They are also called the long and the short dash.)[53]

For purists, the en dash is used to separate date ranges (*1837–1901*) and connected or contrasted pairs of words (*the North–South divide*). The em dash is reserved for breaks in sentences. Many style guides say there should be no space on either side of a dash (although I don't usually follow this typographical convention when I type a document; I think it looks sort of odd).

In the days of the manual typewriter, the em dash was rendered with three hyphens (---), the en with two (--). Typography nerds decry the continuation of this practice in the digital era, but you may have to resort to the "special characters" menu to get the em dash, or figure out some combination of option and shift keys (which eludes me).[54] In common usage, most people use a hyphen for date ranges and word-pairs, and an en dash for sentence-breaks (your computer will generally convert two hyphens into the latter, but not always).

16) Italics

Slanted type like *this*, with some distinct uses.

53 See also, online: https://lawyerist.com/the-enigmatic-em-dash [the original page has unfortunately disappeared, pending 2020 revisions].

54 But see CK MacLeod, "5 Ways to Create an Em Dash" *Tech Tools for Writers* (15 May 2015), online: www.techtoolsforwriters.com/how-to-create-an-em-dash (thanks to François Longpré of BLG for this reference); and Matthew Butterick, "Hyphens and Dashes" *Practical Typography*, online: http://practicaltypography.com/hyphens-and-dashes.html (from Jonathan Cheng of Stikeman Elliott).

Italics are used in these pages to set off a word or phrase that is being discussed. Quotation marks would serve that purpose just as well, although things might look a bit cluttered and fussy. More commonly, italics are used for emphasis. Go easy with emphasis of any kind: if *everything* is emphasized, the force is diminished.

In the old days of manual typewriters with only roman (non-italic) typeface, underlining stood in for italics. Underlining can still be used, especially where you're quoting something that already contains italics but you want to add your own editorial emphasis (indicate that in square brackets with something like *underlining mine* or *underlining added*).

Italics are also used to indicate foreign expressions. In these, the law abounds: *ultra vires*, *sine die*, *cy-près*, *autrefois acquit*, to mention but a few.

Two observations, though. First, you're better off not (or perhaps that should be *not*) using dead languages at all if there is a good English equivalent. Secondly, after a certain point, foreign words and phrases become fully part of English and lose their italics. We don't write *etc.*; it's now naturalized and needs no italics.

In literary writing, there is a new movement to drop the italics for any "foreign" word or expression, on the grounds that differentiating typefaces creates "a monolinguistic culture of othering" that presupposes the primacy of English and fails to reflect the experience of bilingual and multilingual people.[55] That has yet to hit the law, however.

A final legal use of italics is in styles of cause, aka case names. Traditionally, these were rendered like this: *Hadley* v. *Baxendale*. The *v* for *versus* is NOT in italics because when you italicize something containing an element that already has italics, you convert that element to roman type. Because switching back and forth between typefaces was a bit of a pain, we now italicize everything and also drop the period after the *v* (both to the horror of traditionalists). By the bye, the traditional way to refer in speech to a case is *Hadley AND Baxendale*,

55 See Thu-Huong Ha, "Bilingual Authors Are Challenging the Practice of Italicizing Non-English Words" *Quartz* (24 June 2018), online: https://quartzy.qz.com/1310228/bilingual-authors-are-challenging-the-practice-of-italicizing-non-english-words.

not *Hadley VEE Baxendale* or even *Hadley VERSUS Baxendale*. I've heard Baroness Hale of the UKSC say "X *against* Y."

17) Oh, With the Verbing!

Professor Frink says this on *The Simpsons*, but don't you do it.

In simple terms, a verb is an action word. Sometimes there doesn't seem to be a good verb available to express a particular action, so it may make sense to adapt a noun or some other word. This is often fine, but often not. Herewith, some of the pitfalls.

a) Noun as Verb

In *The Sweet Smell of Success*, the 1957 *film noir* classic, Burt Lancaster's character holds up an unlit cigarette and says "Match me, Sidney!" in a particularly venomous speech directed at Tony Curtis. An effective and memorable phrase — but other examples of verbs made from nouns are less happy inventions.

We can do without all the noun-verbs on the list that follows. Some may save you a word or two, but they add nothing useful and they are weaker than what they seek to replace:

- *action* [how about *act*, *implement* or just plain *do*?]
- *credential* [a thing, not an action]
- *friend*, *unfriend* [technical terms from Facebook, but confine them to that platform; in real life, *befriend* or *make friends with* people and then *drop* them]
- *impact* [*affect* is preferable, but presumably people shy away from it because they get it confused with the verb *to effect*]
- *leverage* [there is actually the perfectly good verb *lever*, generally confined to working with some kind of tool; we are now stuck with *leveraged buy-outs*, but try to avoid this verb-form otherwise]
- *medal* [in the Olympic sense; please say *win a medal*]
- *message* and *text* [OK, these are kind of useful, but I still prefer to *send a message*]
- *partner* [in use since the nineteenth century, but not one I'm mad about]

* *plain-language* [oh, the irony of using a piece of jargon to describe taking the jargon out]
* *reference* [awful! it's *refer to* or *mention*]
* *repurpose* [wouldn't *adapt* or *convert* do?]
* *task* [how about the more vivid *charge*, as in *She was charged with compiling the closing books for the transaction* — or you could just say she was *asked* to do this]
* *trend* [in its modern sense of becoming trendy, anyway; well-established to express heading in a certain direction or having a general tendency]
* *trial* [hideous marketing-speak]

Two newish appearances are *permitting* and *permissioning*, which are related — and problematic.

Permit as a noun meaning "licence" is totally fine (*In Canada, we require owners of guns to have permits*), as is the verb form when it means "to allow" (*Smoking is not permitted*).

In legal usage — and I think mostly in US legal usage — *permit* as a verb has come to mean "to license" or "to issue a permit to" (*The permitting of architects is governed by the relevant statute and professional rules*).

I haven't heard how *permitting* in that last sense is pronounced, but I suspect it may more like *PER-mitting* than *per-MITT-ing*. (The latter would be correct in something like *weather permitting*, of course.)

Better to avoid *permitting* in the regulatory context, I think.

Worse is *permissioning*, which you may encounter if you deal with the technical aspects of document security in your legal workplace (*Permissioning can be controlled at a file or matter level, or individually by user*). Avoid this altogether, especially when it's easy (and more elegant) to say something like *Permission can be granted . . .*

Now that we've entered the realm of knowledge management and legal tech, *templating* is something people seem to do. Please don't. Just *create a template* (or *model* or *precedent* or *sample*).

Admittedly, verbs-from-nouns can have their uses: *position*, as a term in marketing or advertising, is convenient shorthand for what would otherwise be a long and unwieldy explanation of promotional techniques.[56] Just use such formations sparingly and thoughtfully.[57]

b) Back-Formation

Please don't ever *liaise* with anyone. The noun is *liaison*, but it comes from the French verb *lier* ("to link or connect"), not *liaiser*. Why don't you just *connect with*, *co-ordinate with*, or *talk to* someone, instead of trotting out this hybrid English-French mess?

Equally bad is *surveil* to describe what spies, cops, and private detectives do from parked cars. The noun may be the French-derived *surveillance*, but the verb is not *surveil*. *Watch* or *conduct surveillance*.

Even worse is to *incent* someone. No! You might be OK to *incentivize*, but you're better off to *create incentives*, *motivate*, or *encourage* — anything but *incenting*, please.

c) The Dreaded *–ise/–ize*

Another way to make a verb is to add *–ise* (*–ize*, if you prefer) to another word. As HW Fowler saith, "Within reason, it is a useful and unexceptionable device, but it is now being employed with a freedom beyond reason."[58]

No one would object to *apologize*, *jeopardize*, or *pasteurize*, but the same cannot be said for *commoditize*, *incentivize*, *moisturize*, *pressurize* (although this is usual in the United Kingdom), *productize*, *randomize*, *slenderize*, *tenderize*, and *volumize*. *Monetize* (in the sense of exploit commercially) is new-fangled and unattractive.

Acclimatize is preferable to the (now mostly US) *acclimate*, however.

18) Past or Present?

A student who is helping a partner with writing a book (I hope he gets due credit) called to ask which verb tense to use in describing cases.

56 See the definition in the *Oxford English Dictionary Online*.

57 See also Brandon Ambrosino, "Why 'Medalling' and 'Summering' Are So Annoying" (25 August 2016), *BBC Culture*, online: www.bbc.com/culture/story/20160825-why-medalling-and-summering-are-so-annoying.

58 *Fowler's*, 2d ed, above note 5 at 389.

My answer was that it depends on context.

I think you would say that a judge *found*, *held*, or *stated* something in a particular case. Perhaps where you are talking about a judge's *obiter dicta* rather than *ratio decidendi*, you would use the present tense: *In this case, So-and-so J discusses the applicable factors.* But you would say, *The judge said* in dicta *that* . . .

Where the description is depersonalized, the present seems more normal: the case *sets out* a three-part test, *stands* for a proposition, *distinguishes* an earlier case.

But let me know what you think.

Just supposing . . .

In a recent email, someone wrote *What am I suppose to do?*

That should be *supposed*, obviously — but was it a typo or a more serious error? It could just be a typo, or else one of those spellings based on oral information only. In colloquial speech, the final *–d* can sometimes drop off. (*Dad said you're not s'pose to do that!*) It clearly needs the past-tense ending, though. One is *assumed*, *presumed*, *supposed*, or *thought* to do or have done something.

Similar is *used*, as in *We used to rent videos but now just watch Netflix*. The final *D* in *used* may also get lost in speech. But *use* in that context could actually be correct. To *use* to do something, meaning to be in the habit of doing, is well-established usage. Archaic, though:

> *In that Season of the Year when the Water* **uses** *to be lowest* (1726)
>
> *All delights which* **use** *to crown princely banquetings* (1819)

Interestingly, this is still current in Caribbean English:

> *How she uses to dress (Dictionary of the English/Creole of Trinidad & Tobago* (2009, citing 1959)

19) The Subjunctive

Did your studies in French get you as far as the subjunctive mood and all its weird variations (*que je sois, que je fusse, que j'eusse été*)?

Things are a little less complicated in English, but still not straightforward. This is partly because the English subjunctive, though falling out of use (since the eighteenth century), isn't dead yet — and was never consistently applied when more alive.

To refresh your memory, the subjunctive is the form of a verb that is used for an action or state that is conceived (but not actual), hypothetical, or prospective; or for expressing a wish or command.

You may use the subjunctive without realizing it:

* *Be that as it may*
* *Come the revolution ...*
* *Come what may*
* *Convention be damned!*
* *Far be it from me*
* *Go away!*
* *I wish I were there*
* *If I were you*
* *Would that it were true*

There are times when you may need to think about it, though. Not every *if* or *though* calls for the subjunctive. *If I were you* does, because I am not (and cannot) be you; but it's *If she eats* [not *eat*] *strawberries, she breaks out in hives* because that's a statement of fact.

The use (or non-use) of the subjunctive can change meaning. *I insist that the contract is signed* and *I insist that the contract be signed* mean different things: the first asserts that the contract has, in fact, been executed; the second, the strong desire that it should be. Fowler's examples in *Modern English Usage* are subtler: *Though all care is exercised ...* (= in spite of the fact that care is exercised) as opposed to *Though all care be exercised ...* (= even on the supposition that care has been exercised ...).[59]

There are also times when we could do without the subjunctive. It sounds antiquated beyond belief to say *If it be no bother ...* or *If I be incorrect about this ...* But the subjunctive can lend an appropriate air of formality, as in the Queen's coronation oath, where she swore to devote her "whole life, whether it be long or short," to the service of her subjects. Nice.

59 *Ibid* at 595.

In 2016, *The Economist* took the view that the following headlines would look stilted (even if classically correct) with a subjunctive: *If Donald Trump was president* [sadly no longer a hypothetical], *If the ocean was transparent*. This prompted many letters from dismayed, subjunctive-loving readers.[60]

Then there is what is sometimes called the "American subjunctive" (and the Yanks do seem to get into the subjunctive mood more than the Brits):

- It is moved that X be appointed secretary
- I suggested that he see a doctor
- We demanded that the other side disclose the contents of the file
- The associate insisted that she be admitted to the partnership

The meeting-minutes subjunctive is well-established, but in other constructions think about adding *should* (*I suggested he should see a doctor*) or using some other, less strained construction (*We asked the other side to disclose*; *I insist that the other party is* [or *should be*] *present*; *The associate insisted on being admitted*). (See also Chapter 2, Section B(7)(b), "*Should* and *Would*.")

20) Cleft Sentences

Know what these are? Don't worry, I didn't know what that term meant either, until it was brought to my attention by a linguistically minded articling student.[61]

It's "cleft" because there is a divide between a main clause and a dependent one, the problem being that the correct way to bridge the clausal divide can end up looking odd.

A couple of examples:

> It's you who has to fill out the form before submitting your application.
>
> It's me who is the problem here, and I'm sorry.

60 "Would That It Were So Simple: The Strange Tale of the Subjunctive in English" *The Economist* (13 August 2016), online: www.economist.com/news/books-and-arts/21704776-strange-tale-subjunctive-english-would-it-were-so-simple.

61 Thanks to Nicholas Arrigo for suggesting this topic.

The grammar nerds will cry foul, because the sentences in question should read as follows:

> It's you who have to fill out the form . . .
>
> It is I who am the problem . . . [two fouls in writing It's me who is]

Constructions with a relative clause beginning with *who* often leave you with an unpleasant choice: you can either be grammatically correct in getting the two clauses to match up, but sound stilted in doing so; or you can sound more normal, but risk alerting the grammar police. Even if we go with the colloquial *It's me*, the correct *who am* still sounds weird, in a way that *you who have to* does not.

The solution is easy, fortunately:

> You have to fill out the form . . .
>
> I am the problem . . .

Or break your sentence up into two.

This won't come up very often, but can cause grammar-nerd anxiety when it does.

21) "Garden Path" Sentences

My sister sent me a fun article about these.[62] They are sentences that you think are going in one direction but which suddenly seem to go off on a weird tangent that doesn't quite make sense. When you read them again, you realize they do make sense but just not in the way you expected.

By way of example: *The old man the boat.*

Your brain probably tells you at first, "Oh, this is about an old man who . . ." but then the path diverges and you have to figure out that *man* is not a noun but an unexpected (and perhaps unfortunately gendered) verb. It's only after a moment of thought that a seeming non-sentence makes sense.

62 Caroline Biggs, "20 Grammatically-Correct Sentences You Won't Read Right the First Time" *Apartment Therapy* (1 October 2018), online: www.apartmenttherapy.com/garden-sentences-262915.

The initial reading process is the mental equivalent of predictive text on your computer or phone screen. Your brain then has to correct its original miscue because it doesn't like the look of a sentence without a proper verb. Better drafting could have prevented confusion with many of the sentences in the article.

The raft floated down the river sank would be better if recast as something like *The raft sank after having been floated down the river.*

Add a comma after the third word of *When Fred eats food gets thrown.* (Actually, that one isn't so bad as is.)

The lesson for legal writers is not to type and simply leave it at that. There will be syntactical ambiguities, errors, stylistic awkwardness, things that don't make sense. Come back to your piece of writing with fresh eyes. Read it aloud. Have someone else read it.

Your first draft is never as good as it could be.

B. THIS, THAT, OR THE OTHER THING?

1) *–ice, –ise, –ize*

Verb endings: a small but tricky point.

If you're from the United States, the *practice* (noun) of law is *practiced* (verb) by lawyers. If you're from the United Kingdom, the *practice* is *practised.* The pattern is the same for *licence* and *license.* Here in Canada, we see both verb forms — but preferred usage (by me, anyway) is to go British.

So, is it *admitted to practice* or *admitted to practise*? Either is defensible: the first means admitted to the practice of law, the second permitted to engage in practising. *Practice* is better in this context, on the grounds the noun is what people probably have in mind (although maybe not in the United States).

The *practice/practise* distinction has the advantage of being consistent with another verb that describes what we do: we provide legal *advice*, but we *advise* our clients on the law. (Distressingly, *advise* is cropping up as a noun, perhaps as a result of the vagaries of spell-check. It's just plain wrong.)

The Brits often use *–ise* for other verbs, too, as readers of *The Economist* will know: *amortise, rationalise, realise,* and the like. The advantage of this over *–ize* is that you don't have to remember the small number of verbs that always take the *–ise* ending (including *advertise, devise, surprise*).[63]

But practice is divided even in the United Kingdom: the *Oxford English Dictionary* (*OED*), the Oxford and Cambridge university presses, and *The Times* all prefer *–ize*. (The editors at Irwin Law do too.)

Whether you adopt *–ise* or *–ize*, do at least get the noun-verb distinction right with *practice* and *practise*, *advice* and *advise*, *licence* and *license*.

2) *–ee, –or*

Not the donkey from *Winnie the Pooh*, but a pair of word endings.

a) First, *–ee*

As in *attendee, bailee, drawee, lessee, mentee, mortgagee, payee, trustee*, and the like.

This ending is common in law, often indicating the indirect object of some action. For example, the person to whom property is entrusted (*trustee*) or leased (*lessee*), the person to whom a mortgage is given (*mortgagee*).

It can also be the direct object of an action: for example, the person you employ (*employee*) or train (*trainee*). *Hono(u)ree*, a North Americanism, is unobjectionable.

So far, so good. But let's not go crazy. *Tippee* (person in receipt of an (illegal) stock tip) is well-established, but not necessary: one could as easily say *the tipped* or *the recipient of a tip*.

Worse are *attendee*, *invitee*, *coachee*, and *mentee*. The first is illogical in relation to *trustee* or *employee*; the person who goes to something attends it, not is attended. Why not just say *guest* or *participant*? *Invitee* passes the logic test, but it's rather ugly; here again, *guest* is preferable. *Coachee* is unlovely. *Refugee*, yes — but as for *asylee*, ugh.[64] *Retiree* is here to stay, but *retired* (*person*) is better.

63 Although readers of Jane Austen will know that the spelling of some of these words has changed over time: her characters are *surprized* not *surprised*.

64 David Yanofsky & Gideon Lichfield, "Southwest Has an Explanation for Why It Kicked an Arabic Speaker off Its Plane" *Quartz* (19 April 2016), online:

I have, with horror, seen *advisee*, *cohabitee*, *escapee*, *evaluatee*, *lendee*, *secondee*, and *sponsee*.

Mentee is the one that really gets my goat, however. It assumes that the word *mentor*, from which it is derived, comes from a verb in the way that other *–ee* words do. Not so! Mentor is the name of the chap (but really the goddess Athena in disguise) who, in Greek mythology, tutored the young Telemachus while his dad went off to besiege Troy and then sail around the eastern Mediterranean. *Mentee* assumes that a *mentor* is someone who *ments*, but that isn't a word at all, and certainly isn't the root of either *Mentor* or *mentor* (see "sponsee" in Chapter 2, Section E "Terms for Lawyers — Juniors in general").

Admittedly, the alternatives for *mentee* aren't great. I sometimes hear *protégé(e)*, but that sounds at once pretentious and faintly creepy. How about just *student*, *associate*, or *junior*?

b) Now, *–or*

Lawyers like this one too: *advisor*, *mortgagor*, *settlor*. In non-lawyer English, *–er* is just as frequent, and sometimes one can use both (*payer*, *payor*). *Adviser* is perfectly correct (and the term of art used in Canadian securities legislation). Sometimes only the *–er* form is possible (*employer*).

One thing that has always puzzled me (OK, I may have time on my hands) is the difference in pronunciation between *mortgagor* and *obligor*. Under the normal rules of English pronunciation, those Gs before the Os should both be hard (as in *gore*). But it's *OB-li-gore* (hard G) and *MOR-gaj-or* (soft G). In the United States, the emphasis is more usually on the final syllable: *mor-gaj-OR* and *ob-li-GORE* — but still those inconsistent Gs.

There are, in fact, the older but now less common variants *mortgager* and *obligeor*. They have the same legal meanings as their *–or* equivalents; an *obligeor* is also someone who does you a good turn. Pronounced *MOR-gaj-er* and *o-BLIGE-er*.

Now you know.

---

https://qz.com/665134/southwest-has-an-explanation-for-why-it-kicked-an-arabic-speaker-off-its-plane.

3) Should That Be *–able* or *–ible*?

Or even *–uble*? Perhaps not one of the burning questions of the day, but I bet you've hesitated over this at least once. I did recently, when trying to google an antiques dealer who had a well-priced early twentieth-century silver snuffbox. The dealer used the form *collectibles* in its business name, it turned out.

This is the (mostly) US spelling of the preferable (but disappearing) *collectable*, which is something that is collected (*Violators are subject to a fine collectable on summary conviction*) or an object that is worth collecting (*Silver snuffboxes are highly collectable — really!*).

Is there a general rule for determining which ending to use? Most of the time it's *–able*, and usually if the stem is a complete word in itself (*bill/billable*, as opposed to *feasible* or *tangible*, which aren't formed from *feas* and *tang*).

The more detailed rules are a bit arcane. The default position is *–able*, unless the word is derived from a Latin verb ending in *–ere* or *–ire*, or where there is a well-established *–ible* form (like *collectible*?) in English already.

If your Latin is a bit rusty, you'll just have to remember a list of words like this:

* *demonstrable* (*–able* replaces the final *–ate* in *demonstrate*, as with *abominate*, *alienate*, *appreciate*, *calculate*, etc.)
* *enforceable* (the final *–e* of *enforce* stays so the following consonant stays soft; same thing for *manageable*, *pronounceable*, etc.) or to keep the initial vowel long (*rateable*)
* *forgivable* (the final *–e* in *forgive* drops out because it isn't necessary for pronunciation; same thing for *movable*, *usable*, and the like — but *tradable* seems to be preferred, at least in securities law)
* *justifiable* (the final *–y* gets converted to an *i*)
* *predictable*

BUT

* *convertible*
* *incorrigible* (compare *uncorrectable*)
* *incredible* (compare *unbelievable*)

* *irresistible*
* *perceptible* (*perceivable*)
* *responsible*
* *reversible*
* *soluble* and *insoluble* (*a soluble substance, an insoluble problem* — although *unsolvable* is also possible for the latter)

Where the stem ends in a hard C or G, or a consonant that gets doubled in the adjectival form, go with *–able* (*amicable, navigable, forgettable*).

New words have tended not to go with the *–ible* ending.

Sometimes there are two forms, not always with the same meaning: *extendable* and *extendible* are interchangeable; but *contractable* (can be caught, like a disease) isn't the same as *contractible* (can be made smaller).

Totally confused now?

4) Is That *in–* or *un–*?

The question of *–able* or *–ible* got me thinking of other spelling conundrums. Is a course of action *inadvisable* or *unadvisable*? Either one — but usage is changing and now seems to favour *inadvisable.*

Is there a rule for determining this? Sort of, but it's not very helpful (like the one for *–able* versus *–ible*). The general rule is where the word is fully English, go with *un–*. Example: *unwholesome.* Where the root is Latin (or more immediately so), the negated form generally takes *in–*, as in *ineffable* or *inevitable.*

This assumes some familiarity with word origins, however — and it may not always be easy to determine whether a word is more Latin than English. In those cases, you might go either way: it could be *insanitary* or *unsanitary*, for example.

The Latinity rule breaks down anyway. The root of both *just* and *justice* is Latin, but it's fully acclimatized in English. This leaves us with *unjust* but *injustice.* Similarly, *unable* but *inability.* Maybe *un–* for shorter words and *in–* for longer ones? And yet, *unexpressive* but *inexpressible.*

Words ending in *–ed* and *–ing* tend to go with *un–* (*unceasing, uncomprehending, undigested*). Words ending in *–ible* usually take *in–* (*inaccessible*), but *–able words* don't follow a regular pattern: *inconceivable* but *unbelievable*. For *–ent*, go with *in–* (*infrequent*).

The following could take *un–* or *in–* (for those marked with an asterisk, the *in–* form is probably in the ascendant):

- communicative
- decipherable*
- escapable*
- substantial*

In the end, you just have to remember.

5) One L or Two?

An assistant called me once, asking whether the other side on a transaction was correct to keep inserting an extra L every time the word *instalment* appeared in an agreement.

The traditional/British spelling is with only one L; the Yanks now generally use two — so I told the assistant to stick to her guns if she felt strongly about it.

Similarly, the classic spellings are *fulfil* and *fulfilment*— but one increasingly sees a doubling of the second L in both. *Fulfill* is listed in the *Oxford English Dictionary Online* only in the usage examples up to about 1600, but is now usual in the United States. Take your pick (but I know which way I'd go).

Are there any rules? Yes, but they're tricky and inconsistent. The Atlantic is (as ever) the great divide — leaving Canadians adrift somewhere in the middle.

a) Verbs

- UK: usually double final L if the preceding letter is A (*befall, enthrall, install*; but *appal*), single if it's another vowel (*distil, instil, enrol, annul*).
- US: inconsistent? Our American spell-check wants *appall, enroll*, and *instill*, but is OK with the other single-L spellings in the previous line.

b) Derivatives of Verbs Ending in L

- UK: double the L, unless it's preceded by a long vowel sound (so, *travelled* but *failed*).
- US: only one L (*traveled, traveler*).

c) Derivatives of Nouns or Adjectives Ending in L

- UK: when you add *–ed*, *–er*, or *–y*, the L is generally doubled (*gravelly, jewelled, jeweller*; but *unparalleled*); before *–ish*, *–ism*, and *–ist*, not doubled (*devilish, liberalism, naturalist*; but either *panelist* or *panellist* — and the *OED* prefers the double-L form).
- US: generally not doubled before *–ed* and *–er* (*jeweled, jeweler*); *panelist.*

d) Before *–ment*

- UK: never double the L (*fulfilment, instalment*).
- US: double away (*fulfillment, installment*).

e) Derivatives of Words Ending in *–ll*

Sometimes the second L disappears: *almighty, almost, already, altogether, always* (but NEVER *alright*; it's two words, *all right*), *skilful* (Yanks want *skillful*), *wilful* (*willful* in the United States).

The second L used to disappear (and still could, really) in *dullness* and *fullness*.

6) U and Non-U

I refer here not to Nancy Mitford's use of these terms in *Noblesse Oblige* (a very funny if dated guide to the sociolinguistics of the English class system, *circa* 1956).[65]

I mean the troublesome letter U that divides US spelling from that in the United Kingdom. As ever, Canada (British North America?) falls somewhere betwixt.

65 In that book, U stands for "upper class" (*napkin*, not *serviette*; *died*, not *passed away*, etc.). Nancy Mitford, ed, *Noblesse Oblige: An Enquiry into the Identifiable Characteristics of the English Aristocracy* (UK: Hamish Hamilton, 1956).

a) The Basic Pattern

Let's start with *honour/honor* as typical.

The word comes from Latin, which spells it *honor* without a U. The word came to English via the Normans (1066 and all that), which meant that when it became acclimatized in England it retained the U of the French *honneur*.

Noah Webster, the nineteenth-century American lexicographer, wanted US English to be closer to its roots in (republican) Rome, so promulgated the non-U spelling that has stuck in the Untidy States ever since.[66]

Canadians, originally more British than Yankee, tended to go with Britannia's *honour* rather than Uncle Sam's *honor* — but one now sees both spellings north of the 49th parallel. The dominance of US spelling in all things computer-related is wearing away the Anglo; the default settings for spell-check and auto-correct are invariably US English, not our Canuck variant. If you haven't, please change this; it's often these little cultural things that really make us different from our neighbo(u)rs to the south, which has lately been more important than ever.

b) Complications

Honour begets *honourable,* and *honor*, *honorable. Hono(u)ree*, a largely North American word, takes a U depending on which side of the Canada-US border you live.

That much is easy. But you would be deluding yourself if you thought English spelling followed regular rules.

Honour, *labour*, and so on weren't always the invariable British spellings. The Elizabethans would often leave out the U if they were feeling Latinate: Shakespeare's play was originally published as *Loues labors lost* not *Love's Labours Lost*. Certain words were routinely spelled with a U until the late 1700s (*governour*, *horrour*, *terrour*) but have now lost it.

And in modern British/Canadian English (as in the United States), the correct form is *honorary*, not *honourary* — although in

66 I've always suspected a motivation based on economy or efficiency as well: *THRU* on road signs and *labor* in newspapers saves on paint, ink, and time.

Canada one often sees the latter (and even *honourarium*) on the part of people who are so keen to wave the maple-leaf flag (or perhaps the Red Ensign) that they ignore (or don't know) what's correct.

The Yanks are not immune to this either: some years back, Ralph Lauren launched a perfume called *Glamourous* with an extra (but incorrect) U that was presumably intended to make the product look British, posh and ... er ... glamorous.

Similarly, one correctly writes:

* *colour*, *colourful*, *colourise/colourize*, and *colourist* but *coloration*
* *humour* but *humorous*, *humorist*
* *odour* but *deodorant*, *deodorise/deodorize*
* *vapour* but *vaporise/vaporize*
* *vigour* but *invigorate*

No one said this was easy.

7) It Could Go Either Way

English is a very difficult language to learn — and not just for those whose mother tongue is something else. Native speakers may, in fact, have a harder time, because they may have picked up the rules (more or less accurately) by osmosis, rather than having them clearly articulated.

This is complicated by English spelling, which is fluid. Before the early 1700s, you could spell things more or less how you felt — which largely meant phonetically. There were, for example, twenty-odd variants of *Shakespeare* in use during the playwright's lifetime (and his own spelling of the name was inconsistent).

Even modern writers are faced with choices, and there isn't always a clearly preferred spelling — as the following examples will attest.

a) *Dreamed* or *Dreamt*?

Many verbs used to have past-tense forms ending in both *–ed* and *–t*. In modern English, one form or the other may survive, or sometimes both. It isn't always clear which one is better: go by instinct.

No one still writes *stopt* or *curst*, but on the other hand you would always use *crept*, *dealt*, *felt*, *kept*, *meant*, *slept*, and *swept*.

Verbs that could go either way: *bereave*, *burn*, *dream*, *kneel*, *lean*, *leap*, *learn*, *smell*, *spell*, *spill*, *spoil*. With some of these, the meaning changes depending on which way you go: *bereft* (deprived of), *bereaved* (having lost a loved one). Sometimes, it may just be idiomatic: *burnt offerings*, *burnt toast*, but *You have burned your bridges*.

Amongst and *whilst* are still with us, although the latter is not often seen in North America. I've used *betwixt* in a jocular way in this book, but don't go there.

b) *Preventive* or *Preventative*?

Both OK, shorter form better? *Preventive measures*, but *a preventative*?

c) *Roofs* or *Rooves*?

Both are correct. My instinct would have been to go for *rooves*, but the *Oxford English Dictionary Online* and *Fowler's Modern English Usage* prefer *roofs*.[67] Not sure I agree.

Similar words that could go either way (and *Fowler's* prefers *–fs* except as noted): *hoof* (*Fowler's*, second edition prefers *hoofs*, but the third edition notes that *hooves* now dominates), *oaf*, *scarf* (*–ves* better), *staff* (*staffs* when it's about personnel, *staves* when musical), *wharf*.[68]

And then, of course, there are the Toronto Maple *Leafs*, for whom there is no linguistic (or perhaps other) explanation — although the plural *still lifes* may offer support. (The rapper Snoop Dogg likes *Leafs* for a different reason.)[69]

d) *Shined* or *Shone*?

The *OED* says *shone* is the past tense and participle for *shine*, relegating *shined* to United States, dialectical and archaic usage, but *I had*

67 *Fowler's*, 2d ed, above note 5 at 673; *Fowler's*, 3d ed, above note 5 at 680.

68 *Fowler's*, 2d ed, above note 5 at 82 and 673; *Fowler's*, 3d ed, above note 5 at 365.

69 Kwan Loh, "Nuthin' but a Leaf Thang — Toronto Maple Leafs Take Issue with Snoop Dogg's Trade-Mark Application for LEAFS BY SNOOP Logo" (22 June 2016), Canadian Trademark Blog, online: http://trademarkblog.ca/opposition-case-toronto-maple-leafs-take-issue-snoop-doggs-application-leafs-snoop.

my shoes shined sounds normal to me. On the other hand, a reference to an Amercian Bar Association report having *shined a light* on whatever the subject was strikes me as odd.

8) Singular and Plural Issues

a) Singular or Plural?

It's surprising that people routinely get things wrong here, or at least don't think things through.

In the latter category, does your law firm have a *student committee* or a *students committee*? To me, the first suggests a committee made up of students (like a *student delegation* at a conference); the second, a committee charged with matters dealing with the students as a group — but both are used.

Alternative Subjects

If there are two subjects to your sentence, separated by *or*, the verb should take the number of the subject that is closest to it:

> The parent company or the subsidiaries are likely to be named in the lawsuit

BUT

> Is the parent or the subsidiaries liable?

You could also rewrite the sentences to avoid the issue:

> The parent or the subsidiaries will be named.
> Will the parent or the subsidiaries be liable?[70]

Collective Nouns

Is it *The committee* ***is*** or *The committee* ***are***? There are two schools of thought.

In the United States, words like *committee*, *firm*, and *board* are invariably treated as singular: the entity, not its constituent parts. There is a good case to be made, however, that these words can take

70 *Fowler's*, 2d ed, above note 5 at 401.

a plural verb when you want to emphasize the members of the group over the totality:

> The [individual members of the] jury *are* casting votes.

BUT

> The jury [the body] reached *its* verdict.
> The board *has* agreed on most issues.

BUT

> The board *are* unable to reach consensus on the thorniest question.

Fowler's Modern English Usage supports this view, with these examples: *The Cabinet* ***is*** *divided* (on the grounds that the whole is a unit before it can be divided) but *The Cabinet* ***are*** *agreed* (because it takes two or more individuals to agree). *Fowler's* notes that this can be a delicate distinction and one that few will bother to make; "any attempt to elaborate rules would be waste labour."[71]

Current practice in the United Kingdom probably goes further than what Fowler had in mind, with results that have some logic but may look outlandish to North Americans. These would be normal in the United Kingdom:

> Apple *are* to release a new version of the iPhone on Tuesday.
> New Zealand [that is, the New Zealand rugby team] *are* likely to win the cup.

In speech, this approach could lead to confusion: *Diversified Industries are acquiring XYZ Co* sounds like a consortium has (have?) made the purchase; but at least on paper or the screen that capital I would resolve the ambiguity.

There is a certain logic to *New Zealand* [the team, as a group] *are*, but one even sees things like *Hungary* [the state, the government] *are threatening to ignore EU directives . . .* , which is pushing it too far.

Whichever way you go, make sure you are internally consistent: don't say *During* ***their*** *time in office, the government* ***has*** . . . (Or, as the

71 *Ibid* at 403.

Saïd Business School posted on LinkedIn, *It's fantastic that Oxford* are *doing this with* its *MBA students* (26 February 2020).)

None

This is singular or plural, depending on the context.

> I looked for books on this subject in the library, but there were none.

BUT

> I asked for a volunteer, but none was forthcoming.

I would say *None of the partners is attending*, on the assumption that *none* is a proxy for *not one*.

Red Herrings

Don't let extra words throw your sense of number off. This sort of thing is wrong (but very common): *One in five Americans have never been outside the United States.*[72]

It should be *One in five Americans* **has** ... because the subject of the sentence is *One*, not *Americans*.

There Is, There Are

There may seem like a singular subject in constructions like *There is no excuse for getting this wrong*, but it's not the subject of the sentence (*excuse* is, actually). *There* is, in grammatical terms, an expletive (but not the NSFW kind).

As a result, whether it's *there is* or *there are* depends on what follows. So, *There is no excuse* but *There are many things to consider*.

In colloquial speech, *there's* is often followed by a plural (*There's so many things I like about you*), as is *here* (*Here's the facts*). Resist the temptation to import this usage into more formal writing (and even to use it in colloquial speech). You wouldn't want to sound like the business school (hint: it's in London, Ontario) that announced in a tweet, *There is still a few spots left in our upcoming workshop*.

72 See, for example, Frida Garza, "One in Five British Kids Who Grew Up with the Internet Believe All of It Is True" *Quartz* (22 November 2015), online: https://qz.com/555755/one-in-five-kids-who-grew-up-with-the-internet-believe-all-of-it-is-true.

Things That Aren't Singular

criteria	We get this from Greek. Singular *criterion,* plural *criteria. Associates are evaluated according to these criteria ...*
data	Latin. Singular *datum*, plural *data. The economic data indicate ...*, as the *Financial Times* and *The Economist* would correctly say. (And it's best pronounced DAY-ta not DAH-ta.) Admittedly, *agenda* has become singular over time (no one talks about an *agendum* any more, although it is a rather elegant alternative to *item on the agenda* or *agenda item*, or as a description for a single-item order of business).
media	More Latin; plural of *medium. The medium is the message, and social media are proving that point.*
phenomena	Greek again. This is plural; the singular is *phenomenon*.

Things That Aren't Plural[73]

biceps	Latin again. Routinely treated as a plural, but it's not. The correct plural is *bicipites*, but your trainer is unlikely to know that; *bicepses* is better (although it may still attract funny looks).
kudos	Those pesky Greeks. It means "praise" (singular), so it's incorrect to say *kudos* **go** *to so-and-so*; and the second syllable rhymes with "loss" not "rose." I have heard, but not seen, *They deserve a kudo for that*. Ugh.
quadriceps	See *biceps*.
shambles	Something is *a shambles* or *in a shambles* not *in shambles* (*shambles* is singular; it means "slaughter-house" or, figuratively, a chaotic state).
triceps	See *biceps*.

73 See David Chaplin, "Modern Data," Letter to the Editor *The Economist* (11 February 2017), online: www.economist.com/news/letters/21716590-shareholders-narcotics-australia-schools-california-data-pop-police-latin; Barry Maletzky, "Data Is No Singular Exception," Letter to the Editor *The Economist* (23 February 2017), online: www.economist.com/news/letters/21717347-kenya-american-law-voting-russia-data-letters-editor.

Things That Could Be Either

forceps	Both singular and plural.
innings	Both singular and plural. The American singular form *inning* is a semi-barbarous back-formation.
lots	*There is lots to do in New York* BUT *There are lots of things to see there.* And *There are a few things I need to talk to you about*, but not *There's a lot of questions* ... That last must be *There are* ...

Things That Don't Have a Singular Form Without -s (or Don't Usually)

Amends, cahoots, clothes, glasses (in the sense of *spectacles*), *loggerheads, pants, scissors, shenanigans, shorts, smithereens, spectacles* (in the sense of *glasses*).[74]

Trousers is not generally seen without a final S, but one does say *trouser-leg, trouser-pocket*, and *trouser-press*; and *thank-offering* is a survival of the obsolete singular *thank* (a grateful or kindly thought).

b) Number

This is the grammatical term for the distinction between the singular and the plural.

Unsurprisingly, a singular noun takes a singular verb (*takes* being an example of that), while plural nouns take plural verbs (that was another example, in case you missed it). Where there are two subjects in the sentence, the verb is generally plural (*Diligence and enthusiasm **are** desirable in an articling student*).

It's easy to lose the plot, however, when the two components of a compound subject are separated by a lot of intervening material. A case in point is a clause a lawyer asked me about. Which wording is correct?

1. The division of this Agreement into articles and sections and the use of headings ***is*** for convenience of reference only and ***does*** not modify or affect the interpretation or construction of this Agreement or any of its provisions.

74 The name of the retailer Sunglass Hut has always troubled me.

2. The division of this Agreement into articles and sections and the use of headings ***are*** for convenience of reference only and ***do*** not modify or affect the interpretation or construction of this Agreement or any of its provisions.

It has to be version 2, because the subject of the sentence is *The division . . . and the use* — so the verbs should be *are* and *do*.

This is the general rule, but there are times when the two elements of a compound subject are inextricable and therefore demand a singular verb: *Scotch and soda* ***is*** *her favourite drink; gin and tonic* ***is*** *mine*. Or where they could be said to constitute a single concept: *Drinking and driving is dangerous* (the subject of the sentence being, in effect, *drunk driving*.[75]

On that rationale, the boilerplate provision about consideration could be *the receipt and sufficiency of which* ***is*** *hereby acknowledged* — but one also sees ***are*** *hereby acknowledged*.

Don't stretch things too far with compound subjects, though.

And where it's *X* ***or*** *Y* rather than *X* ***and*** *Y*, the verb will accord with the nearest element (in this case, *Y*): *Either the company or its directing minds* ***are*** *liable* BUT *Either the directing minds or the company* ***is*** *liable*.

Another common pitfall that has been discussed already (see Section B(8)(a), "Singular or Plural?", above) is the *one in* [larger number] formulation, which often ends up in error. It isn't *One in ten doctors* ***smoke*** but *One in ten doctors* ***smokes***. (The subject of that sentence is *One* (singular) not *doctors* (plural).)

c) Plural Puzzles

Compound Words

For compound words used as titles or descriptions of people, the general rule is to pluralize the noun element: so, *Governors-General* and *daughters-in-law* but *Lieutenant-Governors* and *Major-Generals*.

Where there is no noun, the –s usually goes at the end: *forget-me-nots, knock-offs, knock-outs, lay-abouts, lay-offs, ne'er-do-wells, take-offs*.

75 *Fowler's*, 2d ed, above note 5 at 401–2.

For compounds joined by *and*, pluralize both elements: *ins and outs*, *ups and downs*. (Compound drinks: *gin and tonics*, *whisky and sodas*.)

Other kinds of compounds can be tricky. It should always be *statements of account*, but the plural of *release of guarantee* could be *releases of guarantee* (if *guarantee* is seen as a general concept rather than a specific instrument) or *releases of guarantees* (focusing on the *guarantees* as individual documents).

Latin-Looking Words

It's pretentious to talk about *syllabi and croci*. These words, while derived from Latin, no longer need Latinate plurals; *syllabuses* and *crocuses* will do just fine. Outside a scientific context, opt for *formulas* and *indexes*, not *formulae* and *indices*. *Memoranda* but *factums*.[76] Please, no *premia*.

One that could go either way is *forum*. Your Latin teacher (if you had one), would have insisted on the plural *fora*, of course. Both *fora* and *forums* are correct in English (although auto-correct wants to turn *fora* into *for a*). *Forums* is preferable, and there is judicial authority for this view: see the words of Belobaba J in *Leon v Volkswagen AG*.[77]

If you must use a Latin word (or one that we get from Latin), use it correctly (unlike my bank, which asks in its online advertising, *Are you a U of T alumni?* I also received an email informing me of the death of *an alumni* of the firm where I articled. I was saddened by that news — he was a very nice guy — but also (albeit in a less significant way) by the writer's choice of words.

The Latin singular is *alumnus*, meaning a foster-son — but also any male child who is a ward, charge, or pupil. By extension, *alumnus* came to be applied in the United States to former pupils or students. When universities went co-ed, the Latin *alumna* (foster-daughter, ward, etc.) was available. The plural of *alumnus* is *alumni*; if you have more than one female former student, they are *alumnæ*. Sometimes *alumni* is used to refer to all former students, regardless of sex

76 *Factums* is the officially adopted plural in the courts of British Columbia: see *Johnson v Laing*, 2004 BCCA 364 at para 115.

77 2018 ONSC 4265 at para 40, n 33.

(or gender); *alumni/æ* is also seen. (I'm not a fan of using a slash for that kind of thing, but it's functional.) *Alum* is a nice way to way to be gender-neutral, and I suppose lends itself to the plural *alums*. But *an alumni*? Never.

At Oxford, the old way was simply to call everyone who had left the university (or *gone down*, in traditional parlance) an *old member*, regardless of age. Perhaps because this seemed ageist, *alumnus* and *alumna* are now officially used (after the predictable outcry from traditionalists, who saw it as yet another example of encroaching Americanism). *Old member* does have the advantage of being easier to pluralize if you don't know Latin.

One that pedants love is *octopus*: the plural must be *octopi*, right? Not so; it's Greek, not Latin, so the correct plural is in fact *octopodes* — but you'd be better to use *octopuses* (if that doesn't sound awkward) or the singular as a collective (*The octopus at the fish counter looked a bit off, I thought*).[78]

"Politics" and Other –ics Words

A tricky area, this — and to a certain extent, you need to go by feel.

It probably should be *Politics* ***is*** *not for the fainthearted* but *His politics* ***are*** *offensive*. Similarly, *Acoustics* ***is*** *the science of how sound projects* but *The acoustics at the concert* ***were*** *terrible*.

Singular in relation to an *–ics* word that describes a concept or science, but plural when more specific or in relation to one person?

Singular Words That End in –s

These aren't plural: *corps*, *gallows*, *innings*, *measles*, *mumps*.

This used to be plural but now isn't: *news*.

Surnames

Never, ever use an apostrophe to make these plural. The 1980s band is therefore *The Smiths*, and what you are trying to do vis-à-vis the neighbours is *keep up with the Joneses*. The apostrophe comes in *only* when you need to make a possessive:

78 "Subversive Facts" (17 March 2017), *The Economist*, online: www.economist.com/news/books-and-arts/21718850-describing-language-objectively-need-not-meaning-doing-so-dispassionately-subversive-facts.

The Smiths' last album was *Strangeways, Here We Come.*

The Joneses' new car was parked ostentatiously in the driveway.

Jones' is NOT an acceptable rendition of either *Joneses* or *Joneses'*.

Words Ending in –o

Poor old Dan Quayle, the hapless US vice-president who was ridiculed back in 1992 for thinking that *potato* needed a final E added to it. It sometimes did have one in the eighteenth century, if that's any consolation to the ex-VP, and it always does when you're talking about *potatoes* in the plural.

The plural forms of words ending in *–o* can go both ways, and hard-and-fast rules probably prove elusive:

* *cargoes, embargoes, flamingoes, haloes, heroes, hoboes, mosquitoes, noes* (as in *The noes outnumbered the yeses*), *potatoes, tomatoes*
* *armadillos, cameos, commandos, crescendos, discos, embryos, fiascos, ghettos, photos, pros, Romeos*

9) *The*: Yes or No?

a) Names of Countries

One does still occasionally hear or see *the Ukraine*, but be careful not to use that around people of Ukrainian origin. They can get very shirty about it. Their point is that the definite article *the* makes the country sound more like a region, like *the Midwest* or *the Highlands* — and, by implication, a sub-division of some larger entity. And we all know which larger entity most Ukrainians are not longing to be part of again. This is all fair enough, geopolitically speaking, but perhaps not linguistically.

First, Ukrainian (like other Slavic languages) uses no articles at all (no *a*, *an*, or *the*), so perhaps can't really dictate when English uses them. Secondly, there are countries that do take an article as part of their names: the definite article is part of the official names of *The Gambia* and *The Bahamas*.

The definite article is often — even usually — used with a range of other geopolitical entities, as a matter of idiom. Many are archipelagos or include a form of government as part of the name, but not all: *Central African Republic*, *Channel Islands*, *Comoros*, *Congo*, *Czech Republic*, *Dominican Republic*, *Lebanon* (especially for those who know their Human League back catalogue), *Maldives*, *Marshall Islands*, *Netherlands*, *Philippines*, *Seychelles*, *Solomon Islands*, *Sudan*, *United Kingdom*, *United States of America*, *Yemen*. (*The*) *Congo* and *The Gambia* each takes its name from the river that runs through it. But, if you're likely to be read or heard by Ukrainians, the country is just *Ukraine*. *The Dominican* is also likely to irritate Dominicans, for whom it is always the *Dominican Republic* (or sometimes even the historical *Santo Domingo*).

b) From the Specific to the General

One of the most difficult things to explain to someone whose first language is not English is when, as a matter of idiom, we drop the definite or indefinite article in front of a noun. But even those who learned English first have trouble with the simple matter of *the* or *a*.

Burden

In a recent news release, the Ontario Securities Commission said this: *Most recently, the OSC announced 107 regulatory changes to reduce* burden *for market participants while maintaining critical investor protections.*

Good initiative, but the use of *burden* annoys me. *The burden* or *the regulatory burden* would be better: a specific thing, not a general state of affairs. *A burden* is a discrete load one bears, not the sum of all loads. The load can be figurative, of course, whether it's the weight of duty, blame, sin, responsibility, proof, or securities regulation.

Stigma

Another word that gets used in the same way is *stigma*.

This is a borrowing from Greek, meaning the mark of a pointed instrument like a branding iron. The Greek plural *stigmata* is often used to describe the marks of the nails on the crucified body of Jesus. In figurative use, *a stigma* is a mark or brand of disgrace, infamy, and the like. We used to talk, for example, of *the stigma of illegitimacy*.

But *stigma* is now used as a word to describe the totality of shame-inducing responses to some state of affairs.

The Centre for Addiction and Mental Health in Toronto uses *stigma* in grammatically correct ways, but also less well.

> This is good: *Challenging* ***the stigma*** *associated with mental illness takes understanding, education and a closer look at our own attitudes toward health.*

> Less so: *Take a positive step toward addressing* ***stigma*** *with this online tutorial.*

The sentiment is to be applauded; the usage could be better.

Chattel

The legal term *chattel* is often similarly (mis)used. *A chattel* is an item of movable personal property, with the plural *chattels* denoting a collection of such stuff. Perhaps because of a perceived similarity with the collective *cattle* (and the two words in fact have a shared etymology), *chattel* sometimes gets used as a general/collective rather than a specific term: *Are we just going to be* chattel *for commerce?*[79]

Keep all three of these specific, with definite or indefinite articles attached.

10) A or *an*: Yes or No?

Please don't refer to *a surgery* (for *a surgical procedure* or *an operation*) or to multiple *surgeries*. Similarly, it is not *a litigation* and one should not refer to *being successful in future litigations*, as I recently saw on LinkedIn.

Surgery and *litigation* are general states of being, if you will, not specific instances within those states.

79 Shoshana Zuboff, "You Are Now Remotely Controlled: Surveillance Capitalists Control the Science and the Scientists, the Secrets and the Truth" *New York Times* (24 January 2020), citing a 1997 Federal Trade Commission decision, online: www.nytimes.com/2020/01/24/opinion/sunday/surveillance-capitalism.html.

chapter four

Your Queries Answered

This book originated as a series of emails and then as a blog, and readers have sent questions on miscellaneous points, which are gathered here. (And I've invented a couple of queries, just to round things out.)

So, since you asked . . .

What's with "Esquire"? Does it have some special meaning in law?
In mediæval England, an esquire was one rank above a gentleman and one below a knight; hence the variant *squire* for a trainee knight.

While the precise class of chaps eligible to be an esquire is a matter of intense historical controversy, it seems that you had to be the younger son of a nobleman, the son or grandson of a knight, or an office-holder (possibly including a barrister-at-law). By the eighteenth century, *Esquire* came to be used as a polite substitute for *Mister* on an envelope (and the older use of *Gent*, after a name, faded away). This usage persists in the United Kingdom and more traditional parts of the Commonwealth.

Americans used to use *Esquire* in the same way, but by about (I'm guessing here) the 1940s, it was replaced by just plain *Mister* on envelopes, except in diplomatic and legal circles (conservative, those). By about the 1970s, only lawyers were using it. As a result, *Esquire* came to be viewed as synonymous with "attorney" — and second-wave feminists who entered the legal profession wanted to be able to use it, like their male peers. (Like women barristers and judges in England, who adopted the masculine wigs that their male counterparts have been wearing since the eighteenth century.) To someone in the United Kingdom today, however, *Susan Jones, Esq* looks as bizarre as *Ms Neil Guthrie* would.

Can I begin a sentence with "And" or "But"?

Contrary to what Mrs Snelgrove told you in grade 7, yes. But do it sparingly, for effect.

You can also start a sentence with *Because*, in constructions like this: *Because I forgot to set my alarm, I was late for the client meeting.*

How many spaces after the period at the end of a sentence? One or two?

You've got time on your hands if you're fussing about this!

In the days of the Smith-Corona manual typewriter, two spaces were *de rigueur*. In the digital age, one seems to be the norm.

What's the difference between "farther" and "further," and "less" and "fewer"?

Less and *fewer* are straightforward (although frequently confused). Use *less* for things you can measure (money, time, substances), *fewer* for things you can count (people, objects).

> Example: There are fewer people around in the summer, so there are fewer cars downtown and less traffic.

NEVER say *less people*. Grammar nerds appear to be divided on whether one should use *less* or *fewer* when dealing with percentages, with the preponderance favouring *less*.[1]

The precise difference between *farther* and *further* is hard to pin down, and the two words can be (and are) used more or less interchangeably. The consensus among language mavens is that *farther* is best used for actual distances, *further* where distance is conceptual or not part of the equation at all.

1 See Patricia T O'Connor & Stewart Kellerman, "When Fewer Is Less" Grammarphobia (21 March 2014), online: www.grammarphobia.com/blog/2014/03/fewer-less.html.

EXAMPLES: Edmonton is farther from Toronto than Calgary *but* Don't go any further — I've had enough of your silliness.

I sometimes see in emails that someone is going to "revert" to me. What's up with this?

This expression appears to have originated in business and legal circles in India in the 1970s, spreading from there to the United Kingdom and Australia. It's a bit weird, because *revert* normally means to return to an original shape or form (*The werewolf reverted to human form once the full moon had passed*).

I would avoid the word in business correspondence (unless you mean it in the werewolf sense), and just say *reply* or *answer* (*get back to you* is a bit colloquial). *Revert* just seems fancy for the sake of being fancy, which is never desirable.

Is it "travelled" or "traveled"? "Focussed" or "focused"?

In the United States, it would be *traveled* and *traveler*; *travelled* and *traveller* are more usual in Canada. On the other hand, *focused* is the better way.

Is it "Quebecer" or "Quebecker"?

Traditionally, *Quebecker* is the correct form, although this is less commonly seen nowadays. Logically, the C in *Quebecer* should be soft (C followed by E or I generally is, in English), and the E long as a result. You need that K to make it a hard C sound and to keep the short E. But I may be losing the battle on this one. (And why do I suspect that it's being won by people who pronounce the place name ka-BECK?)

Another troubling one is the *syncing* that our phones do. By rights, that C should be soft, not hard, given the following I; but the phone function is clearly pronounced like *sinking*. Adding the H from *synchronize* doesn't help, as that would be pronounced like the *cinching* that one does with a belt. *Sync'ing* or *synch'ing* gets round the spelling/pronunciation problem, but they both look odd.

I'm never sure whether it's "licence" or "license."

Well, it depends what you mean and where you live. In the United States, *licence* (and *practice*) are both the noun and verb forms. In the

United Kingdom, a *licence* is required for driving, but one is *licensed* to drive — and one *practises* the *practice* of law. I would go British on this one.

Related point: US usage demands *defense* (and *offense*); on the other side of the Atlantic and (generally) north of the 49th parallel, it's *defence/offence* (even though the adjective is *defensive/offensive*). And while we're on the subject, don't say DEE-fence and OH-fence; they really should be pronounced duh-FENCE and off-FENCE.

Additionally: the ugly Americanism *licensure* has been popping up in the context of regulated professions (like the law, and the regulator in Ontario is an offender in using it). This needs to stop: *licensing* is adequate to describe the state of being licensed.

Is there anything wrong with "as per" or just "per"? They seem like useful expressions to me, but I suspect you may disagree.
You are so right about that. *As per* is ugly commercialese from the nineteenth century. In normal English, you would just say *as* or *according to*.[2]

Use *as usual* instead of *as per usual*; *as we discussed* for *as per our discussion* (or *per our discussion*), *as requested* instead of *(as) per your request*.

I'm not sure if it's OK to refer to "the above [or below] paragraph."
It isn't. These are prepositions or adverbs, not adjectives. You could say *see the passage quoted above* [or *below*], or just *see above* [or *below*], but it's inelegant to talk about *the below* [or *above*] *passage*.

I have this feeling that I shouldn't use "hopefully" in the way that I do. Can you shed some light?
Let there be light.

The standard meaning of *hopefully* is "in a hopeful manner." Example: *The articling student started work* hopefully, *confident that she would find the answer*.

2 Robert Hartwell Fiske, *Robert Hartwell Fiske's Dictionary of Unendurable English: A Compendium of Mistakes in Grammar, Usage, and Spelling with Commentary on Lexicographers and Linguists* (New York, NY: Scribner, 2011) at 310.

There is a second — and more controversial — sense to the word, when it's used to mean "It is hoped (that)" or "I hope (that)." As in, *The partner told the associate, "**Hopefully**, you'll be finished this task before midnight."*

Grammar nerds often criticize the second usage, on the grounds that it doesn't clearly refer to the person who is doing the hoping. But *hopefully* in this sense does perform a useful function (although *I hope* would work just as well). There is a reasonable argument that because people use *hopefully* in this way and everyone knows what they mean when they do, it has become acceptable.

Defenders of *hopefully* in the second sense often trot out the analogous German word *hoffentlich*, which means "it is to be hoped," and they note that its English equivalent has been used in the same way since the early eighteenth century (in America, at any rate), with objections only surfacing in the 1960s.

The *Oxford English Dictionary Online* gives both meanings, but says that the second is avoided by many. You may want to do the same, if only not to be called out by a grammar nerd.

Is it to "orient" or to "orientate"? "Oriented" or "orientated"?

Either, although *orientate(d)* is more common in the United Kingdom, and *orient(ed)* in the United States. This is one of those rare occasions when I would side with the Yanks; *orientate* just sounds fussy.

Orient also has the virtue of being the older form of the word, borrowed directly from the French *orienter* in the early eighteenth century.

Is "Will do" an appropriate response from junior people to a request for assistance? I find it kind of annoying.

Will do is both grammatically correct and stylistically traditional. On its own, however, it may seem a bit abrupt, even curt. An exclamation mark could help with that, turning what might seem begrudging into a more clearly enthusiastic expression of willingness.

Sure is similar: just that one word, followed by a period, may come across as the equivalent of "yeah, whatever" or as a downright "I'll be damned if I'm doing that." Here again, an exclamation mark would convey more enthusiasm.

Exercise restraint with exclamation marks, however: too many may suggest the breathless tone of a fifteen-year-old, especially if you use more than one after a single word. There is no place for *Yes!!!* in professional writing.

Context is everything — and tone is notoriously difficult to convey electronically. (Although the tone of the original questioner's email was unmistakable!)

What is the correct plural of "factum"? Is it "facta" or "factums"?
One sees both, but *factums* seems to be preferable.[3]

But what about *memoranda*, then? Even though words ending in *–um* take *–a* as their plural form in Latin, we get *factum* from Latin via French (and civil law). As a result, we've adopted the naturalized French plural *factums*. *Memorandum* comes to us more directly from Latin, so takes *–a* (although *memorandums* is an old plural form (Shakespeare used it) that seems to be gaining traction in modern US and non-legal usage). Who said English was regular?

Factum is, incidentally, not a common word outside the Canadian legal context: the equivalent document is a *brief* in the United States, a *skeleton argument* in England.

I got a mark-up from a US law firm last week that changed "enure" to "inure." I always thought "enure" was the legal term ("this agreement will enure to the benefit of . . .") and "inure" was for getting used to something unpleasant ("After two months backpacking across Asia, I was inured to the rock-bottom conditions of Cambodian hostels."). Am I right?
My research indicates that the UK tendency is to use *inure* in your Cambodian hostels sense, *enure* in the legal sense.

But the two words derive from the same source (the obsolete noun *ure*, which means "use" or "practice"), and ultimately mean the same thing: one gets used to Cambodian hostels; the legal benefit is put to one's use.

3 In British Columbia, *factums* is official: see *Johnson v Laing*, 2004 BCCA 364 at para 115.

The *Oxford English Dictionary Online* prefers *inure*, but its examples of usage go both ways (and *enure* is more frequent in the legal citations). *Fowler's Modern English Usage* says the variant spellings are unnecessary and opts for *inure* only.[4]

I'd still do it your way though, unless pressed by a Yank.

Is it "quaere" or "query" when beginning a question?

Lawyers — especially new ones and wannabe ones — love to pose questions beginning with one or other of these.

In Latin, *quaere* (*quære*, if you want to get fancy with typography) is a verb meaning to inquire, question, or examine. In English, both the Latin and its English derivative *query* are used as a verb (to inquire or ask) and a noun (the question itself).

Both *quaere* and *query* may be used as an introduction to a question or subject of enquiry, typically followed by *whether* (although the *Oxford English Dictionary Online* describes the use of *quaere* as not only archaic but rare — outside legal circles, I guess).

My inclination would be to ditch them entirely, especially when communicating with non-lawyers. They add a layer of unnecessary lawyerish fussiness. Just pose a simple question in plain English. Better yet, provide an answer.

Is there a difference between "toward" and "towards"?

None except geography. *Toward* is general in the United States, *towards* in the United Kingdom — but *toward* crops up occasionally on the other side of the Atlantic too, and one sees both in Canada.

What's your view on "etc."?

Best avoided.

It suggests you didn't have time to think about whatever it is, couldn't come up with another example, couldn't be bothered to dig more deeply. Or even that you're pretending to know more than you do.

4 HW Fowler, *Fowler's Modern English Usage*, 2d ed, revised by Sir Ernest Gowers (Oxford, UK: Oxford University Press, 1983) at 295; RW Burchfield, *Fowler's Modern English Usage*, 3d ed, revised (Oxford, UK: Oxford University Press, 2004) at 410.

I was always told that you shouldn't end a sentence with a preposition. Is that true?

As Sir Winston Churchill famously said of a sentence that studiously avoided putting a preposition at the end, "This is the sort of English up with which I will not put."

The answer is yes, you can. This will generally be in a few scenarios:

- where the preposition is part of an idiomatic expression (like *put up with*)
- with a relative clause (*This is just the thing I am looking for*)
- in answer to *what*, *where*, *which*, and *who* questions (*What is it you are looking for?*)
- in *what*, *where*, *which*, and *who* clauses (*No one told me that's what you're looking for*)
- in some passive constructions (*This has been paid for*)

It's therefore perfectly fine to say *What are you referring to?* rather than the classically correct *To what are you referring?* — especially if that means you won't say *What are you referencing*? [shudder].

Is it ever OK to say use "triage" as a verb?

No.

Is "ain't" ever OK?

Not in legal writing or in current, educated speech; but it was once an acceptable contraction for *am not*, especially among the British upper class in the late nineteenth and early twentieth centuries (as was the dropping of the final G in *–ing* words (*huntin', shootin', and fishin'*). Still fine today in colloquial/jocular expressions like *ain't it the truth.*

You was there would have been acceptable usage up to the middle of the eighteenth century, in reference to one person.

"Quebec" or "Québec"? "Montreal" or "Montréal"?

These have been just fine without the accent for centuries in English, but no one can object if you want to make them look more French.

You should take care, however, that other French names and terms are also properly accented (but you then also run the risk of looking pretentious).

Practice varies in using the local or the historic English version of place names. *Mumbai* is now usual (for the old *Bombay*). *Beijing* prevails for the city, but we still eat *Peking duck*; *Peiping* has gone the way of the dodo. It is either *Lyon* or *Lyons*, with the French s-less form gaining traction, as with *Marseille/Marseilles*; and yet *Florence* not *Firenze*, *Naples* not *Napoli*, *Munich* not *München*. Probably *Livorno* now rather than *Leghorn*, except in reference to poultry. *Frankfurt* ceased being called *Frankfort* by English-speakers a long time ago (but the name of the capital of Kentucky is still spelt that way). When territory and thus naming are actually contested by different constituencies, geographical nomenclature can be a minefield. Tread carefully.

Why do contracts sometimes have pages that say, "This page intentionally left blank" in square brackets?
Beats me. Those pages aren't blank, are they?

Someone has criticized my writing for using "There is" and "there are." What gives?
The US legal writing expert Ross Guberman includes eliminating these as the first of his "Thirty Key Edits."[5] With good reason.

As openings to sentences, they are weak and will force you to write something longer, flabbier, and less effective.

Compare:

> There are no reasons to think that the court will reject this argument.
>
> The court will not reject this argument.

The second version is clearly punchier.

It is as an opener raises the same issues:

> It is apparent that the plaintiff's claim is without merit.

5 Ross Guberman, *The Attorney Toolkit* (LegalWritingPro.com, 2014) at 17.

To what, in these examples, do *there* and *it* actually refer? Nothing, really, which has the effect of making the sentence itself an appeal to something vague, perhaps insubstantial. For this reason, *there* and *it* are sometimes referred to as "dummy" subjects.

Much better:

The plaintiff's claim is without merit.

As Richard Wydick suggests in *Plain English for Lawyers*, your sentences will be shorter — and therefore more effective — when they focus on the actor, the action, and the object.[6] Otherwise, you may be relying on a dummy, which probably isn't a good thing. (See also Chapter 3, Section B(8)(a), "There Is, There Are," in this book.)

Is it "treble" or "triple"?

They mean the same thing: consisting of three parts or things, three in number, three times an amount.

A *treble* is also a singer with a soprano voice, often a choirboy, or a musical instrument in a high key. In the number-related sense, *treble* and *triple* can both can be verbs, nouns, adjectives, or adverbs. Readers of *Private Eye* may recall the frequent cry of "*Trebles* all round!" in the "Corporation Street" series (a satire on the BBC), meaning triple measures of spirits.

Treble seems to be more common in Britain, but it has a strange persistence in North American legal usage. This is thanks to old statutory drafting in the United States, which provides in certain circumstances for *treble damages*. That is, an award of damages that is three times what the trier of fact determines. Examples are found in the *Clayton Antitrust Act*, *RICO* and Title 35 of the US Code (patents).

There are frequent instances in historical Canadian legislation, although the concept does still appear in the *Distress Act* and *Sheriffs Act* currently in force in Manitoba. Federal fisheries regulations also refer to "double or *treble* hooks" (see *Maritime Provinces Fishery Regulations*, SOR/93-55, s 1(1) ("hook")). In the damages sense, *treble*

6 Richard Wydick & Amy E Sloan, *Plain English for Lawyers*, 6th ed (Durham, NC: Carolina Academic Press, 2019) at 16.

actually appears to be more common in Canadian case law (some of it fairly recent) than *triple* (seventy-five hits in CanLII for *treble damages*, thirty-three for *triple damages*).

Take your pick, but unless your statute specifies *treble*, I'd go with *triple*.

Is it "OK" or "okay"?

Not a question that arises in drafting a contract or pleadings (one hopes), but certainly in composing email. Both are recognized forms.

On the traditional assumption that the expression was originally shorthand for *all correct* (rendered in humorous, dialectical, or unschooled US English as *oll* (or *orl*) *korrect*), *OK* has the merit of being closer to the source.

I've always thought there is something fishy-sounding about that etymology, but the *Oxford English Dictionary* (*OED*) and Fowler repeat it. The latter gives some other possible origins and a case reference to *Nippon Menkwa Kabushiki Kaisha (Japan Cotton Trading Co Ltd) v Dawsons Bank Ltd*,[7] where Lord Russell of Killowen calls it a "commercial barbarism" but accepts its usage in business transactions (even if, on the facts of the case, writing *O.K.* on an invoice did not give rise to an estoppel).

The older usage citations in the *OED* have *OK* (the first is from 1839), with *okay* appearing later in the nineteenth century, so *OK* also appears to have age on its side. Spell with or without periods (I prefer to omit them). *Ok* and *ok* are also seen, though probably more in email and text messages.

Okeh is a variant (and the name of a jazz record company founded in 1918 by Otto KE Heinemann, as an obvious play on his initials and the popular expression). *Okey-doke* and *okey-dokey* emerged in the 1930s, Ned Flanders's *okely-dokely circa* 1990.

What is the origin of the expression "trite law"?

To a layperson, *trite* means hackneyed, worn-out, stale from overuse — as in *Greetings cards are filled with trite expressions of cloying sentiment.*

7 [1935] 51 Ll LR 147 (PC (Burma), 1935.

To a lawyer (or a law student after about four weeks into 1L), *trite law* means any legal principle that is "obvious or common knowledge" (in the words of that unassailable authority, the Wiktionary).

The expression *trite law* has an ancient pedigree. Its origins go back to *T Pasch's case*,[8] where Brian CJ says that "it is trite law that the thought of man is not triable, for even the devil does not know what the thought of man is."[9]

In Canada, judges seem to be fond of this particular old chestnut: a search of CanLII yielded nearly 7,000 hits; in the Canadian subscription databases, the figure is closer to 10,000. The phrase is less popular with US judges: not quite 400 hits in the US version of Westlaw.

What does this suggest? Obviously, that the phrase *trite law* is itself trite, hackneyed, devoid of freshness, lacking in novelty (although less so in the United States). A good reason, then, to stop using it.

Another reason to drop *trite law* is that it is, in Richard Wydick's phrase, one of those expressions that lawyers (and wannabe lawyers) use to give their writing "a legal smell," but which mean little to a non-lawyer — and may, more dangerously, "give a false sense of precision and sometimes obscure a dangerous gap in analysis."[10] Don't tell your client something is *trite law*; tell her that it is *well-established that* ... Your advice will be more meaningful.

And less trite.

Do you "lend" someone money or do you "loan" it?

You can do either, in fact.

The verb lend, in the sense of granting someone else temporary possession of something in the expectation of its eventual return, is an old one: Ælfric used it in his *Grammar* more than a thousand years ago.

8 (1478) YB 17 E4 Pasch fo 2 pl 2.

9 Cited in R Haigh, "'It's Trite and Ancient Law': The High Court and the Use of the Obvious" (2000) 28 Fed L Rev 87 at 87 — although Haigh translates the original law French.

10 Richard Wydick, *Plain English for Lawyers*, 5th ed (Durham, NC: Carolina Academic Press, 2005) at 64.

Loan as a verb isn't much more recent, going back at least as far as the early thirteenth century. In modern usage, however, the *OED* says it is mostly American. How we use the two verbs in this northern part of North America is, I think, idiomatic — with *loan* more frequent (but not universal) in a transactional setting:

- Can you *lend* me ten bucks?
- I will *lend* you the book, but please return it.
- She *lent* me a hand when the going was tough.
- The room doesn't *lend* itself well to groups of more than ten.
- Banks *lend* money at interest.
- The finance company *loans* money at exorbitant rates.
- The National Gallery *loaned/lent* the painting to the travelling exhibition.

The noun is always *loan*, and the person who makes one is a *lender*. A *loaner* is something like the laptop you borrow from the IT department for the weekend.

"O" or "Oh"?

On a recent Canada Day, someone on LinkedIn referred to *O'Canada*, which is clearly wrong. (*O'* is confined to Irish surnames, where it is the anglicized version of the Gaelic Ó or *Ua*, meaning "descendant of"; *M(a)c* [or *M'*], as for the Scots, means "son of").

But is it *O Canada*, *Oh! Canada*, or what?

O, not followed by punctuation and closely linked in sense to what follows, is what's called a vocative — and is correct in things like national anthems or hymns.

Oh is usually followed by punctuation and is more like a standalone exclamation tacked on to the rest: *Oh, hell! Oh! What a scoundrel! Oh, no you don't!*

Usage of O and *Oh* has not always been consistent, however (think back to the revue *Oh! Calcutta!* if you're old enough).

But *O'Canada* has never been OK.

Is it "court house" or "courthouse"?

Either, really. Or, better, *court-house*.

The *OED* uses a hyphen, but its examples of usage (mostly from the United States) give all three forms.

The single-word, no-hyphen version is often seen (British Columbia has its Courthouse Libraries), but does suggest an unnatural pronunciation (cor-THOWZE). Perhaps the best way to go is to talk about the Victoria Avenue Court House in Regina, but to say that the parties settled on the *court-house steps*.

Nevertheless and nonetheless — or is that none the less?

Nevertheless and *nonetheless* mean the same thing ("notwithstanding"), so they can be used interchangeably. *Nonetheless* is a more recent coinage.

Both started as three words, but over time have ended up as one. It's now always *nevertheless*, but the three-word form *none the less* is still seen, especially in the United Kingdom. There is a certain logic to *none the less*, if spelling it as a single word might suggest an odd pronunciation (*non-EATHE-less*, with the second syllable rhyming with *breathe*). But you're fine nevertheless with *nonetheless*.

That said, they are both pompous and flabby, best avoided.

What does it mean when you "table" something at a meeting?

It depends on where you live.

For those in the non-US parts of the English-speaking world, *to table* means to submit something formally for discussion or consideration. The expression comes from act of laying your submission on the table of a legislative assembly or other decision-making body (like a board of directors). This usage goes back at least as far as the 1650s. The Canadian *Glossary of Parliamentary Procedure* uses *table* as a noun and verb in these senses.[11] In the United States, however, *tabling* has, since the mid 1800s, meant postponing or even shelving a matter indefinitely.

Winston Churchill noted the difference in the Second World War: British officials wanted to *table* (*i.e.* raise) something as a matter of

11 House of Commons, Canada, "Glossary of Parliamentary Procedure," online: www.ourcommons.ca/About/Glossary/Index-e.html#LetterT.

urgency; their American counterparts thought they meant "putting it away in a drawer and forgetting about it."[12]

In Canada we see both, but the non-US usage makes more sense when you think of the actual table of the deliberative body.

Why do we call a group of lawyers who practise together a "firm"?

The term goes back a while.

In Italian, *firma* has been used since the sixteenth century to describe a commercial enterprise or business; the word also means "a signature." *Firmar* and *firmare* (in Spanish and Italian, respectively) have meant "to sign a document" since the tenth century. All are derived from the post-classical Latin *firmare* ("to sign or ratify").

English had borrowed *firm* in the signature sense by the 1570s. By the eighteenth century, it had come to mean, by extension, the name under which a commercial enterprise transacts business, and also an association of two or more people in business together—what we would now call a partnership. Over time, it came to mean any kind of business or company, although for lawyers the partnership aspect has remained.

Since the early twentieth century, *The Firm* has been a colloquial term for the Royal Family; and since the 1950s for MI6, the British foreign intelligence agency.

The adjective *firm*, meaning "solid or steady" (as in a *firm offer* or *firm handshake*), comes from a related Latin root: *firmus* ("firm, solid, or stable").

One needs a steady hand when signing on behalf of a law partnership.

Agreeance: is that a thing?

I was on a call recently, and someone said "OK, now that we're all in *agreeance*, . . ."

A colleague asked me afterwards if that was an odd word to use. I've seen and heard it occasionally. So I checked out the *OED* (natch), and there it is.

12 Winston S Churchill, *The Grand Alliance* (Boston: Houghton Mifflin, 1950) at 687.

It's a synonym for *agreement*, in the sense of "concord of opinions" (rather than "contract"), and its origin is Scottish, dating back at least to the early fifteenth century. *Agreement* is older, apparently by about a century, and means both the concord and the contract thing. *OED* notes that *agreeance* may now be regarded as non-standard, and the examples of usage are mostly Scottish and American (which is to say, non-standard for an Oxford lexicographer).

I saw "misunderestimate" used recently. Is that a word?

Well, sort of. But it's a useful coinage.

By way of example, John King of CNN cautioned his followers in a tweet not to "*misunderestimate* the relentless base and focus" of Trump supporters in their drive towards November 2020.[13] That word (italicized here for emphasis), attracts red underlining on the screen, signalling an issue, and might therefore attract a raised eyebrow.

The *mis*– prefix is redundant, because you've already got *under*– working to qualify or compromise *estimate*. *Misunderestimate* isn't in the *OED* — but it is in the Wikipedia entry on "Bushisms";[14] that is, the various "unconventional statements, phrases, pronunciations, malapropisms, and semantic or linguistic errors in the public speaking" of an earlier president, George W Bush. The 43rd president of the United States observed of his 2000 election that he had been *misunderestimated* by the pollsters, the media, and the public.

So, King's use of the word is a nice political allusion, as well as a warning not to discount a candidate with longer odds. Looking back from the vantage point of 2020, GWB isn't looking so bad (remember when he was called the "Worst President Ever"?).

The reference to *misunderestimating* is therefore a useful reminder against complacency.

13 John King, "yes, #RNC2020 will keep fact checkers and ethics lawyers very busy, but do not misunderestimate the relentless base and path to 270 focus," Twitter, 25 August 2020, 10:41 p.m., online: https://twitter.com/JohnKingCNN/status/1298450368964198400.

14 Wikipedia, "Bushisms," online: https://en.wikipedia.org/wiki/Bushism.

What are your thoughts on the term "gross negligence"?
This is a term we have imported from US law. Canadian (and English) judges and authors were not keen on it initially.

Linden *et al* in *Canadian Tort Law* (2018) cite Baron Rolfe, a famous nineteenth-century English jurist (later Lord Cranworth LC), who said that *gross negligence* is merely ordinary negligence "with the addition of a vituperative epithet." A skeptical American judge "is reputed to have compared the differences among negligence, gross negligence and recklessness to the distinctions among a fool, a damned fool and a God-damned fool." (Still a fool.)

Over the years, Canadian case law has come to recognize that the term has its uses, however. Sir Lyman Duff CJ thought *gross negligence* usefully described "a very marked departure from the standards by which responsible and competent people in charge of motor cars habitually govern themselves," adding that it is "not difficult of application by a jury whose minds are not confused by too much verbal analysis."[15] As one student suggested to me, it would be *grossly negligent* to leave Homer Simpson in charge of operations at the nuclear power plant, but probably only *negligent* to entrust things to any other employee at the same level.

That made perfect sense.

Did the COVID-19 pandemic raise any linguistic or grammatical issues for you?
Linguistic ones, certainly.

CURBSIDE PICK-UP

All of a sudden, we did a lot of this. It felt like shopping in Bulgaria in the mid-1970s, lining up for the remaining 40-watt bulb on the shelf. If you live in the United Kingdom or other parts of the Commonwealth, you would be doing it at the *kerbside*.

The form *curb* is usual in North America in describing the raised edge of a sidewalk, walkway, or paved area. Both versions are seen in early eighteenth-century examples (sometimes *kirb*). *Curb* actually makes more sense, given that the word comes from the French *courbe* and Latin *curvus*, meaning "curved."

15 *Murray v McCulloch*, [1942] SCR 141.

Why the *K*, then?

The *OED* points to the word *kennel* by way of comparison, which also comes from a C-word: *canis*, which is Latin for "dog." In mediaeval French, a *canaille* was a pack of dogs. Spelling being flexible in the Middle Ages, the word also appeared as *chienaille* or *kienaille*. A *chenil* or *kenil* was the enclosure or structure one put them in. For reasons that aren't entirely clear, British English went with *kennel* and, after a flirtation with *curb*, *kerb*.

The verb meaning "to restrain" is universally spelt *curb*.

FACE MASK

Never write or say this — it is just a *mask*. There is no other kind but that worn on the face (except figuratively). *Face mask* is as silly as *foot shoe* or *head hat*.

As these twenty different senses of *mask* that are listed in the *OED* will attest:

* face-covering
* image of a face worn by an actor
* representation of a human or animal head
* grotesque representation of a face worn at carnivals, etc.
* facial expression concealing emotion, giving false impression
* human face resembling a mask
* protective covering for the face
* surgical dressing for the face
* medical device placed over the mouth and nose
* gauze or fibre covering for mouth and nose
* gas mask
* swimmer or diver's watertight shield for the eyes
* face disguised by cosmetics
* cosmetic preparation for the face
* likeness of someone's face in clay or wax, especially from a mould
* stylized representation of a face
* face, head, or skinned head of a fox or other animal
* mouth of a dragonfly larva
* marking on the face of an animal
* blotchy discoloration on the face of a pregnant woman

Please do wear a *mask*, but refer to it properly.

WHEN WE RETURN TO NORMALCY — OR IS THAT NORMALITY?

Properly, it's *normality*. Just as *formal* leads to *formality* and *final* to *finality*. But one does also see *normalcy*, as in this *New York Times* piece.[16]

You won't see the word *normalcy* as much outside the United States, however. (And whether one saw the concept there from 2016 to 2020 is another question entirely.) Although *normalcy* was used as early as 1857, the word really only came into its own in 1920, when Warren G Harding used "A Return to Normalcy" as his campaign slogan in that year's presidential election. He meant the conditions that had existed before the First World War and the Spanish flu pandemic that came in its wake. Harding was ridiculed by the word nerds of the day, but he won the election handily — and the word gained currency.

Normality has a slight edge in terms of history: the earliest example cited in the *OED* is 1839. But it's also close to the post-classical Latin *normalitas* ("the state of being governed by rules or norms"), seen as far back as the eleventh century.

I'd go with (and hope for) *normality*.

PANDEMIC VERSUS *EPIDEMIC*: WHAT'S THE DIFF?

Coverage, essentially.

You'll need a little ancient Greek here. The *–demic* suffix comes from *demos*, which means "the people," "the community." *Demos* is the root of *democracy* ("rule by the people").

The *epi–* bit comes from the Greek for "upon," "at," "close to." Think of the *epicentre* of an earthquake.

Pan–, on the other hand, means "universal." *Pandemonium* (or *pandaemonium*) is total confusion or chaos; *pantheism* is the belief that the divine is present everywhere in the universe.

An *epidemic* is a disease that touches a fairly localized group; a *pandemic* reaches far beyond the local. One would therefore say *There was an epidemic of meningitis among local highschool students*,

16 "Coronavirus Testing and Tracing: The Path to Normalcy?" Letters to the Editor, *New York Times* (21 April 2020), online: www.nytimes.com/2020/04/21/opinion/letters/coronavirus-testing-tracing.html.

but *The world was severely affected by the Spanish flu, AIDS, and COVID-19 pandemics.*

The earliest use of *pandemic* appears to be 1666 (a year of plague in London); *epidemic* goes back further — to 1603 in its current form, to the late fifteenth century as *epidemy*.

LET'S GET *PHYGITAL*

As long as we don't call it that, though. (In part because "Let's get *phygital*" may conjure up images of Olivia Newton-John in a headband for those of a certain age.)

Phygital is a newish (and unlovely) term for communication or connection that combines the physical and the digital. It comes from the pre-COVID world of marketing and sales. In the pandemic period, if you were hosting a virtual breakfast or happy hour for the summer students in your office using a digital platform, you could make it (ugh) *phygital* by sending participants all the food and drink they need to have an experience that feels a least a bit more like being in the same room with everyone else.

But *phygital*? Please, no. Just send the cereal or the ready-made Negronis and try to have a good time.[17]

Reflections on Language From Confinement

I often feel like a grumpy old schoolmaster, rapping the knuckles of my hapless pupils with a ruler when they misplace a comma or mistake *who's* for *whose*.

A certain amount of knuckle-rapping is necessary, but no one who writes about words and writing can afford to be overly prescriptive.

Language changes over time, sometimes for the better. I like *text* as a verb; it neatly captures a new kind of linguistic transmission we didn't have when my knuckles were being rapped as a schoolboy. Readers of my blog will be well aware of new words I am less fond of (*productise*, *reference* (as a verb), *attendee*, *learnings*, *proactive*, to name but a few).

I also don't like the way *crucial* has changed in meaning from "that which finally decides between two hypotheses" (*crux* being

17 Thanks to Chris Graham of tellpeople.ca for drawing my attention to a word he finds equally unfortunate.

Latin for an instrument of torture and, by extension, a difficult problem) to merely "very important," but there isn't much I can do about it at this point.

What we think of as long-established rules sometimes turn out not to be that old: Shakespeare broke just about every grammatical and stylistic rule you can think of, mainly because it wasn't until much later that many of them came into being (like coherent punctuation and consistent spelling). Many were invented (and were the subject of vigorous debate) by writers of grammars and dictionaries in the eighteenth and nineteenth centuries. Some rules turn out not to be as hard-and-fast as we think (*between* versus *among, none is/are*). Some are arbitrary, if useful for the sake of consistency (the "rules" of legal citation, for example).

This doesn't mean writing is a free-for-all, at least in a professional or business context. You want to write prose that your peers will recognize as technically correct and socially appropriate (in the sense of respecting norms, rather than being polite). A certain amount of conformism is required, so if you want to be a linguistic radical, law may not be the best berth for you.

You don't want to write exactly the way others do, though. That's boring. A distinctive voice, an unexpected turn of phrase, a fresh metaphor, or an unusual word will make your writing vivid and memorable. Heaven knows there are enough dull legal blog posts out there.

Writing like the herd is not only boring; it can also show lack of thought. This is what troubles me about buzzwords and jargon. In an exchange on LinkedIn, a reader suggested that what I call bad business jargon can often be useful shorthand that gets the job done when everybody understands the terminology. OK, but it can just as often be a cover for a problematic lack of actual content or analysis. The *New Yorker* cartoon on my desk calendar for the day of that LinkedIn exchange depicted a guy telling his audience in a business meeting, *Enhanced branding metrics drive robust solutions for scalable monetization of jargon*, which seemed apt. Jargon more often than not means nothing, or not much.

It's important, particularly for lawyers, to think about the meaning of words and to use them with precision and purpose.

When words lose meaning, they can be manipulated and the underlying facts distorted. Think of the Twitterer-in-Chief or his precursors in Orwell's Ministry of Truth.

But perhaps I have just been spending too much time alone in my apartment.

chapter five

Conclusion

A. DON'T BE SMART

A final piece of advice. Lawyers are experts, and that expertise is hard-won. Don't flaunt it, though — a point that was made in a good article in the *Harvard Business Review*.[1]

There are two risks in pitching things at too high a level. The first is that you alienate your audience by a show-offy display of technical information they neither understand nor care about (for example, the difference between *therefor* and *therefore*). You want to avoid being preachy.

The other risk is that you may have ventured into territory which you don't know well, and have got it wrong. Some clever reader is bound to catch you out. A thin veneer tends to chip off easily.

I have probably gone both ways in my time, but I hope not in these pages.

1 Liane Davey, "Stop Trying to Sound Smart When You're Writing" *Harvard Business Review* (5 October 2015), online: https://hbr.org/2016/10/stop-trying-to-sound-smart-when-youre-writing.

Some Recommended Sources

By no means a comprehensive list, but some of the classics and some sources specific to the legal context.

ADLER, MARK & DAPHNE PERRY. *Clarity for Lawyers: Effective Legal Language* (London: London Society Publications, 2017).

BLUMBERG, THEODORE L. *The Seven Deadly Sins of Legal Writing* (Baltimore: Owlworks, 2008).

BUTTERICK, MATTHEW. *Typography for Lawyers: Essential Tools for Polished & Persuasive Documents*, 2d ed (Houston, TX: O'Connor's, 2015).

FISKE, ROBERT HARTWELL. *The Dimwit's Dictionary*, 4th ed (Rockport: Vocabula Communications, 2014).

———. *Robert Hartwell Fiske's Dictionary of Unendurable English: A Compendium of Mistakes in Grammar, Usage, and Spelling with Commentary on Lexicographers and Linguists* (New York: Scribner, 2011).

FOWLER, HW & FG FOWLER. *The King's English*, 3d ed (London, Oxford, & New York: Oxford University Press, 2003).

FOWLER, HW & RW BURCHFIELD. *New Fowler's Modern English Usage*, 3d ed, rev (Oxford: Clarendon Press, 1998).

FOWLER, HW & SIR ERNEST GOWERS. *A Dictionary of Modern English Usage*, 2d ed, rev (Oxford & New York: Oxford University Press, 1983).

GARNER, BRYAN A, ED. *Black's Law Dictionary*, 10th ed (St Paul: Thomson Reuters, 2014).

———. *LawProse Blog*, online: www.lawprose.org/lawprose-blog.

———. *Legal Writing in Plain English: A Text with Exercises*, 2d ed (Chicago: University of Chicago Press, 2013).

GRIFFIN, SIMON. *Fucking Apostrophes: A Guide to Show You Where You Can Stick Them* (London: Icon Books, 2016).

GUBERMAN, ROSS. *The Attorney Toolkit* (Np: the author, 2016).

———. *Deal Struck: The World's Best Drafting Tips* (Np: the author, 2014).

———. *Legal Writing Pro*, online: www.legalwritingpro.com.

GUTHRIE, NEIL. "Lawyers and Greengrocers" (2007) 25 *Advocates' Society Journal* 11.

LASKIN, HON JOHN I. "Forget the Wind-Up and Make the Pitch" (1999), Court of Appeal for Ontario, online: www.ontariocourts.ca/coa/en/ps/speeches/forget.htm.

MACRAE, PAUL. *Business and Professional Writing: A Basic Guide* (Peterborough: Broadview Press, 2015).

MAINE STATE LEGISLATURE. *Maine Legislative Drafting Manual*, online: http://legislature.maine.gov/doc/1353.

METZLER, JACK & THE OFFICE OF THE SOLICITOR GENERAL, US DEPARTMENT OF JUSTICE. *The Solicitor General's Style Guide*, 2d ed (Washington: InterAlias Press, 2015).

MOWAT, CHRISTINE. *A Plain-Language Handbook for Legal Writers*, 2d ed (Toronto: Carswell, 2015).

NUNBERG, GEOFFREY. *Going Nucular: Language, Politics, and Culture in Confrontational Times* (New York: PublicAffairs, 2004).

Oxford English Dictionary Online, The, online: www.oed.com (available for free to cardholders of some public libraries, including the author's in Toronto).

PARTRIDGE, ERIC. *Usage and Abusage: A Guide to Good English* (Harmondsworth, UK: Penguin, 1973).

——— & JANE WHITCUT, EDS. *Usage and Abusage: A Guide to Good English*, new ed (New York: WW Norton, 1995).

PINKER, STEVEN. *The Sense of Style: The Thinking Person's Guide to Writing in the 21st Century* (New York: Viking, 2014).

PLAINLANGUAGE.GOV. Resources, online: www.plainlanguage.gov/resources.

SECURITIES AND EXCHANGE COMMISSION. *A Plain English Handbook: How to Create Clear SEC Disclosure Documents* (Washington: SEC, 1998), online: www.sec.gov/pdf/handbook.pdf.[1]

STRUNK, WILLIAM & EB WHITE. *The Elements of Style*, 4th ed (Boston: Allyn and Bacon, 2000).

UNIVERSITY OF CHICAGO PRESS. *The Chicago Manual of Style*, 16th ed (Chicago: University of Chicago Press, 2010), online: www.chicagomanualofstyle.org.

UNIVERSITY OF LEICESTER. *Grammar Guides*, online: https://www2.le.ac.uk/offices/ld/all-resources/writing/grammar/grammar-guides.

WYDICK, RICHARD C. *Plain English for Lawyers*, 5th ed (Durham: Carolina Academic Press, 2005).

——— & AMY E SLOAN. *Plain English for Lawyers*, 6th ed (Durham: Carolina Academic Press, 2019).

1 See also, online: US Securities and Exchange Commission, "Plain Writing Initiative" (13 April 2016), SEC.gov, online: www.sec.gov/plainwriting.shtml, "Federal Plain Language Guidelines" (March 2011, revised May 2011), online: https://plainlanguage.gov/media/FederalPLGuidelines.pdf.

Index

About the Author

Neil Guthrie is a lawyer and writer. He was educated at the universities of Toronto (BA, LLB) and Oxford (D Phil). He is director of professional development, research, and knowledge management at Aird & Berlis LLP.

Printed and bound by CPI Group (UK) Ltd, Croydon, CR0 4YY

15/09/2026

14962402-0001